the structure of awareness

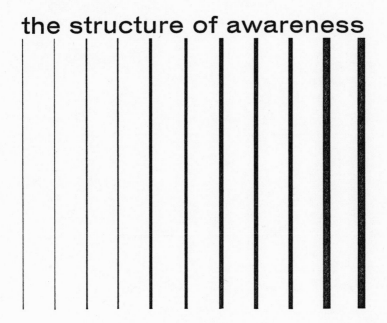

the structure of awareness

the structure of awareness

THOMAS C. ODEN

𝄞 abingdon press—nashville and new york

THE STRUCTURE OF AWARENESS

Copyright © 1969 by Abingdon Press

Standard Book Number: 687-40075-9

Library of Congress Catalog Card Number: 75-84711

SET UP, PRINTED, AND BOUND BY THE
PARTHENON PRESS, AT NASHVILLE,
TENNESSEE, UNITED STATES OF AMERICA

To the one who through human care
first mediated to me the unconditional care of God
my mother, Lily Clark Oden

*Non faciat ad disputationem theologicam, modo faciat ad
vitam theologicam.*—Erasmus

*Vivendo, immor moriendo et damnando fit theologus, non
intelligendo, legendo, aut speculando.*—Luther

contents

abbreviations

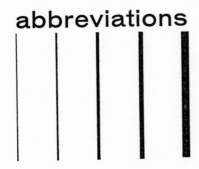

BN	*Being and Nothingness*, Jean-Paul Sartre
BT	*Being and Time*, Martin Heidegger
CD	*Church Dogmatics*, Karl Barth
CS	*Childhood and Society*, Erik H. Erikson
CTP	*Contemporary Theology and Psychotherapy*, Thomas C. Oden
KC	*Kerygma and Counseling*, Thomas C. Oden
KM	*Kerygma and Myth*, Rudolf Bultmann
MA	*The Meaning of Anxiety*, Rollo May
NDM	*The Nature and Destiny of Man*, Reinhold Niebuhr
NHG	*Neurosis and Human Growth*, Karen Horney
OBP	*On Becoming a Person*, Carl Rogers
OED	*Oxford English Dictionary*
PSS	*Psychology: The Study of a Science*, Sigmund Koch
RMWC	*Radical Monotheism and Western Culture*, H. Richard Niebuhr
ST	*Systematic Theology*, Paul Tillich
TMAV	"Toward a Modern Approach to Values," Carl Rogers
TNT	*Theology of the New Testament*, Rudolf Bultmann
WG	*Waiting for Godot*, Samuel Beckett

introduction

To be aware is to be awake to reality, to recognize the situation in which one exists. *Awareness* is a word that functions with especially powerful connotations in the English language. It implies the full use of one's tactile and sensual resources in knowing where one stands.

With a long Anglo-Saxon prehistory, which centers on the connotation of being *on guard* against danger, the modern usage of awareness still suggests keen sensitivity to one's environment. If one is *wary*, he is cautious, circumspect, alert to subtle movements in his presence; if he is *aware*, his full bodily faculties are sensitized to whatever is being encountered. The nearest French and German correlates (*attentif, vigilant, Gewahrsein, Gewissen*) all suggest certain aspects of the English word, but none succeeds in combining the multiple nuances of keen consciousness, attentiveness, vigilance, sensitivity, care, and organismic responsiveness as well as our remarkable English term *awareness*.

This book is addressed to the one who lives in a passionate quest for deepened awareness, who hungers to touch and taste human existence more intimately, who delights in the celebration of now. The emerging generation often finds it necessary to "drop out" of routinized, conventional society in order to resensitize

13

awareness, discover intimacy, resurrect the capacity for responsiveness. However much it may offend the passing, production-oriented generation, the children of abundance seem determined to pursue their special historical vocation of learning to live now, embracing life more awarely, experiencing more concretely than their fathers what it means to be a human being: bodily, sexually, interpersonally, inwardly, socio-politically, morally, and aesthetically. The quest for awareness is structured into our times.

The best way to get a glimpse of the overall direction of this inquiry is by the chart (pp. 16-17), which summarizes the seven categories of the human condition, both in their dysfunctional and functional aspects.[1] The longest part is understandably the first, where many issues are explored which do not need to be repeated in subsequent parts. Once the analogical patterns are established,

---

[1] The nucleus of this argument was first presented in May, 1960, at Perkins School of Theology. In 1961, for a regional youth conference at Mount Sequoyah, Arkansas, I wrote a series of dialogues between an artist, a Marxist, a psychotherapist, and a theologian which were focused on six of the seven categories presented here. (I had not yet developed the category of desecration.) In 1962, when asked by the Methodist Student Movement to write a study in biblical theology for University study groups, I again turned to the same structure around which to organize *The Crisis of the World and the Word of God*, portions of which have been reworked for this discussion. After finishing *Radical Obedience* in 1963, I began to develop an elaborate research project which I conceived under the overarching title of *Authenticity*, which would have included both a discussion of the dialogue between theology and psychotherapy, and a précis of the categories of the structure of awareness. What was first proposed as a single, unified effort has now turned into three books, since the dialogue with therapy has already demanded two separate books, *Kerygma and Counseling* and *Contemporary Theology and Psychotherapy*, (The Westminster Press, 1966 and 1967, hereafter *KC* and *CTP*). At some future time it may become desirable to spell out in more detail the concisely summarized patterns of Part IV, in which the last four of seven categories of the structure of awareness are condensed. For now, however, I am leaving it to the perspicacity of the reader to employ his own analogical imagination in the last part in hopes that further elaboration will prove unnecessary.

Portions of these proposals were presented in several series of special lectures whose audiences have given me helpful criticisms: the 1961 Arkansas Christian Minister's Institute; the 1963 Phillips Lectures for the Oklahoma Christian Minister's Institute; the Texas Methodist Student Movement, 1966; the 1967 Willson Lectures at Centenary College, Shreveport, Louisiana; and the 1968 Parkhurst Lectures, Southwestern College, Winfield, Kansas. I have profoundly benefited from responses of my students in interdisciplinary seminars at Phillips Seminary, Enid, Oklahoma, 1960-69. Special thanks are due each of my student assistants over these years for faithful help with the manuscript at various stages of its development: David Livingston, Roger Hall, Doyle Dobbins, Roger Barker, Coletta Reid Holcomb, James Laing, and Don Anderson.

the reader will be able to apply them easily to subsequent sections. Hence each succeeding portion is shorter than the previous part, and in fact the last four of the seven categories are summarized in the concluding quarter of the book. There was a time when I seriously considered dividing up this discussion into two separate volumes, one on the structure of awareness in time (past, present, and future) and the other on the structure of the awareness of being (God, self, neighbor, world). As the argument developed, however, it became clear that once the analogical patterns were secured, each succeeding section could be more spare.

When I first began to conceive this argument, I thought of it as an exercise for the "spiritually serious." There are seven unavoidable existential relationships in which every man exists:

Past	God
Present	Self
Future	Neighbor
	World

These seven dimensions, I thought, could form the foci around which a seven-day retreat in self-examination could be undertaken, asking about the predicament and possibility of contemporary man in each of these modes. Although as the argument has grown it has taken on many complexities, I nevertheless hope that it may lend itself to a certain kind of devotional study for secular, moral self-examination.

When I speak of the "spiritually serious," I have in mind not just the classical pattern of self-examination literature such as William Law's *Serious Call* or Edwards' treatise on the affections, but instead the new breed of spirit-questers amid the maturing twentieth century: those involved in psychotherapy, the flower people, those struggling with responsible political decision amid immense historical ambiguities, the university student wrestling for his own identity in a twisted world of masks and phoniness, the over-forty mother whose now-grown children leave her forty more years in which to despair or create, the technocrat in a computerized bureaucracy who wonders where it is all going, the unionized electrician who has started to read Kafka in his spare time off his thirty-hour work week. These are the "spiritually serious" to whom this book is addressed.

I find myself thinking about this project as an architect thinks

15

THE STRUCTURE OF AWARENESS

Part & Chapters	Orientation of Awareness Toward Time and Being	Inclusive Types of Existential Relationships	Access to Awareness	The Human Predicament, Dysfunctional Awareness	Self-Actualizing Awareness (*therapeutic categories*)
I Chs. 1-5	*Past* the already actualized	remembered relationships	Memory	*Guilt* awareness of irresponsible value negation	*Forgiveness* in spite of guilt
II Chs. 6-8	*Future* possibility, not yet	anticipated relationships	Imagination	*Anxiety* awareness of threats to values considered necessary to one's existence	*Trust* (openness)
III Chs. 9-11	*Present* current actualization	experiencing relationships	Experience	*Boredom* awareness of current blocks to value actualization	*Responsiveness* amid emptiness (respons-ability)

AWARENESS OF TIME

IV Ch. 12	*God* and the gods, centers of value	transpersonal (I-Thou) relationships	Valuational Consciousness	*Idolatry* deification of finite, contextual values	*Faith* in God, beyond the gods
IV Ch. 13	*Self* I	intrapersonal (I-I) relationships	Self-Consciousness	*Despair* awareness of impotence of self-actualization, identity diffusion	*Self-Discovery* transcending despair (self-affirmation, new man, new identity)
IV Ch. 14	*Neighbor* other persons, order of society	interpersonal (I-you) relationships	Social Consciousness	*Interpersonal Alienation* awareness of estrangement from others in overdependency, depersonalization, withdrawal, and aggression	*Love* overcoming alienation (covenant concern, care for others)
IV Ch. 15	*World* nonhuman creation, natural environment	subpersonal (I-it) relationships	Spacio-physical Consciousness	*Desecration* abuse, defilement of natural environment	*Reclamation* amid desecration (new creation, consecration)

AWARENESS OF BEING

about a building. He looks for symmetry, organismic wholeness, functionality, interconnection of all parts, and aesthetic beauty. It is not that I presume to build such a system *de novo*, but that I see it already in operation in human awareness and want to try to give it adequate expression. The construction of this argument is something like the composer who hears the rich chord but has difficulty putting it down on paper, or the painter whose eye glimpses a magnificent setting but who must now decide how to organize it on canvas.

There is another sense, however, in which my method of operation has been more like that of a mathematician who works with complex equations and geometric proportions, moving from knowns to unknowns, extrapolating, inferring, hypothesizing, hunching. My endless exercises with odd-looking diagrams (which have helped me to visualize key elements in my equations and work analogically with their relationships) have at times seemed to take on the character of an intricate algebraic task, working from perceived elements in the equation toward the clarification of the opaque and enigmatic elements.

The Greek word for discover is *heuriskein*, from which we derive our word *heuristic*. If thinking serves a heuristic function, it serves to stimulate investigation. Philosophers use the term heuristic to refer to that form of argument which is not demonstrable but which nevertheless commends itself as a fruitful hypothesis tending to invite further creative reflection. It is in this sense that I think of this whole discussion as an exercise in heuristic reflection. My search is offered as a heuristic device to invite the reader to reflect upon his own experiencing of awareness, its structure, dynamics, form, and content.

I am braced for understandable criticism on two grounds: that the project is too neat and oversimplified, on the one hand; and that it is too complex to be useful, on the other. I can only ask that the reader walk patiently with me through each stage, step at a time, and all the way, before prematurely dismissing the argument in either of these directions. In McLuhan's terms this exercise is "cool" communication[2] which demands a good deal of the reader, without whose imagination, memory, and experiential reflection the argument will doubtless appear to be bare bones, innocuous structure, abstract speculation without blood, passion, joy, or conflict. In any event the project intends to be a summarizing précis of a very complex mode of inclusive thinking.

In the era of the multiversity with its fragments of introverted expertise, it does sound absurdly ambitious to make an integrative attempt at synoptic reflection, seeking to conjoin disparate insights from developmental psychology, psychotherapy, ontology, epistemology, ethics, phenomenology, the fine arts, jurisprudence, linguistics, theology, hermeneutics, liturgics, history, and the philosophy of history. For those who regard these fields as their own private domain with their own fixed language and gaming rules, I can only hope that they would hear themselves addressed first as human beings instead of specialists. Whatever one's particular gifts, he is a human being before he becomes an expert, and he continues to share the dilemmas of human existence amid his specialized forms of knowing. Admittedly it is not because I am an expert in any or all of these fields, but instead a human being—a single, experiencing, time-bound, warm-bodied human being— that emboldens me to speak with any assurance about the human situation. More than most other academic bailiwicks, my own academic discipline (theological ethics) invites and demands such integrative reflection on man, culture, time, being and value, dysfunctional and constructive human behavior.

Our thesis: The structure of human awareness emerges directly out of man's temporal situation and his relation to being. Both his seven-dimensional human predicament and his sevenfold possibility for authenticity develop as an expression of his sevenfold existential relation to being and time.

Properly defined and qualified, these seven categories present themselves as inclusive of the human condition: *past, present,* and *future* are inclusive of all human relationships to *time.* There is no fourth. Although inseparable (no future is conceivable which is totally disrelated to the past), they are constantly distinguished in our common language, which organizes itself in tenses. Similarly, if properly understood, the relations of the self to *God,* to *itself,* to *others,* and to the *world* are inclusive of all fundamental existential relationships to being. There is no commensurable fifth. Anyone who deals seriously with the human condition touches these four bases or their symbolic equivalent somewhere along the way. Our purpose is to ask how the three inclusive time categories interpenetrate the four inclusive categories of being. How is man's sickness embedded in these fundamental relationships, and how is his authentic existence possible within this specific frame of his meeting with being and time?

A sharp transition from a phenomenological to a theological method is in store for the reader between chapters three and four. I only ask that the descriptive effort of the first three chapters be carefully assimilated before one plunges into the radically different language of the fourth; otherwise it will seem quite meaningless and perhaps archaic. I am convinced, however, that if the entire argument of Part I is read well and understood, the reader can sail through the remaining portions with little difficulty. With this I will leave him to ponder the twenty-one categories of man's awareness of being and time, his predicament and his promise, with which this spiritual exercise for secular moral self-examination is concerned.

part one

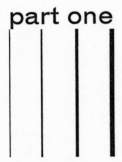

the burden of the past

chapter I

CHOICE DEMANDS NEGATION

1. Framing the Question

Every man exists in a relation to the past. To imagine ourselves without a past is to imagine ourselves being born again.

While we do not know the future at all, we know the past all too well. Since human existence is a choosing existence, it is also a value-negating existence and therefore an existence bound up in guilt.

We ask: What is the essential structure of the burden man must bear in relation to his own past and to the cosmic past?

1.1 The Descriptive Task. In accounting for my own method of inquiry, I rely heavily upon a curious maxim which I first encountered in Carl Rogers: *What is most personal is most general.*[1] Repeatedly I have found, to my astonishment, that the feelings which have seemed to me most private, most personal, and therefore the feelings I least expect to be understood by others, when clearly expressed, resonate deeply and consistently with their own

[1] Carl Rogers, *On Becoming a Person* (Houghton Mifflin, 1961; hereafter *OBP*), p. 26.

experience. This has led me to believe that what I experience in the most unique and personal way, if brought to clear expression, is precisely what others are most deeply experiencing in analogous ways. This has encouraged me to search intensely for an appropriate articulation of my own experience of guilt and its recurring structure, in the hope that others will recognize the same structure in their own experience.

I am thus searching for both concreteness and structure in my own experience. But how is this possible, when it would seem that the uniquely personal, concrete experience is the opposite of formal structural analysis? Is not actual experiencing quite different from the formal account of the structure of experience? I have found, to the contrary, that it is precisely amid the concrete, situational experiencing of guilt that the structure of guilt is most clearly revealed. Admittedly the focus of our inquiry is on the identification of the formal, consistent structure of guilt, so that any self-aware person might recognize that structure in his own experience, but that does not imply that we are diverting our attention away from concrete experiencing, since it is just there that we see the structure operating.

With this understanding in mind, I am now ready to introduce a term which will recurrently be used to describe our method of inquiry: *phenomenology*. Regrettably aware that phenomenology is used in differing ways, ranging from a strict empiricism to the broadly based moral phenomenology of Nicolai Hartmann, I am employing it in the tradition of Husserl, Heidegger, Sartre, and van den Berg to refer to the description of the concrete contents of consciousness, without presupposing or superimposing diversionary assumptions about what is given in consciousness, but rather learning clearly to *see what is given immediately in the phenomenon of awareness*.[2] The phenomenological method, as opposed to

---

[2] *Ideas: General Introduction to Pure Phenomenology* (Collier, 1962), pp. 91 ff.; Martin Heidegger, *Being and Time*, trans. by John Macquarrie and Edward Robinson (London: SCM, 1962; hereafter *BT*), pp. 49 ff.; J. H. van den Berg, *The Changing Nature of Man* (Dell, 1964), *passim*; Jean-Paul Sartre, *Being and Nothingness: An Essay on Phenomenological Ontology*, (Philosophical Library, 1956), trans. by Hazel E. Barnes (Philosophical Library, 1956, hereafter *BN*), pp. 107 ff.; 233 ff.

deductive logic, consists simply in pointing to what is given in consciousness and elucidating it in a step-by-step intuition of the structure of awareness. According to Husserl, phenomenology differs from psychology, which as an empirical science deals with "facts," in that phenomenology is concerned with the intuition of the *essence* of experience, or as I prefer to say, the structure of awareness. It is in this sense that the following inquiry is to be understood more as a phenomenological than a psychological investigation.

The focus of phenomenological interest centers not in other persons' opinions about the phenomenon, but intently upon the phenomenon itself as it appears directly to awareness. Consequently there are fewer footnotes in an inquiry of this sort. My task is to clarify the consistent features and cohesive pattern of the ordinary human experience called guilt. If I allow the experience of guilt simply to be described and clarified in its basic, formal structure, a structure to which no exceptions can be found, I will have accomplished my task. From another point of view, however, my quest might equally be designated an ontological inquiry searching for the structures of man's special mode of being in the world, attempting to look at the specific being-there (*Dasein*) of man, the structure of human awareness in time, in terms of which guilt emerges.[3]

1.2 The Initiating Observation. I have been led into this elaborate inquiry by one elementary observation which appeared to me as simple as it is suggestive: *Guilt and anxiety perform directly parallel, analogous functions.* Guilt and anxiety are dialectical opposites. It is the simple observation that *guilt is directed toward the past and anxiety is directed toward the future* which first aroused my curiosity and led me to an exploration of its implications.

So fundamental is this observation to human awareness, in fact, that it seems incredible that it might be neglected by the hungry eye of scientific investigation. One would imagine that it

[3] Heidegger, *BT*, pp. 67 ff.

would have by now received careful and explicit analysis by phi-losophers, therapists, and behavioral psychologists. Despite an enormous quantity of literature on guilt and anxiety, however, their elemental relation to temporal categories has not been com-monly recognized, and in fact it is very difficult to find any ref-erence to it at all.

Yet, if it should be the case that *guilt and anxiety work in exactly opposite temporal directions, but formally analogous ways*, then I was led to suspect that a clearer understanding of either one would reveal and illuminate the structure and dynamics of the other. It was in an attempt to explore that hypothesis that the ensuing inquiry was born.

This initiating observation could be presented in this way:

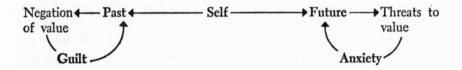

Thus, when the self relates to the future so as to symbolize its possibilities as a threat to values considered necessary for one's existence, then one experiences anxiety. Oppositely and analo-gously, when the self relates to the past so as to symbolize remem-bered events as irresponsible negations of values considered neces-sary for one's existence, then one experiences guilt.

My curiosity aroused by this initiating observation, I found myself drawn into a vast, hidden, magnetic field of inquiry into the psycho-temporal structure of awareness which seemed to lie under it. One intriguing hypothesis which captured my interest was that if guilt is directed essentially toward the past, then *it is literally and ontologically impossible to be guilty toward an empty, future possibility*. It seemed comforting to me to know that guilt has its ontological and temporal limits. Guilt simply has no power to extend itself beyond its own specific territory, which is the past, and we understand ourselves improperly if we think otherwise. Likewise, the corollary hypothesis suggested itself, that if anxiety is directed essentially toward the future, then *it is literally and ontologically impossible to be anxious toward an irretrievably fixed, immutable, certain, past actuality.* To one as anxiety-prone as I, it was profoundly comforting to know that anxiety operates only under this strict ontological limitation. Later I will show the reasons why this hypothesis, properly qualified, can be supported. Now I wish merely to indicate that such elementary findings on the antiphonal relation of guilt and anxiety have remained dim and unexplored because of our neglect of simple, careful, phenomenological investigation of the structure of temporal awareness as a clue to psychic dysfunctioning.

It is only when guilt is compared point by point with the structure of anxiety that its deepest reality is grasped. If man's predicament in relation to the future is his anxious attempt to control the uncontrollable, in relation to the past his predicament is the burdensome attempt to change the unchangeable.

Whereas we have absurdly desired to predetermine the future which is undetermined, we have desired to disestablish the past which is established. Man's predicament in time is that he wants to *form the future and reform the past.* Neither is possible. However pride or anger may protest it, the past remains forever formed, and the future remaines forever unformed.

In order to support this parallel theory of guilt and anxiety, it is necessary to show how the analogous patterns are structurally different. For in order to be analogous, two things must be different; otherwise they would be exactly alike and therefore not analogous.

I have been led to hypothesize, on the basis of this initial observation, that an integrated field theory of the human predicament and possibility must build upon these ontological and temporal foundations, and that it may be perhaps extrapolated from the structure of guilt and anxiety by means of what might be called a calculus of the structure of awareness. That is the ultimate hope which has guided the entire effort, however inadequately realized. Although I do not presume to suggest that what follows has in fact effectively developed such a field theory, it is in quest for it that I have set my feet upon this path.

2. Limitations of the Current Literature on Guilt

Although much has been written about guilt from many different perspectives, the enigma of guilt has hardly begun to be penetrated. From four major perspectives in particular—psychology, law, literature, and theology—persistent efforts have been made to unravel the mystery of guilt; but despite significant achievements by each discipline, we have not seen any credible consensus emerge as to the essential nature of guilt. Acknowledging a profound indebtedness to each of these perspectives, I wish not merely to reiterate the insights of these traditions, but to build upon them, correcting certain neglected dimensions, and to integrate them into a new formulation which would freshly clarify the basic structure and dynamics of guilt.

2.1 The Psychotherapeutic Perspective: Its Achievement. Through revolutionary proposals on the dynamics of repression, the unconscious, Oedipal interaction, and psychosomatic illness, the psychoanalytic and psychotherapeutic traditions have profoundly illuminated the complex, deceptive, vicious, and subversive modes of the operation of guilt in the subjective sphere. Prior to psychoanalysis, the study of guilt was pursued primarily in the objective and moral sense of defining "real guilt" against objective norms. Under the tutelage of psychotherapeutic practice, the concept of guilt has come to be employed more in the sense of "guilt-*feelings*," focusing upon the internal experience of self-loathing, especially as it emerges in the history of one's primary relationships with parents and siblings. A therapeutic stratagem aimed at resolving guilt conflicts has developed which utilizes dream interpretation, transference, psychometric devices, and other therapeutic means in order to clarify and reconstruct the primitive history of guilt-creating patterns and to redirect them toward new patterns of self-fulfillment.[4]

[4] Sigmund Freud, *The Basic Writings of Sigmund Freud*, trans. and ed. A. A. Brill (Modern Library, 1938), pp. 39 ff., 181 ff., 532 ff.; Clara M. Thompson *et al.*, eds., *An Outline of Psychoanalysis* (rev. ed.; Modern Library, 1955); Clara M. Thompson and Patrick Mullahy, *Psychoanalysis: Evolution and Development* (Hermitage House, 1950); Patrick Mullahy, *Oedipus: Myth and Complex* (Grove Press, 1955).

Its limitation. Without allowing myself to be diverted into a discussion of competing types of therapy or the dubiety of the success of various therapies, I wish to acknowledge the remarkable achievement of this whole multifaceted tradition of therapeutic interpretation of guilt, especially respecting the psychogenesis of guilt. The persistent inadequacy of this perspective, however, has been its stubborn unwillingness to examine its basic philosophical commitments and assumptions, which in the case of its treatment of guilt have often been decisive. In particular, psychotherapy has neglected what might be called an ontology of guilt, i.e., an analysis of the relation of guilt to the structures of being. Often psychotherapy has been caught in the anomalous situation of directing a general polemic against moral norms, while at the same time it has presupposed certain unexamined moral norms in its therapeutic operations.[5]

2.2 The Legal Perspective: Its Achievement. The Western legal tradition, including both Roman law and Anglo-Saxon common law, has for many centuries been nurturing and refining its concept of guilt, in the sense of the violation of established law.[6] It has provided rules for the gathering of evidence, the determination of guilt or negligence by a jury of one's peers, and the determination of appropriate penalties for offenses against the law. Much is to be learned from this venerable system of jurisprudence with its care and precision of language and with its meticulous, stated procedures for determining guilt and the criteria for guilt. I only regret that the medical, theological, and philosophical discussions of guilt have not achieved such great clarity and consistency of language.

Its limitation. The incompleteness of that distinguished legal tradition is a limitation which it has placed upon itself;

[5] Cf. Abraham H. Maslow, *Toward a Psychology of Being* (Van Nostrand, 1962); Heinz Hartmann, *Psychoanalysis and Moral Values* (International Universities Press, 1960); J. Masserman, ed., *Psychoanalysis and Human Values* (Grune & Stratton, 1960); Sidney M. Jourard, *Personal Adjustment* (Macmillan, 1958).

[6] Edmond N. Cahn, *The Moral Decision: Right and Wrong in the Light of American Law* (Indiana University Press, 1955).

namely, it has not concerned itself with the internally experienced feeling of guilt in the subject self, but rather, quite opposite from psychotherapy, it has focused exclusively upon the objective, legal definition of guilt and upon appropriate public procedures for dealing with guilt in the administration of justice. The law does not deal with feelings but only with legal principle and its application. Our focus is quite different. Although I would aim toward the same kind of clarity and precision in my attempt to clarify the internal structure of experienced guilt, I have not found adequate resources in the legal tradition alone to describe guilt at the highly personal level at which it actually exists.

2.3 The Literary Perspective: Its Achievement. Much closer to my descriptive interest in guilt is the act of literary creation, in which the skilled novelist or playwright creates intensive value conflicts in and between characters in an imaginal situation intended to be vicariously experienced, felt, and explored by the reader or audience. Such an "indirect communication"[7] of the truth of human existence, as distinguished from the direct communication of a systematic treatise, enables more immediate contact with the phenomenon of guilt than wordy tomes. For it portrays man concretely as a value-negating chooser, with subtle complications and specific images appropriate to a particular situational conflict. Elemental to all good literary creation is the invention of believable value conflict and value negation, and therefore the implicit and indirect discussion of the problem of guilt. If so, then the saga, the poem, the drama, or the cinema may yield profound insights for the understanding of the dynamics of guilt. A lively production of *The Beard, No Exit,* or *The Master Builder* will doubtless thrust the beholder into a more immediate existential encounter with the reality of guilt than the reading of a systematic treatise on guilt.

Its limitation. Our task is to reflect consistently upon the essential structure of the phenomenon of guilt which is revealed

---

[7] Søren Kierkegaard, *Concluding Unscientific Postscript,* trans. David F. Swenson and Walter Lowrie (Princeton University Press, 1941), pp. 225-67.

with so much more imaginative concreteness in dramatic conflict. The limitation of literary creation is precisely this: It does not attempt any such formal interpretation or structural analysis. It is not philosophy, much less literary criticism. It is more like situational phenomenology. That is its value. It is a dramatic linguistic event which explores an imaginative situation in which certain value conflicts implicit in human existence can be examined and perceived for what they are in that situation.

2.4 The Theological Perspective: Its Achievement. Virtually every religious tradition in the history of man has attempted an analysis and therapy for guilt. As a whole, the one special contribution of these varied traditions is clear and decisive: It consists in a radicalizing of the whole issue of value negation under final accountability before the ground and giver of life. The religious imagination has not been content to view guilt merely as violation of civil law, or as an internal psychological process, or a fictional portrayal of existence caught in the ambiguities of value negation. Rather, it has cast the question of guilt upon the cosmic scale of ultimate responsibility to the source and end of being itself. Through mythological media, the Judeo-Christian tradition in particular has perceived the issue of guilt, not merely as a negation of limited, finite, contextual, historical values, but as involving one's total stance before the giver of finitude and history. Through eschatological and apocalyptic images, the question of guilt has become an "end-time" question, with man at the end of days being called to radical accountability before the Judge and Lord of history for his irresponsible value negations. This is a mythological way of radicalizing the question of guilt.

Its limitation. While we can acknowledge the profound importance of this contribution, it is regrettable that the theological interpretations of guilt have often been rejected by modern man because of their tendency to become enslaved in petty legalistic interpretations of that radical accountability and to absolutize what later appear to be relative, culturally determined mores, social norms, taboos, and rules of cultus. This has caused critics

31

to dismiss the entire theological radicalization of guilt as merely another fraudulent effort at static institutional survival amid changing historical contexts.

Furthermore, it is precisely the theological achievement of the radicalization of guilt which is actually a part of its incredibility and offense to modern man. For it has so tended to absolutize guilt as to neglect discriminating judgments about specific contexts of value negation, with which the literary tradition deals so adeptly and concretely. The theologian often does not know what to do with the concrete situation, but only what to do with the cosmic and eschatological totality. It is therefore not surprising that theological views of guilt often have not been taken seriously by those practical moralists enmeshed in the situational analysis of value conflicts (writers, lawyers, and psychotherapists), who might otherwise have benefited from them most profoundly.

2.5 Recent Interdisciplinary Perspectives. Widespread interest has recently been shown in the question of guilt among an astonishing variety of psychological, philosophical, and theological writers. My discussion proceeds in dialogue with several of these, including the wide-ranging discussions by the British psychologist John McKenzie, *Guilt: Its Meaning and Significance*, and the Swiss psychiatrist Paul Tournier, *Guilt and Grace*. The more controversial proposals made by psychologist O. Hobart Mowrer in *The Crisis in Psychiatry and Religion*, and the attempt to apply that thesis to contemporary Protestant pastoral care by David Belgum in *Guilt: Where Psychology and Religion Meet*, are also significant partners in dialogue. The most serious pastoral and liturgical treatment of confession by Protestant thought in our time has been *Confession*, by Max Thurian, brother at Taizé, the monastic Protestant community in France, whereas the most significant phenomenological analysis of guilt by a theologian has been in the works of Paul Ricoeur, *Fallible Man* and *The Symbolism of Evil*.[8] Older psychoanalytic treatments of guilt by Freud,

[8] McKenzie (Allen & Unwin, 1962); Tournier (Harper, 1962); Mowrer (Van Nostrand, 1963); Belgum (Prentice-Hall, 1963); Thurian (SCM Press, 1958);

Horney, Menninger, and Binswanger, as well as philosophical and *Daseins*-analytical interpretations in the tradition of Husserl, Heidegger, and Sartre, are my steady companions along this way.[9] My argument has emerged in appreciative dialogue with each of these perspectives but in the conviction that no one of them by itself adequately expresses the necessary and consistent features of the structure of guilt.

Although I will not attempt any ambitious historical typology of views of guilt, my search for the structure of guilt has been pursued in keen awareness that this has been a recurring question in man's intellectual history as well as his social and religious history. Numerous historical questions present tempting diversions from my main course, which has a descriptive and experiential focus. For the interpretation of guilt has occupied an astonishing variety of thinkers, from primitive cultures through Hebrew and Greek traditions, Roman law, Stoic philosophy, medieval and Reformation thought, Enlightenment rationalism and empiricism, philosophical idealism, and in the development of the social and behavioral sciences to the present time. The great historic options, however, stand inconspicuously behind my phenomenological descriptions, and have been in various ways internalized in my language.

3. The Living Past

3.1 The Temporality of Awareness. Awareness exists in time. *Temporality gives to human awareness its specific character.* Although human awareness always quite literally *exists* exclusively in the present, it never exists without some latent awareness also of former and future times. In fact, it may become so

Ricoeur, *Fallible Man*, trans. Charles Kelbley (Regnery, 1965); *The Symbolism of Evil* (Harper, 1967).

[9] Freud, *Basic Writings*, pp. 807 ff.; Karen Horney, *Neurosis and Human Growth* (W. W. Norton, 1950) hereafter *NHG*; Karl Menninger, *Man Against Himself* (Harcourt, Brace and Co., 1938; Ludwig Binswanger, *Being-in-the-World*, trans. Jacob Needleman (Basic Books, 1963); Edmund Husserl, *The Phenomenology of Internal Time-Consciousness*, trans. James S. Churchill (Indiana University Press, 1964); Heidegger, *BT*, pp. 67 ff.; Sartre, *BN*, pp. 107 ff.; 233 ff.

preoccupied with its anticipative imagination that the primary awareness comes to focus tenaciously upon the future with its unmet possibilities; or it may be so encumbered by remembered time that primary awareness is fastened firmly upon the living past. Human awareness cannot escape time and in fact finds itself indefensibly molded by the categories of time's curious procession of unfolding reality.

Everything that occupies space, as a matter of fact, requires temporality. Space demands time in order to be space. If awareness is to be awareness *of* anything, it must presuppose both time and space. It is quite easy to point out the spatial character of awareness of an object (let us say the book you are reading), but much more difficult to grasp the temporal character of that awareness (that the process of reading can exist only as a movement through time). An enigmatic movement of being in time is presupposed even in the most ordinary human acts.

We have tended to think of the self quite abstractly as if it were not in time, in process, always already concretely engaged and fully enmeshed in temporal continuities. When we deal with the self as if it were abstracted out of time, we deal merely with an abstraction. For the self not only has time, it *is* itself a relation with time and is undefinable without the categories of time.[10]

3.2 The Power and Powerlessness of the Past. The sparest definition of the past is nonfuturity. It is time which has gone by. To *pass* something spatially is to go by it and leave it behind. We use this spatial image of passing to express the character of time. We experience our present moments as *passing* into time past. Our comprehensive phrase, *"the* past," is our way of expressing all former times which once were but now are no longer. *"My* past" is something quite different. It is that small part of the total, cosmic past in which I have directly participated, that arena of time in which I have shared with my freedom in the shaping of the destiny of the whole, for which I am in some sense account-

[10] Heideger, *BT*, 274 ff.

able. My past does not remain past. Through memory it haunts present decision.

The essence of the past is best understood by direct contrast with the future. The future is empty, nothing; completely unactualized, undetermined being; open, void possibility. The past, in itself, is its opposite: fixed, immutable, closed, determined actuality. If the future is the nothingness of possibility, the past is literally filled with actualized being, impossible to redo or even revisit except in memory. The only sense in which man can change the past is at the level of changing his perception or interpretation of it. Indeed what we call "the past" is constantly undergoing revision through our reinterpretation of it. But reinterpretation takes place only within the strict confines of the present, and the past as such remains immutable.

Often it seems that the past is dead and inert, while at other times it seems that the past is very much alive, making its impact upon the present. Each viewpoint needs the correction of the other. For it is precisely the inert, inaccessible, immutable, "dead," fixed character of the past which lays its most compelling moral claim upon the present, calling man to radical responsibility and decision now, and exerting its unique power over memory and decision.

Note carefully: If the past were revisitable and changeable and eternally repairable, then present decision would be meaningless, since any irresponsible act in the present could be revised and there would be no present accountability. It has been persuasively argued that if there were no death, man's life would be utterly meaningless, since he could postpone any decision indefinitely.[11] Present decision can have significance only on the basis of the fact that life has a definite terminus. Apply that argument to the past, and the result is surprising. For if the past could at any moment be redone, if any decision could be remade, if every human judgment were always accessible to revision, then human existence would be neither free nor meaningful. For what

[11] Viktor E. Frankl, *The Doctor and the Soul*, trans. Richard Winston and Clara Winston (Knopf, 1957), pp. 72 ff.

we call "free" exists only under finite limitations, and what we call "meaning" emerges only under the conditions of finite freedom. If any negated value could be revoked and revised, there would be no accountability, no guilt, no consciousness of genuine value negation.

When we say something is past, we mean quite seriously that it has *passed* beyond our grasp. A moment once present has passed beyond human recoverability. Suppose every "now" were a marble statue being created for all time to come. That occurrence would never be changed or be subject to retouching. For that is the nature of the past. Even if it should exist in the mind of God as an eternally beheld object, it can never exist again in our minds, except through the precarious, twisted, and ever-elongating access route of man's poor memory.

3.3 The Precarious Access to the Past. Although human awareness is always new in the now, it is never merely thrown *de novo* in the now without sustained interactive continuity with what has been and what is yet to be. Human existence is an existence in continuing recollection. Human existence without memory would be unthinkable. To imagine a man without memory is to imagine a man without language, imagination, or rational reflection.

Just as the anticipative imagination explores the future in expectation, searching empty possibilities for options for self-fulfillment, likewise memory explores the past in retrospective awareness, searching out the actualized occurrences, meanings, and relationships for whatever message they bear for present self-understanding. Memory is best understood as the direct, dialectical opposite and therefore the analogous counterpart to the anticipative imagination:

Past ←————— (memory) ——— Self ———(imagination)————→ Future

Just as the self's only access to the future is the anticipative reach of imagination into possibility, its only access to the past is the retrospective reach of memory into actualized being.

Our knowledge of the past is fragile and tenuous, since the capacity for recall is subject to many distortions. Memory does not necessarily re-image the past accurately or objectively. It may distort the actual event in the service of present needs, perceptions, and demands. Although memory may retain certain elements of "what happened," there always remains an unnavigable and ever-broadening ocean between the actual occurrence and the present memory of it. For it is impossible to remember anything without bringing it into some present self-understanding. The self always finds itself placed at an increasingly widening distance between now and the remembered event. Every known past event is a remembered event. Every remembered event is an event which is constantly being reconstrued in the light of the always new situation in which one exists.

However fragile, memory nonetheless remains our only access to the vast ranges of past experiencing so important to present self-understanding. Artifacts, geological formations, and written documents serve as aids to human memory to enable an expanded, scientific remembering of human history and prehistory. Through astronomy and associated sciences, an expanded memory of cosmic history is even being achieved. But the temporality of awareness leaves us with the embarrassing certainty that all that exists is now, and whatever else may have come to pass can never again be actually observed, but only remembered.

3.4 Re-imaging the Past. To remember is to call into present awareness some past event or relationship which bestows significance upon one's present. However dimly or sharply, memory seeks to re-image the past deed so that it may impinge meaningfully upon current perceptions and decisions. Memory thus enables man to grasp his existence as a historical and therefore a responsible existence and to become aware of his movement through time as not only accountable to the now but responsive to past meanings and values as well. Memory thus lends to human awareness its specific character as awareness in temporal continuity and responsibility.

What I remember reveals what I value. Conversely, what is

37

unimportant is not remembered. If seemingly "unimportant" things are remembered, their actual importance is concealed from awareness. And when important experiences are repressed, there are important reasons why they are later "unremembered." Repression, like memory, is the servant of the valuing self.

Thus, merely by entering the arena of the question of memory, we are already deeply involved in the question of value: what is good, what ought to be remembered, what is important. Such questions (of worth, good, value, obligation) are all ethical questions. Memory does not function without some presupposed ordering of values, however vague or inarticulate it might be. Thus is would seem ineffectual for psychotherapy to attempt to understand how memory functions without at the same time attempting to understand how memory functions on behalf of some value orientation. The long-estranged fields of psychology and ethics are called to reconciliation by the very dynamics of memory. The question, "By what criterion does a person remember?" actually implies the question of who that person is, what he values centrally, how and why he loves. His memory is shaped by his eros, what he desires, adores, worships. Hebrew psychology forcefully symbolized this by viewing memory as an act of the heart.[12] What one wills comes through the heart, the center of volition. What one remembers therefore penetrates to the heart, to the level of total organismic responsiveness.

If time is important for the healing of any psychological or physical wound, it is especially so in the healing of guilt, since the tenaciousness of guilt depends upon the memory of it. If time continues to separate the memory from the guilt-creating event, then time itself is an awesome force working against guilt-consciousness.

4. Internalizing Value

4.1 The Internalizing of Values.
From the day we are born, we are being invited into a remarkable learning process. Life

[12] Brevard S. Childs, *Memory and Tradition in Israel* (Allenson, 1962).

calls us to be valuing beings and ushers us into the pursuit of multiple goods. Parents, peers, pedagogues, and pundits all point out potential goals, values, goods, and ideals to be incorporated into the growing self. Acculturation is an extended learning process in which one weighs, sorts out, and organizes various values and goals into some self-shaped, internalized whole.

When G. H. Mead speaks of the internalized alter ego, or Freud of the superego, they refer to this process of becoming acculturated, receiving and internalizing values or ideas of values through social traditioning. To grow up means to accumulate a fund of these voices inside us, which in the last analysis becomes our own voice. The parental voice that repeatedly warns me to beware street traffic may at one time have been my father's voice, but finally it becomes, through my own choice, my own voice, in such a way that I cannot distinguish between the various sources. This is what is meant by conscience—the total accumulation of stored concepts of value or ideas of good behavior which have become internalized from other voices and have finally become my own voice.[13]

Understood as an internalized fund of accumulated values, conscience is a universal human phenomenon and is recognized as such in the varied languages of man. If we had no word for conscience, we would have to invent one, even in a highly permissive or altruistic society, since human existence as we know it cannot be lived without reference to some sort of shared consensus concerning what is importantly to be valued. Although the specific content of such values and norms may differ widely from society to society, it can hardly be convincingly argued that human life could proceed totally without reference to any forms of shared values. In this sense conscience is elemental to the chemistry of human experience. It belongs to the temporality of awareness and to the ontological structure of human existence.

What do I know when I know my conscience? Quite simply, myself. I know what I value and how I share in a valuing community. In many languages the word which we translate "con-

[13] Erik H. Erikson, *Childhood and Society* (2nd ed.; W. W. Norton, 1963), pp. 247 ff., hereafter CS.

science" maintains the connotation of "knowledge *with*." The Latin *conscientia*, the Greek *syneidēsis*, the German *Gewissen* all share the notion of a knowledge which one has with oneself, that which one knows in knowing oneself, a dimension of awareness which is given in and with human selfhood. It is, to be more precise, the awareness that I stand under norms or concepts of value or goods which I identify with my very self, which make my life worth living, which give meaning to my existence. In conscience, what I "know" (*science*) is internalized patterns of valuing which I regard as necessary for my well-being. It is possible, at least temporarily, to not listen to one's conscience. When I do not know my conscience rightly, clearly, then I do not recognize that which I regard as most deeply akin to my authentic self-fulfillment.

Insofar as man is man, he is a creator and recipient of value.[14] His values compete with each other in endless new configurations, and as life emerges more complexly, his valuing process becomes more complex. The self confronts delicately subtle, infinitely complex, competitive constellations of values in each new situation, which can only be understood concretely by the person experiencing them.

To simplify the matter, however, let us suppose that in a particular moment a certain individual is confronted merely with two competing possibilities for value actualization. Admittedly there are always subtle shades of value that combine and change even in an instant, but in an oversimplified sense let us suppose that only two values are in play and that both are regarded by the individual as immensely important. The character of human decision may be understood essentially in this way: *Decision means to affirm one value at the price of the negation of the other*. To decide is to elect one optable configuration of value in lieu of another and never without some sense of loss of some genuine good. We have now come to the threshold of the next phase of our argument on defining the essential structure of guilt. The human self, as a deciding, self-determining organism, lives con-

[14] Frankl, *The Doctor and the Soul*, pp. 72-134; *Man's Search for Meaning*, trans. Ilse Lasch (Washington Square Press, 1963).

40

stantly amid its own value negations. Given the structures of temporal awareness which we have delineated, the burdensome memory of value negation is elemental to human decision. Or, compressed into a simpler formula: Choice demands negation.

4.2 The Judicial Review of Legislative Actions. Government undertakes three functions: It creates *legislative acts* to bring the law into being; it performs *executive enforcement* to implement the law in specific situations; and it has the power of *judicial review* to ensure that the law is properly administered and to judge between conflicting claims under the law. It has been convincingly argued that every government short of anarchy must in some sense render these three services and that every conceivable governmental action belongs either to the category of legislative action, executive enforcement, or judicial review, or some combination of them.

There is in human awareness a tension among three decision-making functions analogous to the tension among the three basic functions of the body politic:

Governmental Decision	Orientation in Time	Individual Decision	Evaluating Functions
Legislative Task	Future Possibilities	*Self-Legislation:* Exploring and choosing the best possible maxims for self-direction and fulfillment	Value Envisioning
Executive Task	Contextual Present	*Self-Direction:* Current actualization of the good envisioned in the maxim	Value Actualization
Judicial Task	Remembered Past	*Self-Review:* Judging the adequacy of the maxim and its contextual actualization	Value Judging

In this way the basic governmental functions are directly related to man's stance within *time:*

41

THE STRUCTURE OF AWARENESS

(a) The *legislative* task is concerned with exploring *possibility*, seeking to envision what ought to be done, how the human *future* might better take shape, what might be possible for greater human fulfillment. The imaginative legislator looks ahead toward reformulating the human situation, venturing toward possibility for unactualized options more likely to bring human fulfillment into being.

(b) The *executive* task is focused more so upon the *now*, the existing context with its possibilities and limitations. The realistic executive strives to actualize the good which is envisioned in legislation within the stubborn limits of the current situation. His task is to see that the envisioned good does not remain in the limbo of vague possibility but comes into being and lives in time. Without an executive, even the most inventive legislature is like a factory without a distribution and sales operation, or like a gifted artist without paint and brush to execute the masterpiece he envisions.

(c) The *judicial* task has a reflexive function, focusing upon *already* actualized decisions and *past* responsible actions now up before the bar of conscience. Having envisioned the legislative action and having executed it in a decision related to some specific context, one then *reflects back* in order to judge the adequacy of the intent and performance of the law. It is in this way that the threefold function of government is related to the threefold movement of the self in time.

4.3 Judgment and Conscience. It is I who bring myself to the bar of conscience, set forth evidence against myself, call upon myself to defend my actions, very much like a courtroom drama. The case is argued internally, and I am my own prosecutor and defense attorney. I judge myself both in terms of the adequacy of my self-legislative acts and in terms of the way they have been executed in certain contexts. Both prosecuting and defending voices within me appeal to various values or systems of value which claim to be identified with my own well-being. I listen carefully to their accusations and defensive arguments.[15]

[15] Cf. Helmut Thielicke, *Theological Ethics*, I, ed. William H. Lazareth (Fortress Press, 1966), 298 ff.

Both sides appeal ultimately to what might be termed "the constitution" of my existence, the basic presupposed self-understanding or undergirding self-image out of which particular actions and decisions proceed.

The summons of the judging self comes to my awareness from within the inner recesses of my valuing self. It summons me, whether I like it or not, often unexpectedly, to accountability before my cherished values and relationships. It calls me to be who I am as one bound up in various covenants with other persons, ideals, and valued relationships. I may not like its verdict, but I submit to it, feel it intensely, acknowledge its immense importance, since it is really in the most literal sense *me* judging myself.

It is impossible for me to be a well-functioning person without this continuing judicial review of my actions. How else could I move self-correctively toward the goals which I identify with my basic welfare and ultimate good? Without it I am crippled, and denied that self-critical capacity to redirect my actions toward more realistic self-actualization. I cannot turn it off or on at will, except at the price of radical, neurotic denials to awareness of valued relationships. Since these values are internalized (their voice having become my own), I cannot run away from them, anymore than I can run away from myself. When I negate values I identify with my self-fulfillment, I must live with the painful memory that I have failed to be myself, failed to actualize my deepest intention. This pain performs the therapeutic function of rechanneling me toward more adequate fulfillment of my presupposed value structures.

The more precious is the value to me, the deeper will be the pain. It can be so intense, in fact, as to render temporarily inoperative the whole will. At times, the judging function may become sick and neurotic, so as, for example, to review again and again one particular value-negating action. It becomes fixated upon a single event which so powerfully symbolizes value negation that nothing else seems so important, though viewed objectively that event may seem bizarre or insignificant. Since cherished values are at stake, however, the act is compulsively and repetitiously submitted for review, so as to rehearse the act of self-punishment again and again.

An opposite malady of the judicial function is the psychopathic neglect of any norms or maxims for self-fulfillment. The psychopathic mind is different in that it seems at times to have no law or value to which it can summon itself in responsibility, or to which others can appeal to it for accountability. Wisely or foolishly, sagaciously or unfairly, however, the judicial function of memory continues to call the self to its own commitments to values.

4.4 The Tragic Choice. Since it is never possible to actualize all the goods we can envision, and never possible even to envision all the possible goods which with greater perception might be actualized, there is always a tragic dimension to the judging memory. We execute laws which do not serve our genuine well-being, and we create laws which cannot be meaningfully enforced. Our capacity to conceptualize fulfillment works at a much faster pace than our actual ability to embody those conceptions.

Moreover, whenever I choose to actualize one set of values, I neglect other potential values. Every pursued good implies a dozen unpursued goods. Every moment spent on the achievement of one goal is time lost on the achievement of numerous other potential goals. I cannot be a chooser without being a denier. I cannot be a self-legislator without being an obstructor of potentially good alternative self-legislation. I have a friend who has distinguished himself as a floor leader in a state House of Representatives, who concedes that his most difficult task is to find ways of tabling or blocking the flood of mediocre or partly good bills which must be stopped in order that the truly excellent legislation can be passed and administered. Many fine legislative ideas must go down the drain in this process of creative obstruction, in order that the legislative organism move forward with what it thinks is the best and most achievable alternative.

So it is with individual decision, where I must deny many valued relationships in order that the one most valued may be contextually actualized. If this is so, however, then I must live

44

constantly with many forms of painful memory that I have failed to be what I might have been and that repeatedly I have had to deny numerous values which I earnestly embrace. As keenly as any judge who sits on the bench and adjudicates highly competitive claims, I, as individual self-legislator, painfully feel the tragic sense of value-negation in every good choice.

4.5 Recapitulation. Having clarified our descriptive method, the motivation for our inquiry, and the limitations of currently available literature, we have now laid the foundation upon which we intend to build our analysis of the structure of guilt. The foundation lies in the temporality of awareness. Time gives to human awareness its specific character. The self does not merely *have* time but *is* itself a relation to time. It moves through the present always with a retrospective glance toward the past. Ironically it is the stubborn immutability of the past which causes its claim to impinge so forcefully upon the present. Yet if the past could be revisited and redone, then human freedom would find itself no longer accountable in the present, since any choice could later be undone and revised. Our only access route to the past is the precarious route of memory, which is always being reshaped under the demands and needs of the present. The guilt about which we are soon to speak maintains a lively dialogue not with any real or objective past, but only with a remembered past, burdened by all the deceptive distortions and limitations of finite memory.

Decision functions in ways similar to the legislative, executive, and judicial functions of government; envisioning values, actualizing values, and judging value actualization. Whether on the individual or governmental level, however, we learn that value selection implies value negation. Pursuit of one good involves the denial of others. Thus we formulate the central thesis of chapter one: Given the temporal structure of human awareness, the claiming power of the immutable past, and the valuational structure of the judging memory, human decisions must bear the constant burden of remembered value negations. Choice demands negation.

45

chapter II

THE STRUCTURE OF GUILT

We are now ready to pass from a general exploration of the temporality of awareness into the analysis of certain forms of dysfunctioning which emerge directly out of the special shape of man's awareness of the past. We are searching for a structure of guilt which admits of no exceptions.

5. Awareness of Value Negation

Every choice in a sense is a tragic choice, since it is impossible to be a human being without choosing and it is impossible to choose without the negation of value and it is impossible to negate values without guilt. This is the simple thread of our argument. The tragedy of human decision is that repeatedly we find ourselves caught in the denial of things we deeply value. Every human choice, with no exceptions, seems subtly to be implicated in the negation of value. For this is what choice means—to select between potentially desirable alternatives. But in any selection something must be left behind. This is the root meaning of decision. The Germans have a forceful word for this, *Entscheidung*, implying separating in two parts, from the verb *scheiden*, to separate. When you decide, you separate the potential alternatives, affirming the one and cutting off the other.

5.1 The Definition of Guilt. That is a very simple thought, but it forms the core of our definition of guilt, which in its most elemental sense is precisely *the awareness of irresponsible value negation.* Guilt is a form of awareness in which we are painfully conscious that we have said a tragic no to some valued relationship amid the process of attempting to say a self-actualizing yes to some other valued relationship.

That which makes a certain person feel guilty thus depends entirely upon his own unique ethical frame of reference. A thief might feel guilty that he cannot steal successfully. An anarchist might feel the burden of guilt simply by living in an ordered society. A pusher of dope might feel guilty that he could not make a sale to an innocent teen-ager. Whatever form guilt takes, however, it is always shaped by the contextual values at stake. Its essential definition is the awareness that one has failed to actualize a value considered necessary for his existence. This formal definition leaves wholly undecided the profound issue as to what values indeed are necessary for one's essential self-fulfillment.

5.2 Response and Reality. Guilt is not merely a generalized awareness that values are being lost, but the specific awareness that *my* values are being denied due to *my* irresponsible decision. Regret and remorse constitute other types of awareness of value negation which do not necessarily contain the dimension of irresponsibility. In contrast to regret, guilt involves value loss through my own decision. Although I may experience guilt over a situation in which other wills have set the conditions in which I had to make a bad choice, nevertheless there is ordinarily thought to be some element of willed behavior in any guilt-creating deed.

This leads me to comment more specifically on one pivotal term in the vocabulary of guilt: *irresponsibility,* or better, *non-re*-sponsibility, i.e., a lack of responsiveness to what is really there, what is actually being presented to us. Guilt remembers that it has failed to respond to the special, unrepeatable invitation to

47

value discovery in a given situation. Just as we will later define authenticity as full and open responsiveness to the moment, the readiness to receive and re-create what is given in the now, we must at this point define guilt as the awareness of some non-responsible action in which one has failed to answer the rich reality of situations which are now remembered as irretrievably past.

It should not miss the notice of the careful reader that our whole conception of responsibility is deeply bound up with a certain understanding of revelation. By *revelation* in a general sense, I mean that being discloses itself in time, freshly in every now, offering itself ever anew in distinctly contextual gifts and demands to be received and re-created.

Reality, which under this definition is the *now* face of revelation, is likewise a cardinal term in the vocabulary of guilt. For guilt is the awareness that one has failed to respond to *reality*, to what is *there* in the given context, to what is revealed in being now.

5.3 Inconsistency with Self-image. The picture I have of myself is intimately bound up with the values that render my existence meaningful. I define who I am essentially in terms of what I value most importantly. Every man lives in terms of some composite self-image, before which he is constantly measuring the adequacy of his behavior.

From time to time I must bear the pain of remembering myself as one who has denied the very values most closely identified with my self-image. Guilt may be sparely defined as the memory of some past action which is inconsistent with my present self-image. I experience guilt when I do something which is inconsistent with my picture of who I *am!*

Who am I? As a teacher I must carry the burden of remembering myself from time to time as a very inadequate teacher caught up in unteacherly moments in which it becomes quite clear to me that I am failing to actualize this self-image which I associate with my name. As a father I bear the memory of unfatherly moments which are inconsistent with my picture of myself as a father. As a friend I remember unfriendly occasions which

48

remind me of my inconsistency with my own self-image as a friend. So guilt strikes right at the heart of who I am. It asks me to *be who I am*. It forces upon my consciousness the discomfort of comparing my concrete actions with my self-image. Presumably in the interest of greater responsibility, it makes me restless with the terrible inconsistency between goal and deed.

But before we too hastily applaud the service which guilt renders, we should not forget what Karen Horney so ably showed, that the self's image of itself may be absurdly idealized, neurotically distorted, so that no actual behavior is ever good enough for its perfectionistic demands.[1] Under the compulsion of an idealized self-image, value conflicts are intensified, and even moderate value actualization is undermined.

The inconsistency of value actualization and self-idealization is forcefully portrayed in Shakespeare's arresting characterization of Lady Macbeth, whose circumstances have caught her in a passionate conflict of values. On the one hand, she desperately desires to be the queen, to have power, which was her way of viewing herself as a potentially valuable, honored person. On the other hand, we learn later that human life, which she has to sacrifice to the god of her ambitiousness, is also of tremendous value to her. When confronted with the moment of decision, when one or the other value must go, so overwhelming is her passion for glory that she puts the weight of her persuasive personality behind the assassination of the king.

The character portrayal of Lady Macbeth in the rest of the play centers on her compulsive awareness of her murderous deed, symbolized by blood on her hands. So intense is the burden of guilt that she hallucinates the focal symbol of the guilt-creating event. In her perception of herself as one who has destroyed life, she experiences profound self-loathing, a radical disjunction between her irresponsible act and her self-image. "All the perfumes of Arabia will not sweeten this little hand." [2] So acute is this crisis that she loses touch with reality and goes beyond the pale of the medical practice of the day.

[1] Horney, *NHG*, pp. 17 ff., 64 ff.
[2] II, *Macbeth*, Act V, Scene 1.

49

What one feels in guilt is that he is inconsistent with himself. The depth of that cleavage is the measurement of the intensity of guilt, which may differ widely with valuing persons and valued situations. A psychopath may murder his sister with only a twinge of guilt, whereas a wrongly dialed telephone number might be much more guilt-creating for another person who is passionately concerned with the correctness of his behavior. But whatever its situational content, guilt is always formally the awareness that what I have done is inconsistent with who I understand myself to be, that my image of myself is challenged by my own behavior.

5.4 The Pursuit of Good in Value Negation. If guilt involves value negation, however, we cannot deny the corollary argument that every time we commit an offense against some value, we are thereby attempting to choose some perceived good or aiming at some envisioned value. Even in a most heinous crime, such as premeditated murder, some good is sought. In his choice to take another's life, the murderer is attempting desperately to choose some other configuration of value which to his twisted vision seems circumstantially better—perhaps an intolerable obstacle is thought to be removed, or his consuming need for recognition is distortedly fulfilled, or some terrible wrong has allegedly been righted by his act. Seen exclusively from his internal standpoint, at the moment of his decision he is choosing some perceived value which to him is worth the terrible risk and cost of murder. So important is that value to him that he is willing to hazard being caught, imprisoned, hated by society, and perhaps even put to death. In every value-negating deed, therefore, some positive value is being sought, an argument whose formal statement may be classically found in Plato.[3]

6. Toward a Parallel Theory of Guilt and Anxiety

6.1 The Ontological Limits of Guilt. Traditional psychoanalysis has tended to view guilt as a subcategory of anxiety.

[3] *The Dialogues of Plato*, II, trans. B. Jowett (Random House, 1937), 343 ff.

Freud proposed that guilt had its origin in the anxiety of the child over the loss of the mother's love amid the threatening specter of the father's power.[4] Even the sharpest critics of the psychoanalytic interpretation of guilt, such as Mowrer, have nevertheless followed Freud in continuing to view guilt as merely a type of anxiety. Mowrer defines guilt as "the fear a person feels *after* having committed an act which is disapproved by the significant others in his life, before that act is detected or confessed. Guilt, in short, is the fear of being found out and punished."[5]

Against this whole line of thought espoused by Freud and his critics alike, I argue that guilt is of a fundamentally different genre from anxiety and in fact is its precise dialectical opposite, analogous in every major aspect. For guilt always refers through memory to something which is already past, just as anxiety always refers oppositely to some possibility which has not yet occurred. They function consistently with the curious parallelism of opposites. They work in opposite ways, one through memory, the other through imagination, to alert the self to possible or actual negations of value considered necessary to its existence. Although they move in opposite temporal directions, they function formally under the same logic. It is a wholly inadequate observation to see one as absorbed by another or to reduce guilt merely to a form of anxiety.

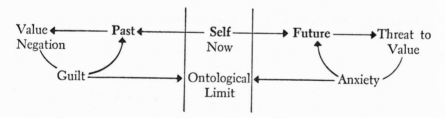

When the future is symbolized as a threat to value, one experiences anxiety; when the past is symbolized as a negation of value,

[4] Sigmund Freud, *A General Introduction to Psychoanalysis* (Washington Square Press, 1960), pp. 255 ff.; *The Problem of Anxiety* (W. W. Norton, 1936); *New Introductory Lectures in Psychoanalysis*, trans. James Strachey (W. W. Norton, 1965), pp. 113 ff.

[5] O. Hobart Mowrer, *The New Group Therapy* (Van Nostrand, 1964), p. 226.

one experiences guilt; but the ontological limit of both guilt and anxiety is the now; guilt can only indirectly penetrate to the future and anxiety can only indirectly penetrate into the past; guilt and anxiety function in directly parallel, analogous, dialectically opposite ways.

This observation can be tested by asking whether it is even possible to become anxious over a past occurrence. Strictly speaking, I think not, although this needs to be qualified as follows: admittedly one may become anxious over the future consequences of some past occurrence, but in that case the object of one's anxiety is again possibility, not actuality. One cannot anticipate the past. If anxiety is anticipation of threatening possibility, it may associate threat with a past event, but the source of the threat remains possibility. Its ontological limit is reached when future threats are exhausted.

Conversely, is it possible to experience guilt over a future (merely possible) situation? Strictly speaking, no. Again one may feel guilt over having imagined oneself in a possible value-negating circumstance, but in that case again guilt is directed toward the past, toward the *remembered* image of oneself as a potential value negator. One cannot remember the future. If guilt is, as we have described, the awareness of already actualized value negations, then it may be projected toward the future from the past, but in that case it is only in an indirect way oriented toward the future. Its ontological limit is reached when the claims of the past are exhausted.

Suppose I know a disturbed person who I think might commit suicide tomorrow. Already I feel guilty that I have not been able to help this person, and already I experience guilt over the anticipated suicide even though it has not yet occurred. In this case it is possible to feel indirectly guilty over an anticipated value negation, but only in the limited sense that it is a projection of remembered relationships toward the future. That over which one feels guilt remains one's past remembered relation with the neighbor. Thus, although it is possible to feel indirectly guilty over events which have not yet occurred, such guilt-associated possibilities are merely anticipated extensions of past relationships. They do not acknowledge the present or future as occasions for decision but assume that they are already fixed and bound by the past.

Thus, it is formally impossible to be anxious over something that is past. It is possible only to be anxious about its future consequences. Likewise it is formally impossible to be guilty about something that is still future. It is possible only to be guilty about past value negations. These are strict ontological limits of guilt and anxiety.

If so, it becomes an infinitely comforting thought [6] that one *cannot experience the pain of anxiety with reference to anything that is past even if one wanted to, and one cannot experience the pain of guilt toward anything that is still future, because of the ontological structure of human awareness.* Anxiety toward the past and guilt toward the future are logical, psychological, and ontological impossibilities. Persons suffering from guilt and anxiety have a right to understand the ontological limits of their tormentors.

6.2 The Anxiety-creating Consequences of Guilt. Hopefully having secured this point, we are now prepared to make another which seems to be in tension with it: *Anxiety is an inevitable consequence and companion of every guilt-creating deed.* Wherever there is remembered value negation, there lives alongside it the anxiety of being discovered as a value negator. Thus one must bear the dual burden not only of guilt but also of anxiety which centers in the threat of being perceived by another valuer as a negator of value.

Although anxiety and guilt can be distinguished, they cannot be separated. Anxiety follows upon guilt with dogged inevitability. For the valuing individual fears being discovered as a value negator by others who share these same cherished values. Consequently, a major preoccupation of the guilt sufferer is his corresponding battle with anxiety. The sufferer runs, hides, deceives, tries to prevent detection as a value negator. He may de-

---

[6] Cf. Søren Kierkegaard, *The Gospel of Suffering,* trans. David F. Swenson and Lillian M. Swenson (Augsburg, 1947).

THE STRUCTURE OF AWARENESS

velop elaborate strategies by which he can conceal his past from view.

This is why guilt tends not only to intensify anxiety, but also to erect subtle barriers toward others. Duplicity toward the neighbor and self-deception are two sides of the same game. In this way guilt becomes a seriously malignant force separating man from man. All of this occurs allegedly in the interest of the pursuit of the good and the attempt to live a virtuous life. Guilt drives us away from others into loneliness. Like criminals trying to escape the vision of the administrators of justice, we feel uncomfortable in the presence of others who might discover us as value destroyers.

From this point it is easy to see how guilt in very complex ways becomes bound up with other forms of the human predicament. For although guilt emerges essentially in one's dialogue with his past, it should not be forgotten that that past exists in a temporal continuum which intimately involves the shaping of the present and the anxieties of the future. So, although we have artificially abstracted guilt out of these relationships in order to examine it more deliberately, it in fact always exists enmeshed in complex future and current relationships which are always modifying its specific content.

6.3 Related Modes of Value Negation. There is a deep kinship between *guilt and grief* which has been noted by perceptive inquiries into the psychology of bereavement.[7] It is not accidental that in almost every grief situation there is some residue of guilt feeling. The reason: Both guilt and grief involve an intimate memory of the irretrievable loss of valued relationships.

Grief, like guilt, is a response to value loss. When a loved and valued person is totally removed by death from all further possibility of value transactions, one experiences intense value loss. But if guilt and grief are alike in their awareness of value loss, their difference lies in the fact that in guilt one understands himself as being in some way responsible for certain elements of the

[7] Paul E. Irion, *The Funeral and the Mourners* (Abingdon Press, 1954); Edgar N. Jackson, *Understanding Grief* (Abingdon Press, 1957).

loss. When another valued life is terminated by death, one suddenly becomes aware that there is no future possibility of redressing past wrongs. That is a part of the shock of death. Death is a final closing of the question of the possibility of rapprochement of estranged relationships. When an entire society experiences such a profound loss as we did in the case of the assassinations of John and Robert Kennedy, for example, it is understandable that we should all be inclined to raise the question of our corporate guilt and ask how our laws, our police, our attitudes, might have contributed to it or might have prevented it. Doubtless, in some vague or indirect way most all of us feel negligent and feel particular anger at those most negligent.

Guilt differs from regret, in that regret may refer to some event for which one has had no direct responsibility. I regret, for example, that India and Pakistan have been embroiled in bitter conflict. It is a regrettable situation, but I do not feel directly guilty or feel that I am a responsible party myself. Although I do not experience much direct personal guilt, however, I may feel a general sense of corporate participation in the destiny in which both India and Pakistan participate and in a sense share in the tragedy of the human situation in which they are enmeshed.[8]

7. Images of Guilt

7.1 Owing, Falling, Blaspheming, and Damaging. Every language has words that refer to the awareness of irresponsible value negation. In words from other languages which translate into English as "guilt," four images in particular recur:

The guilt-creating deed is like owing a debt. In fact, the Old English word for debt is *gilt.* Even today the German word for money is *Geld,* to which our term "gold" is closely related. There is a close linguistic kinship between the experience of guilt and the demand for payment of a debt. We can translate this etymological insight into our categories as follows: the self lives in terms of certain values to which it *owes* its significance, its meaning, its

[8] U.S. arms supplies to both parties make even this example debatable.

worth. The value I place upon my behavior is conditional according to my capacity to actualize these values. You might call them "conditions of worth," the basis upon which I judge myself to be a worthwhile person.

In effect, I make a contract with my center of values: I will be loyal to you, *provided* you will bestow upon my life beauty or significance or pleasure or some other desired good. If it happens later that I must negate that loyalty on behalf of some other potential value, then I find myself in debt, I owe something to myself which is unpaid, and life asks me to pay up.

The experience of guilt is like falling. The Greek *sphalma*, translated "guilt," has the connotation of losing one's balance and falling. A step is misjudged and the whole organism collapses. It is not only the Hebrew-Christian tradition which has spoken of the *fall* of man from his original condition of uprightness in the garden of paradise to the depths of demoralization, but also the very character of human language that intimately associates guilt with the image of falling. Guilt is essentially the awareness that one has fallen from one's exalted, idealized self-image. To the extent that the self-image is exaggerated, it is constantly vulnerable to this experience of falling into an awareness of one's inadequacies.

Guilt is like being blamed for wrongdoing. One of the most powerful visual images associated with the etymology of guilt is the notion of blame, which is made all the more interesting because of its kinship with the whole image of blaspheming (*blasphemein*, to speak ill of another). When we negate values broadly shared by others with whom we live, we feel the finger of blame shaking in our faces, as children experiencing the correction of their parents.

A guilt-creating event is like damaging something valuable. The Latin *noxia* and the Greek *enochos*, both of which translate into English as "guilty," convey the notion of damaging something valuable. A *noxious* act is one which is harmful, unwholesome, pernicious. It is in this connotation that we meet the notion of the destructive character of guilt, both to others and oneself, which we will develop later.

56

All four of these images—owing, falling, blaming, and damaging—are recurrent connotations in the etymological history of the concept of guilt.[9] Each image is implicit in our English word "guilt" and may be directly integrated into the special vocabulary we have employed in our discussion of the structure of guilt.

7.2 The Legal Image of Guilt. The rendering of the verdict of "guilty" by a court of law seems to be the principal model of our English usage of the term "guilt." [10] With the legal images so determinative for our vocabulary of guilt, it is appropriate that we take a special look at the means by which guilt is determined by our courts. If our previous discussion has suffered from the neglect of the discussion of "real" guilt, or objective guilt before publicly acknowledged standards of behavior, we now turn to the process of criminal prosecution as a resource for understanding guilt.

First of all, it is always under the *presumption of innocence* that the law proceeds, placing the burden of proof upon the prosecution to bring evidence of a criminal act. Even in the most heinous crime, "an accused is presumed to be innocent until his guilt is proved beyond a reasonable doubt by legal evidence in a fair trial." [11] "The presumption of innocence is a conclusion drawn by the law in favor of the accused, by virtue whereof, when brought to trial on a criminal charge, he must be acquitted, unless he is proved to be guilty, and the prosecution is required to introduce evidence establishing the guilt of the accused beyond a reasonable doubt. It is an artificial presumption both of fact and of law, which may not be ignored. It is founded on the first

[9] Gerhardt Kittel, *Theologisches Wörterbuch zum NT* (Verlag von W. Kohlhammer, 1949 ff.); C. D. Buck *et al.*, *A Dictionary of Selected Synonyms in the Principal Indo-European Languages* (University of Chicago Press, 1949); *Funk & Wagnalls Standard Dictionary of the English Language* (Funk & Wagnalls, 1961); *Oxford English Dictionary* (Oxford University Press, 1931), hereafter *OED.*

[10] Typical dictionary definitions are somewhat prepsychoanalytic in their emphasis upon the objective dimension of offense against law and in their neglect of interior and unconscious aspects of guilt feelings. The *Oxford English Dictionary* defines guilt as "the state of meriting condemnation and reproach of conscience, of having willfully committed an offense against some duty, law, or obligation."

[11] *Corpus Juris Secundum*, XXII, 893.

principles of justice, and is intended, not to protect the guilty, but to prevent, so far as human agencies can, the conviction of an innocent person." [12]

Significantly, our courts use the harsh term "guilty" only in criminal cases. The softer and yet more discriminating term *negligence* is used in all civil cases, which constitute the majority of litigations before our courts. The law is very reluctant to pronounce a man guilty and only does so after a detailed procedure of investigation and trial. Whereas criminal law is punitive, civil law is compensatory. Its task is not to punish but to compensate for damages to injured parties caused by the negligence (not the criminality) of a defendant. In civil cases, instead of rendering a verdict of guilty or not guilty, the court renders a judgment or a decision by which the court seeks a remedy for certain damages which have been determined from the facts. The judge interprets the law, the jury decides what were indeed the facts of the case upon hearing both the prosecution and defense. If the defendant is judged guilty, the next step is sentence to punishment, or if the defendant is judged civilly negligent, damages must be paid. After the punishment has been served, the guilt is canceled and the accused is free.

Through this linguistic exercise, comparing various images and models for understanding guilt through diverse cultural strata and historical traditions, I have attempted to sharpen a defensible definition of the structure of guilt. Upon this foundation, it is now possible to ask: How does guilt escalate in the sensitized conscience from the small deed to the heavy burden?

8. Paradigmatic Guilt

8.1 Minor Clues to Major Cleavages. A paradigm is a model. Seemingly insignificant events may become broadly symbolic of the total situation of man as value negator. What I am calling *paradigmatic guilt* is the awareness that some minor, other-

[12] *Ibid.*, pp. 894-95.

wise inconspicuous, deed has become sweepingly symbolic of one's total situation of persistent and abominable value negation:

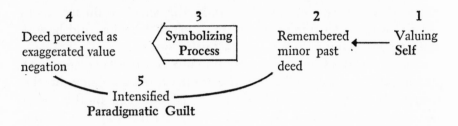

When the valuing self (1) remembers some past deed (2) as extravagantly symbolic (3) of major, continuing, irresponsible value negation (4), then that deed, however innocuous, escalates the awareness into intensified paradigmatic guilt (5). One minor event communicates an urgent message, reminding the self of its bungling of its whole existence.

Paradigmatic guilt is thus a situational symbolic focusing of the total human situation as if everything were burdened with inexorable and dreadful value negation, on the basis of an extrapolation from some more limited guilt-symbolizing deed. To a person acutely sensitive to idealized values and thus more vulnerable to paradigmatic guilt, almost anything can prick the conscience so sharply as to be temporarily immobilizing: an overdue bill, an approaching police car, the collection plate at church, a cool glance from the boss—you name it; any event in an instant can come to symbolize one's radical situation of value negation.

Paradigmatic guilt is the *sudden* dawning that, by George, I haven't done it! Or have done it! It has a sudden character because its symbolic impact hits the consciousness with instantaneous force, exploding in every direction to the ends of the cosmos. I remember a forgotten appointment which I had solemnly promised to keep (oh good grief!); I peel a parking ticket off my windshield, my third one this year (now I'm in for it!); again I am late mowing my grass, and again I will have to hear my neighbor call the place Tanganyika (oh my God!). In each case I am hit by the abrupt, staggering awareness that my behavior is inconsistent with my self-image. The paradigm only points beyond itself to what is really significant to me: the gulf between who I have been and who I ought to be. I need no dramatic occurrence to shout this message in my ears—only the small, ordinary, daily occurrences which remind me of my typical behavior, and how it fails to correspond with my idealized value system.

I suspect that *despair* over one's guilt is a regular component of all paradigmatic guilt. For the symbolic exaggeration of the minor deed into a major predicament is grounded in the vague awareness that things will probably always be this way. I will keep on breaking promises, keep on trying to beat parking meters, and keep on allowing my grass to grow to jungle proportions.

8.2 The Symbolizing Process. How one selects paradigms for guilt is wholly unique to one's own special value orientation. In every case, however, the symbolizing process tends to work overtime, exaggerating any minor flaw, on behalf of the need to improve one's behavior and make it match better one's self-image.

I happen to be a lousy fixer of things around the house. My dear wife and her entire family have always been expert, I would say almost professional, do-it-yourselfers. Whenever anything falls into disrepair, I am called (in very subtle and humane ways) to the bar of judgment. The law (in this case my wife) gives me the strong impression that I could use a little more imagination in keeping things working. I am keenly conscious of that law impinging upon me. But the truth is, I am not interested in mechanical nonsense—I'm far too busy doing more "important" things. The result is that even the most minor maintenance tasks, always delinquently undertaken, remind me of my stubborn neglect of responsible duties.

Fortunately I enjoy very good health, but whenever I am a bit sick so as to cut into my work time, I begin to feel miserably guilty, because I like to think of myself as an efficient, productive person. My whole self-image is built around the assumption that my fulfillment lies in the creation and sharing of meaningful ideas or helpful actions. But when I am cut off from this process of productive action, I am keenly aware that I am not being the person I ought to be. When I cannot fulfill my perfectionistic image of myself as a productive, active, meaning-bestowing human being, I feel guilty. Let even some minor incapacity, a rotten headache or a sprained ankle, slow down the pace of my activity, and I easily oversymbolize it as an intolerable neglect of my responsible commitments.

The symbolizing process works toward paradigmatic guilt in curious ways. My chronic occupational disease as a teacher is not wanting to hand back papers. Students have to wait till papers are yellowed and stale before seeing them again. The reason I do not return the papers is that I do not like to make these kinds of decisions, since it involves the pain of saying no to others for whom I care. It reminds me not only of the fact that my lectures are not getting through to them, but also that I am not a very self-confident decision-maker when it comes to fixing an academic judgment where criteria are often ambiguous. Furthermore, when I was a student, I greatly appreciated those few efficient professors who handed papers back promptly. When I decided to make teaching my profession, I made a conscious decision that I was going to get papers back on time, since that had meant so much to me. Well, here I am now, fairly deep in the ruts of a teaching role which is already locally famous for this minor form of irresponsibility. I receive a set of papers, set them on my desk, look at them for several days, hope they will go away, and only after much annoyance from students do I face the music and give them their marks. The moment of paradigmatic guilt for me is the instant a student knocks on the door and asks if the papers are graded. At that moment it seems as if I stand before the whole of heaven and earth condemned as guilty of persistent negligence.

8.3 The Unending Continuum. Human existence is literally an unending continuum of value choices and consequent value negations. One can find tragic value losses at any point where decisions are being made.

The fact that you are now reading assumes that you have had to say no to certain other valued relationships in order to actualize this one. Perhaps you have had to say no to your political party or to your children or to a sick friend in order to do what you are now doing. But you say those no's in order to say a single yes to time committed to your reading, in hope of some special form of value actualization known only to yourself. Suppose your telephone should now ring, calling you immediately to an undesirable but very important responsibility. You would have to lay down your reading in order to answer the call. If you value your reading intensely, then you might experience a tinge of regret or even guilt that a certain value had to be negated.

Human existence consists precisely of these kinds of value choices in an unbroken continuum. Responsible decision involves being awake to the real values at stake in any given context, being free to affirm and negate, being free to dare to make decisions, having the courage to make value denials, knowing already the deeper imperfection of all our affirmations and negations.

Guilt is painful inasmuch as it is ourselves saying no to ourselves with deep inner seriousness. In excess it will cause severe depression, withdrawal, and inner demoralization. With maturity we learn to protect our awareness from multiple simultaneous unfulfillable requirements. Although properly speaking no reasonable requirement ever demands more of us than we are able to fulfill, we imagine ourselves constantly under multiple demands which, if we fulfilled them all, would take an infinite amount of time each day to do adequately. When sixteen different demands impinge upon one narrow, frail moment, it is hard enough to meet just one of them, but often we feel constrained to bear the guilt for not meeting the other fifteen as well. I am not sixteen people, but only one person. I can say only one yes; so often I must say fifteen implicit no's within the limits of a particular moment. Reality calls us to the one yes, however much our disparate values may presume to require the other fifteen affirmations.

chapter III

THE IDOLATROUS INTENSIFICATION OF GUILT

Having argued that all men presuppose values which make their lives worthwhile, the negation of which causes guilt, it is now possible to show how the guilt-creating process becomes perverted in self-destructive directions. It is at this point that a major hinge in our argument turns on the concept of idolatry.

9. Idolatry Demythologized

The language of idolatry was born in a primitive cosmology which modern men find not only uncomfortable but inaccurate. It is understandable therefore that any talk of the "gods" causes confusion, since we assume that such talk belongs to a prescientific world view. But however remote the notion of idolatry may seem to modern man, I propose that its essential meaning is not only perennially germane to the analysis of human existence, but in fact is *necessary* in order to clarify the essential dynamics of guilt at its most profound level of operation. What follows therefore might be understood as a demythologized reappropriation of the ancient Hebrew command, "Thou shalt have no other gods," in this-worldly value categories.

9.1 The Difference Between a Value and a God. A god is a value elevated to ultimacy, imagined as a final source of meaning. A god is some ordinary, limited value which becomes necessary for one's self-justification. A *value* is anything in creation which is regarded as good, any idea, relation, object, or person in which I have an interest, from which is derived some pleasure or significance, or in relation to which I feel some sense of obligation. A *god* is an overvaluing of a limited value in such a way that it is regarded as pivotal for one's entire self-definition.

In short, *a god is a center of value by which other values are judged to be valuable.*[1] Anything can become a god. Any good thing in the created order is subject to potential idolatry. In fact, it must be good, or it is not even a candidate for idolatry. If it promises no fulfillment, it has no power to tempt us to worship it or order our lives around it. If education were not a profound source of human enrichment, then it could not become a source of idolatry; but precisely because it is of great value to us, it is subject to potential idolatry. If "the American way of life" were not a rich milieu for value actualization, then it could not become for us a source of idolatry; but precisely because it is of great value to many, it is most tempting for us to idolatrize it. If my relation to my mother were not an affectionate source of cherished good, it could not become an idolatry for me; but precisely because it is of great value to me, it is potentially subject to idolatry.

The difference between a value and a god is that a value is known to be a limited, creaturely good (subject to death and the erosion of time), whereas a god is regarded as a final and absolute source of good and is therefore worshiped, adored, and viewed as that without which one cannot receive life joyfully, that by which existence seems justified.

9.2 The Added Burden of Idolatry. The process of taking good things (education, America, art, a Porsche, the stock market,

---

[1] H. R. Niebuhr, "Faith in Gods and in God," *Radical Monotheism and Western Culture* (Harper, 1960), pp. 100-127, hereafter *RMWC*.

high ideals, the sales chart, the gang, etc.) and viewing them *as if* they were enduring and ultimate sources of value is crucial for understanding the deepening predicament of guilt. *For when we elevate limited values to the level of ultimate givers of meaning, we reinforce and increase the power of guilt.* Guilt becomes demonic, destructive, unmanageable, tyrannical.

Insofar as I regard limited, contextual values as *necessary* for my self-definition and yet fail to actualize precisely those values, I feel under the increasing, uncompromising pressure of demonic guilt. *Demonic* is another image borrowed from a prescientific cosmology which dramatically expresses the picture of being a captive to alien powers, being in bondage to mysterious forces seemingly outside my volition but which insidiously work to control my volition.[2] The deeply idolatrous person, who has persistently taken many finite goods and regarded them as ultimate meaning givers, is the most vulnerable to demonic, self-destructive guilt.

It is eminently appropriate that we describe guilt as a *burden,* inasmuch as we have no choice but to carry it around with us in our daily awareness, in addition to the weight of our daily tasks. It is as intimate to us as our very memory of ourselves. It is as heavy as our current memory of past value negations. The burden is the inner division we experience between our self-image and actual behavior. We cannot flee this cleavage, since it is our very selves. Only when we go deeply to sleep are we in some sense freed from the burden, but even then we are strangely still condemned to play out in fantasy our basic relationships of guilt and lost innocence.

9.3 The Demonic Reinforcement of Guilt. It is evident that a strictly nonreligious, phenomenological analysis of human awareness could reveal that the only way to deal effectively with intensifying guilt is to reduce the idolatrizing tendency, to not

[2] Paul Tillich, *Systematic Theology,* II (University of Chicago Press, 1957), 163-72, hereafter *ST.* Cf. Bultmann, "New Testament and Mythology," *Kerygma and Myth,* ed. H. W. Bartsch (S.P.C.K., 1957), hereafter *KM.*

overvalue limited values, or put differently, to obey the Hebrew's first commandment. It does not take any special religious language to show that. We could learn it from a Heidegger or a Horney in our time just as we might earlier have learned it from a Socrates or a Sophocles. Commonsense self-awareness can discover, as did Israel, that our centers of value are subject to idolatrous exaggeration and that they intensify guilt.

We learn from ordinary experience that our gods are vulnerable to the erosion of time. From time to time we are forced to give up values which we have regarded as absolutely crucial for our existence. Life takes them away from us. Any wise man whose face is weathered by time knows that all created things are like grass and flowers—alive today, withered tomorrow, as the ancient psalm so poignantly observes. The nations we love may collapse. The good health we have enjoyed may deteriorate. The children we adore grow up and sometimes reject us. The wealth we amass is vulnerable to depression and dissipation. *Life* is the teacher who constantly instructs us on the vulnerability of our gods.

Put differently, in a Hebraic style of imagery, God the creator, the giver of creaturely values, is a jealous God. He is jealous of *our gods!* We experience him as the slayer of our gods. All the goods of creation are finally to be received as what they are— limited, finite goods, not God. No matter how much I value my child, my social order, my economic ideology, my technological comforts, my ideals and norms, I find that everything in the temporal order has the character of being given and being taken away. If I pretend these values are unlimited, I live under a dangerous, self-destructive, and tenuous illusion.

But it is just under such an illusion that idolatrous guilt proceeds to its slippery and disastrous consequences. *For the more we make an idolatry out of limited values, the more powerfully and demonically is guilt reinforced.* We must live with increasing inner division and the internal burden of escalating guilt. When relative values are taken with absolute seriousness, the demonic grip of guilt is intensified, and we find ourselves in human bondage.

10. Constructive and Destructive Guilt

But is all guilt disruptive and unhealthy? Have we spoken of guilt as if it were only a deteriorating force in human existence? Is it always? Does it not provide certain creative functions for the developing self, without which one would be engulfed in miserable and unbridled value negation?

10.1 The Healing Function of Guilt. It is only now that I am prepared to make a long-delayed but crucial distinction between constructive and destructive guilt. For the irritating awareness of value negation may be a constructive force in the growing self, and guilt is not necessarily evil, harmful, and destructive. The distinction between constructive and destructive guilt is directly parallel to the distinction just made between values and gods.

Through its painful prodding, memory alerts the self to the consequences of continued value negation and strives to redirect its efforts toward increased value actualization. Normal or constructive guilt is the constant pressure which the self places upon itself for improved functioning. Although it is painful and causes inner division, it is good and necessary, and without it the self would sink deeper into the mire of its predicament of choosing poorly. The self needs this stinging reminder that valued relationships are still valuable even though negated. Conscience is the call to authenticity, as Heidegger has rightly said, even though it is preoccupied with making us aware of our inauthenticity.

10.2 The Malaise of Conscience. When does the guiltcreating function of conscience become unhealthy, distorted, and dysfunctional? *Precisely to the extent that limited values are elevated to ultimacy, they increasingly exert a demonic, self-destructive force upon the consciousness.* Demonic is a mythic way of talking about a relationship which, although at one time may have been freely chosen, now has come to lay hold of the volition as if it were an outside power, an alien force, which determines the will toward inauthenticity and destructiveness. As idolatry is in-

67

THE STRUCTURE OF GUILT

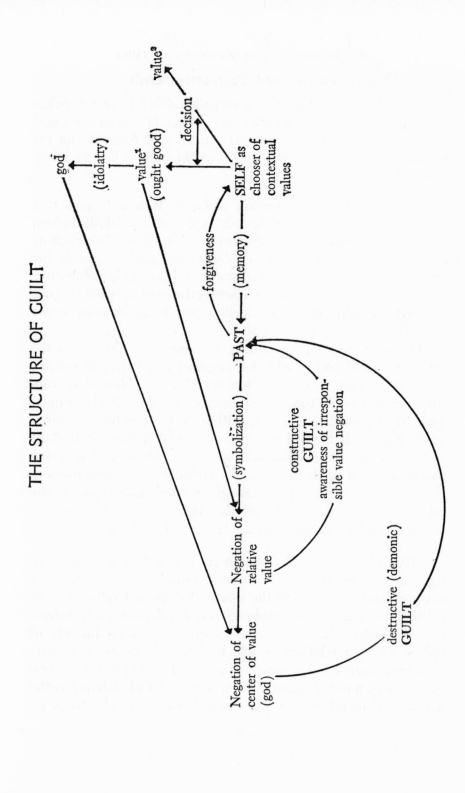

creasingly reinforced through repeated decisions, it tends to grow to compulsive and gargantuan proportions, gets out of hand, and this is what is meant by demonic.

Thus what was intended to be a constructive force comes to exert compulsive, tyrannical power within the self, racking us with inner torment, keeping us from actualizing the very values we idolatrize, depressing us with the unrelieved burden of unresolved guilt. Neurotic guilt is just this destructive form of guilt which has finally manifested itself in symptoms which curb normal functioning, attacking at subversive levels of distorted awareness, crippling rather than improving value actualization.

10.3 Proportional Valuing. To learn to value limited, created, finite goods without idolatrizing them is to let guilt function in its most constructive and normal pattern, so that negated values may be judged in a spirit of proportionality, or judged according to their real value. But the question then becomes: What is their real value? By what measure are relative values to be appropriately valued? The question cannot be answered abstractly or nonsituationally, but only concretely, contextually.

In a formal sense it must be minimally stated that on the one hand no finite good is ever absolute, and on the other hand no finite good is ever entirely valueless. We can at least reject the two extremes by which finite goods are either absolutely valued or absolutely disvalued. Learning the art of making conscientious, discriminative, contextual value choices, as the experienced shopper in the market does, is a major part of what we call maturity or healthy self-actualization.

Much overly idealistic thinking, especially of the moralistic bent, keeps on prodding us to overestimate certain values, ideals, rules, moral injunctions, categorical imperatives—to an infinite degree. It is impossible for the feminist to value women's rights highly enough; it is impossible for the prohibitionist to value sobriety highly enough; it is impossible for the racial activist to value minority progress highly enough; it is impossible for a superpatriot to value patriotism highly enough; so that in each case any other values are viewed as relatively less significant. Christian preaching, somewhat confused and unsure of exactly what it is called to be and do, has often become entrapped by just such idealisms and moralisms, so that many have erroneously come to think of preaching itself as merely the attempt to heighten and intensify the level of one's valuing of selective ideals.

Am I then put in the curious position of asking my hearer merely to value good things a little less? Am I calling for a reduction of the intensity of guilt by a general devaluating of the currency of acknowledged ideals, so as to live a bit more comfortably with an easy conscience? That would miss the point. Although I argue that no finite relationship is of infinite value, it does not follow that I am thereby taking an ascetic or Buddhist view that the source of happiness lies simply in the *reduction of desire*. All ascetic strategies for achieving happiness center in the subjugation of the desires, the mortification of the flesh, the de-escalation of all values so as not to allow the loss of any one to become the source of disappointment. Accordingly, the less one values, the happier he is.

Quite the contrary, I am proposing that love, desire, and appreciation of limited values be adjusted (whether increased or decreased) to the measure of their own real contextual value. I certainly am not arbitrarily calling for a devaluation of all goods merely as a preventive measure against disappointment. I am asking that persons and goods be valued in terms of their real, contextual, finite, historical, and therefore relative value. I am calling for a *love* of good things with an awareness that they exist within the boundaries of finitude and therefore under the judgment of the giver and source of all value.

In fact, as long as one is trapped by the overvaluing, idealizing tendency, it is not possible truly to celebrate even the elemental goodness of creation. For idolatry is not a genuine valuing of goods, but an overvaluing of them so as to miss the richness of their actual, finite value. If, for example, I adore and worship my tennis trophy, my child, or my bank account, then I do not really receive the valued relationship for what it actually is as a limited, historical, finite good which is vulnerable to being taken away from me by time and death. I pretend that it is something

70

more than it is, and thus I value it less appropriately than it deserves. I am not therefore proposing an attitude of cynical, uniform disvaluation of created goods, but rather of genuine valuing of goods at their appropriate proportional, situational value.

10.4 Guilt as Inevitable but Not Necessary. It is just in connection with this distinction between constructive and destructive guilt that I wish to focus upon a very knotty perplexity, which if left neglected could undermine the entire argument, particularly at the crucial point of the nature of human freedom. I have been speaking as if guilt were a universal human phenomenon. The question emerges: If guilt is inevitable, is man's freedom therefore predetermined or necessitated to value negation? Is guilt predestined by the temporality of awareness?

I answer: Guilt is inevitable, but not necessary. I am following a rich tradition of anthropological reflection from Augustine and Calvin through Kierkegaard and Tillich, but best represented in recent times by Reinhold Niebuhr's Gifford Lectures.[3] Although I will not develop this theme in detail, four points deserve special notice:

(a) *The awareness of value negation is a universal and inevitable implication of the temporality of human awareness.* To choose any value is to negate others. Guilt, in this sense, is the inevitable consequence of human freedom. I have affirmed the constructive function of guilt which calls the self to the bar of judgment in order to redirect it to renewed efforts at value actualization.

(b) The more pressing question becomes: Is destructive, demonic guilt universal and inevitable? Here we follow the fine line suggested by Niebuhr. Self-deceptive, idolatrous, demonic forms of guilt are only present insofar as idolatry is present. But is idolatry universal and inevitable? It should be perfectly clear that idolatry, as we have defined it, is not necessitated by the very structure of man's created being. Consequently, *demonic guilt is not necessitated by the very structure of man's creation.* It is

[3] Niebuhr, *The Nature and Destiny of Man* (Scribner's, 1949), pp. 241 ff., hereafter *NDM*.

chosen. Man himself, despite powerful social and environmental determinants, remains in some measure responsible. Man is not *by nature* consigned to demonic, idolatrous guilt. That would be an unbearable embarrassment to any cosmology which essentially affirms the creation as good (Gen. 1–2).

(c) Man's propensity to idolatry seems to lead him into temptations which make demonic forms of guilt a persistent and, to my observation, universally experienced dimension of human existence.[4] *Although freedom is never from the outset strictly predetermined to idolatrous guilt, it chooses modes of reliance which inevitably make idolatrous guilt the self-chosen fate of man.* Of course, such idolatry is not actually a genuine expression of man's authentic freedom, but finally a denial of it. Authentic freedom would be to live a nonidolatrous life of value actualization without self-idealization, an existence for which the Christian community in its own way hopes. But idolatry is never properly understood as an expression of the true nature of man or a part of the essential structure of his existence, but always as a denial of his true nature. Thus if demonic guilt appears to be everywhere observable in the human scene, it is only a regrettable witness to the vulnerability of man's freedom, but it cannot be asserted as a necessary dimension of the structure of man's freedom without a grave misunderstanding of the human predicament.

(d) Man can only be guilty over that for which he is first responsible. There is no guilt without responsibility. But the decisive question unclarified by that affirmation is: What do you mean by "man"? An isolated individual or a participator in the social processes of history? Just as man cannot be viewed realistically as an abstract individual, likewise *responsibility cannot be understood individualistically, as if a single man were abstractly accountable apart from his historical context.* Just as the Judeo-Christian tradition has spoken of the sin of "Adam" (mankind as a whole), so has social psychology spoken of the human predicament in terms of the social transmission of distorted forms of con-

[4] Niebuhr, *NDM*, pp. 251 ff.; cf. Tillich, *St*, II, 31 ff.; Bultmann, *KM*, pp. 2 ff.; *Theology of the New Testament*, I, trans. Kendrick Grobel (Scribner's, 1952), 232 ff., hereafter *TNT*.

sciousness and ideology. Likewise we must now learn to view guilt in complex ways as a corporate as well as an individual matter, rejecting the simplistic notion that guilt can ever be unambiguously or unilaterally assigned to a single individual.[5] Since each individual participates in an environmental context which is always already distorted by guilt, which tempts him into further value negations, we must assert the universality of guilt in every nook and cranny of human history, as an unnecessitated, self-determined corporate denial of genuine human freedom and community.

11. Stratagems of Self-deception

11.1 Masking Self-perception. A curious aspect of the dynamics of idolatrous guilt is its tendency to conceal its trail, to lead directly toward mounting self-deception and distortions in awareness. Why does guilt become so embroiled in self-deceptive strategies?

Precisely to the degree to which one has exaggerated his self-image, he finds it necessary to protect himself from realistic appraisals of his value negations. The last thing he wants to know in full, sharp awareness is his failure to actualize his self-image. So all sorts of tricks and deceptions must be employed in order to prevent full self-recognition. Psychotherapy may help us to see the subtle, subterranean operations of deceptive guilt. The essence of the therapeutic process has even been described as similar to the role of a detective in pursuit of the evidence for the crime.[6]

Guilt which has been pushed out of awareness, however, comes back in more destructive ways through the back door of neurotic symptoms. It may come in disguise in asthma, migraine headaches, and other psychosomatic illnesses. We "punish ourselves," so to speak, with physical pain. Plato rightly observed that the guilty soul "runs to meet its judge." Punishment, even un-

[5] Thomas C. Oden, "The Alleged Structural Inconsistency in Bultmann," *The Journal of Religion*, XLIV (1964), 197-98.
[6] O. Hobart Mowrer, *The Crisis in Psychiatry and Religion* (Van Nostrand, 1961), pp. 86 ff.

consciously administered, seems to atone for the guilt and reconcile us with the internalized values against which we have offended.

11.2 The Exaggerative Tendency. One reason why the trail of guilt is so difficult to track is that it often is directed toward no specific deed, but only generally toward the past. Just as anxiety (as contrasted with fear) does not have an object, guilt likewise is often experienced as a vague and diffuse sense of value loss, without being tied to identifiable times and places.

Closely connected with this generalizing propensity of guilt is another curious feature, the tendency of the guilty memory deliberately to search out the most damaging, horrifying experiences, the deepest breaches of value, the most rending remembrances of value negation, to hold up before the present awareness. Neurotic guilt scans the horizons of the past seeking out the most deplorable, hideous, and culpable acts which are least consistent with one's self-image to call to the attention of the self (analogous to the tendency of idolatrous anxiety to seek out the worst conceivable possibilities in order continually to alert the whole organism to danger). To the extent that values are idolatrized, it is understandable that there is a consequent tendency to oversymbolize value negation. Powerfully motivated, the guilty memory seems to display an unquenchable lust for the most regrettable paradigmatic abuses which most sharply symbolize the denial of the basic self-image.

11.3 Axiotherapy. The Greek *axios* refers to value, or that which has worth. *Therapeia* is also a Greek word referring to a skillful, helping service rendered to one in need. *Axiotherapy* would be a therapeutic service which is rendered to the valuing self, which brings to awareness the value structure itself out of which guilt emerges and directs it toward fuller functioning. It is evident, from what has been said, that the person suffering under intensive forms of guilt stands in need of something like this, an axiotherapy which would enable a basic reappraisal of the idolatrized values which intensify demonic guilt.

To help another guilty man, one must first be sensitive to the universality of guilt, its structure, its subtlety and deceptiveness, and its dynamics in his own personality. Only when one is freed to bring his own distortions into awareness is it possible for him to nurture in another the capacity openly to bring these distortions into awareness.

Then one must learn to identify the values or gods which are at stake in a guilt-creating situation. Only when the values or gods lurking behind guilt can be identified is the individual free to choose whether or not he wants to regard them as such.

A central facet of effective therapy is thus the process of becoming clearly aware of just what it is that one actually values. It is only on this basis that one can choose anew what he wishes to value. The therapist's task is not so much to give the individual values, but to free him to choose how he is to value, to put him in a context in which he can think through his value negations, and to help him work through conflicts between various values which impinge upon him simultaneously.

There is a sense in which if I understand what you value, at the deepest level, I understand you. If you understand where my values center and what values I choose to negate, you understand who I am. This is an intimate sense in which I am what I value. To learn through empathetic imagination to understand another person's structure of values and to help him to see it too is to become a therapeutic agent. Axiotherapy may be defined as any interpersonal encounter which gives special attention to clarifying the specific values at stake in any troublesome situation, ask how they are functioning or dysfunctioning in relation to the long-range fulfillment of the self, and how they might be open for review and behavioral change.

12. The Neonate Prototype of Innocence

I have not dealt with guilt in developmental terms, i.e., its genesis and development through varying stages of the child's growth, since that can all be found easily enough in textbooks in developmental psychology. Before leaving the subject of guilt, however, I do have some observations on the genesis of guilt in the neonate (the newborn), which will serve as a means of transition from this chapter on guilt to the following chapters on the ontology of forgiveness.

12.1 The Priority of Innocence. Our thesis in this section is that *the prototype of innocence is the neonate situation, prior to the development of memory and acculturation.* The original condition of man, the predevelopmental or primordial situation of consciousness, is one of total lack of awareness of value negation and thus one of radical guiltlessness.

In most Western languages the opposite of guilt is innocence. In Latin *noxius* (guilt) is the antonym of *innocens,* and both derive from the same root, just as in German *Schuld* (guilt) has its opposite in *Unschuld* (innocence). It is a curious etymological fact that the notion of innocence in many different languages bears a connotation of harmlessness, naïveté, credulousness, simplicity, and even foolishness, so as to imply that a state of innocence is lacking not only in guilt but also in knowledge—knowledge of oneself and of the nature of things.

My essential argument may be stated in the form of a syllogism: (first premise) If guilt is the awareness of irresponsible value negation; (second premise) and if there is a stage of development prior to value awareness; (conclusion) then there is a stage of development prior to guilt. Although there may be a limited sense in which a knowledge of guilt is prior to the idea of innocence, in every other sense *innocence is ontologically, psychologically, chronologically, and logically prior to guilt.*

Consequently guilt must be learned. *Innocence, in the sense of unawareness of irresponsible value negation, is unlearned, native, natural, spontaneous behavior for the neonate, whereas guilt can only emerge in human consciousness after a lengthy and complex learning process of value internalization.* Innocence, therefore, is given in and with the organism itself, and is the natural condition of the organism in its most primitive chronological sense. Although this observation has been long expressed in theological

76

symbolism, it has been too long neglected by empirical observation.

Into the primordial embryonic situation of innocence, the intrusion of birth occurs. The environment is radically mutated. Prior to the disengagement of the umbilical cord, there was no independent, self-determining past. *Suddenly, with birth, the self begins to have a past and to exist in relation to its past!* Some form of protomemory may extend back into the embryonic stage. But with birth begins the conscious, personal history of the organism, which moves increasingly toward self-direction, acculturation, memory, responsibility, and guilt.

It has already been persuasively argued that the newborn organism is a reliable model for healthy psychic functioning (Rogers).[7] I wish to inquire whether and how the neonate model for health might be related to the neonate prototype of innocence.

Although at present this exercise is still proceeding strictly in a phenomenological fashion, without deliberate theological assumptions, we cannot fail to note certain theological analogies which might under other methodological procedures be explored. One pivotal text, upon which our whole discussion might be viewed as an extended commentary, is the messianic injunction: "Unless you change your whole outlook and become like little children you will never enter the kingdom of Heaven" (Matt. 18: 3 Phillips). To put the issue of that text in current language, we are asking how human self-actualization and authenticity (entering the kingdom) are analogous to the process of turning again (*metanoia*) and becoming repatterned after the neonate model of health and radical self-acceptance. The neonate is open to his experience, astonishingly so. There is no self-deception, no distortion in awareness as with intensified guilt. If the infant experiences the loss of some desired value, he expresses his feelings loudly. He does not conceal his feelings from himself, as later the guilty self learns to hide certain feelings from awareness.

[7] Carl Rogers, OBP, pp. 391 ff.; "Toward a Modern Approach to Values," *Journal of Abnormal and Social Psychology*, LXVIII (1964), 180 ff., hereafter TMAV.

12.2 The Radical Parental Verdict of Unconditional Pardon. We are seeking to identify, if possible, the basic transition from this innocent and open experiencing to the burden of developed guilt. How does the organism "fall" developmentally from innocence to guilt?

The neonate finds himself in the presence of persons who seem to affirm him radically and value him unconditionally. It is only on this basis that he learns to venture, to trust, to explore his environment. Let us express this with a juridical image: *The neonate is freed to move toward the frightening environment of reality-testing on the basis of what he perceives to be a total, overarching juridical verdict of pardon for all his inadequacies.* If such an unconditional pardon is not there, or if he does not perceive it as being there, he is crippled and unable to receive the world trustingly. If it is there, there is nothing the child can do which could cancel it out or undermine it. Not all, but many new parents are unbelievably accepting of the inconvenient behaviors of their newborn offspring. If a six-year-old were to slobber, yell at 3:00 A.M., or wet his bed, he would be in real trouble. But not a new baby—*it seems as though absolutely nothing he does is wrong!* The verdict of pardon seems unconditional.

Only subsequently, after a prolonged period of living under this radical verdict of pardon, does the growing infant learn to discriminate and internalize various values. Later, as the process of acculturation and value assimilation proceeds, he develops a self-image largely shaped by learned, introjected values.[8] It is only on the basis of this slow developmental process that the conditions for guilt emerge. At a much later stage he learns that the pain of value negation causes him to feel a deep split in himself, so that he must finally learn to distort his awareness of guilt in order to preserve his idealized self-image. He then learns to cast out of awareness events which otherwise earlier would have been acknowledged and received into awareness. The dynamics of guilt

[8] Rogers, *TMAV*; cf. Rogers, "A Theory of Therapy, Personality, and Interpersonal Relationships, as Developed in the Client-Centered Framework," *Psychology: A Study of a Science*, ed. Sigmund Koch (McGraw-Hill, 1959), III, 184 ff.; hereafter *PSS*.

only then become problematic and destructive, when the symbolization of experience is no longer congruent with his experienced feelings. Finally, elaborate defensive strategies must be erected to protect these distortions in symbolization. Depth psychology shows the difficulty of reconstituting this tangled web of self-deception, evasion, and hardened defenses.

12.3 The Limit of Phenomenology. Having delienated the fall of the organism from neonate innocence to guilt, we now ask this question: How is it possible to recover what was lost? How does one regain the capacity for receiving the environment ever afresh without the crippling burden of self-deception? Or if recovery of lost innocence is not possible, what might at least partially unloose the self from the rigidities of demonic guilt? Upon what grounds might a new self-affirmation be achieved in spite of one's negations? How does one become free to embrace his past if the past is clearly unacceptable in terms of his presupposed norms and values? This is the point at which psychotherapy begins its task.

It seems evident that it is only possible actually and wholeheartedly to accept the past if it is actually acceptable! But who is to say what is *really* acceptable? An individual by himself, or his friends, or his social history, or his cultural environment? It is here that a phenomenology of guilt tends to run its course. Here it encounters its limit. Here we propose, from a theological commitment, that the past is really acceptable only if it has made itself known as acceptable. The meaning of that must be explored in greater depth. We seem to be coming to the end of our phenomenological study of guilt, only to reach the edge of a profound theological issue, the solution of which is crucial for any further development.

There is no solution to the problem of guilt if the past *is* in fact unacceptable, if the past in fact *is* the permanent concretion of negated values upon which our human well-being truly depends. A clearheaded phenomenology knows its own limits. There is in fact no solution short of a cosmic, juridical verdict by which the past reveals itself as reconstituted or re-formed by some trans-

79

historical power or cosmic volition. Genuine self-acceptance is possible only on the basis of the fact that the past *is* in fact acceptable and has made itself unambiguously known as such. If the past *is* actually forgiven, however, it would be better for our sakes if it made itself known as such in a way which did not invite our further irresponsibility, license, and lawlessness, but rather communicated to us the pardoning nature of temporal reality with profound constraints upon us to future responsible action.

It would be quite cheap and easy here to say that it is precisely of such a verdict that the New Testament proclamation speaks. Already I am overstepping the bounds of a strictly phenomenological investigation to frame the question in this way. But this is precisely the direction toward which a thoroughgoing phenomenology of guilt moves. To explore this in greater detail is the task of the next chapter, where my method of inquiry decisively shifts to theological assumptions.

12.4 The Therapeutic Analogue of Justification. Before making this methodological transition, however, it is relevant to ask these questions: What can we learn from the process of secular psychotherapy about man's own heroic battle against demonic forms of guilt? How does it happen that persons who have been ensnared by neurotic guilt patterns come by means of psychotherapy to increased self-actualization and self-direction? What makes for constructive behavioral change in the therapy of guilt?

In effective psychotherapy the individual finds himself in a situation in which his own organismic valuing process is radically trusted by another person. He experiences the unconditional positive regard of another congruent human being.[9] The healing of demonic guilt is made possible when someone enters empathetically into his frame of reference, supports his efforts to unravel his wretched distortions in awareness, receives and clarifies them. Only then does he increasingly experience the capacity to embrace his own organismic experiencing process. Effective psychotherapy frees the individual from the burden of demonic guilt, not by

[9] Rogers, *PSS, passim.*

making him innocent, but by freeing him to accept his lack of innocence and to act within the tragic ambiguities of his own personal history without the crippling deceptions of idolatrous guilt.

Thus, in psychotherapy interpersonal dialogue proceeds on the basis of a juridical verdict which in some ways is much like the good parents' verdict of pardon. A context is created in which all feelings and behavioral expressions are brought into accepting awareness. Strictly speaking, the distortions of value are not accepted: only the distorting person is accepted. According to the most varied practitioners (Freudian, Rogerian, or behaviorist), the therapeutic process would not function well at all if it did not in some sense nurture an interpersonal context in which all repressed and distorted experiences are permitted to be freshly received into awareness. Psychotherapy thus strives in a sense symbolically and proleptically to regain the fallen innocence, to find its way back through the flaming swords of Eden to a recapitulation of the primitive paradisiac situation of neonate innocence.

12.5 The Implicit Ontological Assumption of Therapeutic Acceptance. What one learns while undergoing effective psychotherapy is not that another person accepts his value system, but that he is valued as a person even amid his past value negations. But the learning of that cannot happen merely as an idea— it must happen in a living relationship in which another person actually mediates to him such unconditional positive regard that its impact comes through to keen awareness. Clearly we are not speaking of the therapeutic effect of the *idea* of acceptance, but only of the concrete *relationship* in which I find myself radically and thoroughly accepted and understood amid my twisted self-awareness by one who trusts his own organism and mine.

Hidden underneath this therapeutic acceptance is the implicit ontological assumption that *being itself* is accepting, that reality is not just a void, nonrelating, nonintentional surd, but that reality itself in some sense is reaching out to affirm and support the healing process. In order to be effective, psychotherapy must in some sense mediate an active acceptance rooted in reality itself. If it fails here, it does not reach its deepest intention. It is not finally the therapist himself as a person who is the source of acceptance. He is only a mediator of an acceptance present and self-revealed in reality itself. He is only performing the representative ministry of making that accepting reality known and felt in a specific interpersonal relationship.[10]

If this is so, then there is no real ontological need—that is, no need in being itself—for destructive and demonic guilt. One is constantly being freed by being itself to embrace the past. If this is so, then to live as if we were necessarily enslaved to neurotic guilt feelings is therefore to live under an absurd assumption which has lost touch with the center of reality itself.

The final step of our argument on the structure of guilt leads us directly to the theological analysis which we are now about to undertake. For it is precisely this implicit ontological assumption that reality is accepting which is made explicit in the Christian proclamation concerning the forgiving verdict of God in the Christ event. Christian worship celebrates and Christian preaching announces a radical once-for-all divine verdict of pardon which has been rendered upon the totality of history. If so, it is now not only possible but necessary to conceive of the past in a new way. A new birth of memory is permitted and demanded. It is now possible to relate oneself anew to the past because the past is not what one at first thought it to be. It *is* something quite different. In reality it exists under a juridical divine verdict of pardon.

---

[10] Thomas C. Oden, *Kerygma and Counseling: Toward a Covenant Ontology for Secular Psychotherapy* (Westminster Press, 1966), ch. 1.

chapter IV

THE ONTOLOGICAL IMPOSSIBILITY OF GUILT BEFORE GOD

13. The Vulnerability of Theological Language

13.1 From Phenomenology to Theology. Everything I have said to this point can be derived from an experiential, psychological analysis of human awareness. Very little could not be echoed as well by a strict empiricist, a Hindu, or an ethical humanist whose eyes were open to his own experiencing self-awareness. But I have now come to the point of a major transition. I am no longer concerned to examine the phenomenon of guilt from the viewpoint of *man's self-perception.* From now on, I am trying to view guilt from an entirely different point of view, viz., *God's perception of man,* as it is witnessed to by the Judeo-Christian tradition.

If heretofore I have been delineating a humanistic, existential (*Daseins-*) ontology, simply describing man's special way of being in the world, I am now attempting to develop something quite different: *a covenant ontology* which would inquire into man's being as he exists before God. The preceding discussion has assumed that the self-aware man is capable of analyzing and understanding, without deliberate appeal to any alleged divine revelation, much of the essential, formal structure of his own experience. A covenant ontology works in an essentially different direction, attempting to grasp the being of man from the vantage point of his being grasped by the love, judgment, and grace of God, who allegedly makes himself known in history. So this is indeed a major transition, not only in the content of the argument, but in methodology as well, from phenomenological to theological inquiry. Instead of exploring the way man *experiences* reality, we are now inquiring into that *reality* which man in fact actually experiences, as it is understood by a particular community of discourse, the Judeo-Christian tradition.

Quite candidly, this new direction involves immense hazards which were not disturbing to our previous inquiry. For I am now presuming to speak not merely about the structure of man's awareness of reality, but instead about the structure of reality itself, which may or may not be adequately appropriated by human awareness. Such an audacious project is vulnerable to all sorts of perplexities and limitations and perhaps is from the beginning doomed to only partial success, and that only in the minds of a few. For I am alleging as a Judeo-Christian consensus that reality itself is finally clarified only in the light of God's self-disclosure, which appears through scandalously historical events in the history of a particular people.

So I am prepared to admit the immense difficulty of the task at hand. In this sphere we are constantly vulnerable to the charge, probably never to be adequately answered, that our language about God actually does not refer to anything and therefore does not finally mean anything.[1] Why then do I persist in pursuing an inquiry into the alleged actual situation of man in the light of God's action, which has only a meager prospect of success? Precisely because I am persuaded that the truth of the human situation is adequately revealed only through such an effort and that only by reference to the self-disclosure of being itself is being really knowable and therefore man's being really under-

[1] Paul van Buren, *The Secular Meaning of the Gospel* (Macmillan, 1963), pp. 13 ff., 81 ff.

standable. If human responsibility finally means responding to reality, we cannot endlessly neglect the question of the meaning of *reality* in favor of the more tame question of the empirical, phenomenological study of self-awareness.

13.2 The Possibility of Knowledge of God. But how can we presume to speak or know about God? Really to come clean on this question would involve spelling out an entire theory of religious knowledge, a prolegomenon to Christian doctrine. Admittedly I cannot in this context treat of all the relevant questions which such a prolegomenon might entail since that would require a time-consuming diversion from the central thrust of the argument. But a brief and modest outline of my theological method deserves to be clarified, and it involves these focal points:

The Judeo-Christian tradition is a community of worship and witness which unapologetically proceeds on the assumption, rightly or wrongly, that God is making himself known. As the Hebraic tradition remembers and celebrates the exodus event as the focal act of deliverance through which the covenant God makes himself known, Christian worship remembers and celebrates the events surrounding the life, ministry, death, and resurrection of Jesus of Nazareth as the focal constellation of events through which God makes himself known. In these pivotal events of exodus and messianic fulfillment this tradition has come to see not only the meaning of universal history mirrored more adequately, but the very reality in which we stand, so much so that no human question is left unrevolutionized by this upheaval in all human reflection. That revolution indeed is what theology is all about: the attempt self-consistently to clarify the meaning of God's self-disclosure as it illuminates the human predicament and possibility.

We know nothing of God except and until he makes himself known. Just as I can know nothing of you (except perhaps a few externally reportable facts) unless you decide to reveal yourself to me, or to speak to me some word about yourself which discloses who you are, likewise we know nothing about God if he

THE STRUCTURE OF AWARENESS

does not disclose himself to us.[2] If he is truly and adequately known as the giver and ground of being, it is only because he has made and is making himself known as such. If he is known as love, it is only because he has made himself known in loving deeds. If he is known as a covenant God, it is only because he has made himself knowable through covenant relationships.[3]

Doubtless a frustrating obstacle in our path is the predictable revulsion of many perceptive individuals toward all this seemingly archaic talk of revelation. I intend to be wholly aboveboard in clarifying *the* pivotal presupposition out of which the ensuing theological argument is now to proceed. Any Christian discussion of God can speak only of the God who has made himself known. Christian faith does not worship a God for whom it still is searching, but it lives out of the assumption of its being found by God. Thus Christian theology, which is the servant of the worshiping, witnessing community, is not out looking for God, but proceeds boldly upon the unconcealed presupposition of its being already addressed by God. It now finds itself searching for means of self-consistently expressing its being found. It is, after all, a *fides quaerens intellectum*, a faith which is questing for intelligibility.[4]

In honestly setting forth this presupposition, however, I am not proceeding any differently than would any science which proceeds from certain axioms and postulates which heuristically enable the inquiry to proceed. No keen scientific mind would argue that scientific reflection proceeds without such elemental assumptions (concerning causality, the reliability of sense experience, etc.) which have the same unproven logical character formally as the Judeo-Christian presupposition that God has made himself known.

The task of Christian theology is to reflect self-consistently upon the Christian faith, faith being understood as man's af-

[2] Oden, *KC*, pp. 41-46.
[3] Martin Luther, *Works of Martin Luther*, II (Muhlenberg Press, 1943), 351 ff.; John Calvin, *Institutes of the Christian Religion*, I (James Clarke & Co., 1953), 50 ff.; Karl Barth, *Church Dogmatics*, I/1 (T. & T. Clark, 1936-62), 11 ff., hereafter *CD*.
[4] Karl Barth, *Anselm: Fides Quaerens Intellectum*, trans. Ian W. Robertson (Meridian Books; World, 1962).

firmative response to the self-disclosure of God in the Christ event. Faith can only be understood from its own center, since it is a response to an event which is only meaningful in the full sense to those who respond to it.[5] Theology differs from phenomenology, which is concerned to clarify the concrete contents of consciousness. For theology seeks rather to clarify faith's understanding of the particular idea of God peculiar to the Christian community, the idea of God as revealed in Jesus Christ. Since faith understands itself not as existing on its own initiative but only as response to something which has gone before it, viz., revelation, then in order to grasp the meaning of faith one must come to grips with the revelation to which faith witnesses. If revelation appears in history, then faith must always be traditioned through a witnessing and worshiping community which acts, wisely or foolishly, as the guardian of the authenticity of that tradition.

Although Christian faith celebrates God's self-disclosure in nature and history generally, it does not regard either nature or history as synonymous with revelation. For in neither nature nor in history is the will and purpose of God unambiguously disclosed.[6] In order more sensitively to perceive the self-presentation of God in nature and history, the Christian faith invites men first to encounter it in an alleged once-for-all event of divine self-disclosure in Jesus Christ. At its best, Christian theology does not pretend to speak of any other God than that God who is made known in the history of the people of Israel and the Christ event.

13.3 Four Sources of Theological Authority. My authority for speaking of God therefore is fourfold: *scriptural* truth *experienced* in life, made intelligible and self-consistent through

---

[5] Gustaf Aulen, *The Faith of the Christian Church*, trans. Eric H. Wahlstrom and G. Everett Arden (Muhlenberg Press, 1948), pp. 3 ff.

[6] Since history is not finished, it is difficult to see its total meaning without some end-time event which anticipatively reveals the meaning of the whole. Here, despite my continued use of the language of faith as response to revelation, I see great merit in the proposal of Wolfhart Pannenberg, *Offenbarung als Geschichte* (Vandenhoeck & Ruprecht, 1963), that God's revelation is expressed in the totality of universal history, the end of which is proleptically anticipated in the resurrection.

reasoning, and mediated through the historic Christian *tradition.*[7] All talk about God in the Christian community is called to be responsible to these four criteria. Each exists in responsive dialogue with the alleged self-disclosure of God. None exists wholesomely without the correctives and balancing features of the others. It is only through a *traditioning* community that faith hears and responds to the word of God. The writing and canonizing of *Scripture* is itself the act of a traditioning community. The witness of Scripture and tradition becomes intelligible, however, only when symbolized in terms that are *experientially* meaningful to oneself and others and only when one self-consistently *reasons* about them.[8]

Thus we cannot focus our affirmations about the self-disclosure of God exclusively upon narrow scriptural literalism (fundamentalism), nor upon an ambiguous ecclesiastical or cultic tradition, however rich, which would claim to have an infallible interpretation of it (ecclesiastical archaism), nor strictly upon our own capacity to make sense out of it or order it into a self-consistent whole (rationalism), nor upon merely our experiencing the benefits of it (pietism). To focus upon one resource so as to exclude the others is to subvert a wholesome theological method.

13.4 Decision and Proof. So we are proceeding candidly with the special assumption that God has made himself known. Who says so? Finally *I* must take responsibility for saying so, but I do so with the companionship of a whole community of men spanning most of the cultural varieties of mankind and twenty centuries of history. Christian faith is not just a private judgment, although it certainly and unavoidably is a personal decision and commitment upon which one stakes his fundamental self-understanding.

But could it all be based upon a hoax? Yes. It is possible that Christian faith is a gigantic conspiracy or mockery. But this is just

---

[7] Cf. Albert C. Outler, ed., *John Wesley* (Oxford University Press, 1964), Introduction ; Oden, *KC,* pp. 31 ff.

[8] World Council of Churches, Commission on Faith and Order, *The Old and the New in the Church: Two Interim Reports: Tradition and Traditions, Institutionalism and Unity* (Augsburg, 1962).

where a whole community of men have been willing to take a risk. Christian preaching announces the promises of God. Every hearer finally has to decide for himself whether these promises are in fact true.

Do we then finally have no proof? We must ask, proof in what sense? Our way of looking at the world is always molded by the community of discourse in which we live or in some community of self-understanding. Christian faith exists in such a community, just as the Marxist participates in a community of ideological discourse, the artist lives amid a community of aesthetic meanings, and the scientist lives out of a venerable scientific tradition. If you ask for proof, you ask for verifiability in terms of some tradition of discourse, some community of understanding. Since we grow up in different communities of discourse, we appeal to different criteria for truth. It is in this way that Christian discourse, not differing from scientific or aesthetic discourse, lives primarily out of a community of commonly shared meanings based upon Scripture, tradition, reason, and experience.

But could not all of these ideas about God merely be, as Feuerbach said, a projection of our own needs? [9] There is much truth in that. Most of our ideas about God *are* merely human wishes. But the Christian faith begins with the audacious assumption that God has in fact revealed *himself* precisely *against* our illusions about him! It is on *his* initiative that the Christian community has been called forth to witness to *him*, not merely our preconceptions about him.

14. Being Unconditionally Valued amid Value Negations

14.1 The Judeo-Christian Contribution. Our focus now is not generally upon the larger question of God's encounter with history, however, but more specifically upon the relevance of God's pardoning verdict for a personal reassessment of the past and guilt. How does the Judeo-Christian memory of God's

[9] Ludwig A. Feuerbach, *The Essence of Christianity,* trans. George Eliot (Harper, 1957).

forgiveness, God's alleged canceling of the human indebtedness of sin, present us with a radical new possibility for reconceiving the very being of the past? And what might this have to say about the reality of guilt? For if it should be the case that God himself has acted so as to take up an attitude toward the total cosmic past, or if it should happen that the divine verdict has in effect reconstituted the past or juridically reestablished the goodness of the past, despite its distortions and value negations, then what might that conceivably mean for my reconceptualizing of my own experience of guilt?

My central thesis: *No man can avoid being forgiven by the God who elects to love the world in Jesus Christ.* The same thesis may be formed in several ways: It belongs to man's being to be forgiven by God. Divine pardon is elemental to the human condition. Man cannot be otherwise than forgiven by God, if God determines to forgive. If such a pardoning verdict is addressed to all humanity, then forgiveness belongs to human existence as such and cannot finally be negated by human rejection or misunderstanding of it. From God's point of view we are forgiven, whether we know it or not, and whether we receive it or not. This is the thesis which we will attempt to support and clarify exegetically.

In demythologized language this means: *We are being unconditionally valued by the giver of values amid our value negations.* Christian worship celebrates and Christian proclamation announces a delivering action of God in which we have come to know that we are being prized, positively affirmed, received, and accepted by the source and slayer of all finite goods, even and precisely amid the most intensive consciousness that we have negated certain valued relationships in order to actualize others.

14.2 The Event of Pardon. The Christian community does not merely teach the *idea* that we are being valued despite our value negations. It celebrates and proclaims a particular historical *event* in which we are once and for all unconditionally valued amid our value negations. Valued by whom? By the ground of reality itself. By the unconditioned source and end of all finite values. The *idea* of being unconditionally valued amid our value negations can only be developed understandably on the basis of some actual relationship to being or some *occurrence* in which we are concretely, unconditionally, as a matter of fact *valued* amid our value negations!

Man's subjectively experienced situation, from his own self-perception, may be as one who *feels* profoundly guilty before his own negated values and gods; but his ontological condition, the way he *is*, from the point of view of the ground and giver of values, is one of existing in an established and unnegatable covenant with an unconditioned valuer. I am distinguishing sharply between how man *feels* about himself (the phenomenological chapters I-III) and who he *is* from the vantage point of the divine verdict (the theological chapters IV-V). However clearly or unclearly man may perceive himself, he is perceived by God, according to the Christian kerygma, as a pardoned man. He is forgiven, ontologically, despite the tenacity of his subjective guilt feeling. Ironically, therefore, the human predicament consists in man's failure to *be who he is*.

How does forgiveness enable freedom from demonic, self-destructive guilt? If the action of God frees us from idolatry, it frees us from the very wellspring of demonic guilt. But how are we freed from idolatry? By being shown that the one who gives both creaturehood and finitude, and finally the one who takes it all away in death and destruction, has made himself known as trustworthy. If I am unconditionally valued amid my value negations, I am enabled to determine myself more freely toward situational values. The self-deceptive rigidities under which guilt has carried on its clandestine operations are themselves undermined.

The pardoned man is in a sense *liberated to fail* without intolerable damage to his total self-understanding; free to be inadequate, free to foul things up, and yet affirm himself in a more basic sense than the moralist or idealist can affirm himself amid his value negation. He is free to be a man who chooses and negates values, free to take guilt upon himself and to see it as an inevitable and constructive part of his human condition.

I have now come to the threshold of my fundamental proposal on the healing of guilt, not previously possible on the basis of pure phenomenological observation, but only now possible as a specifically kerygmatic affirmation.[10] It is set forth not as a finished systematic statement but instead as a heuristic exercise intended to lead to further inquiry, a proposal open to review, and one which deliberately welcomes further critical clarification.

15. Guilt Exists Only Before the Gods

15.1 The Ground of Guilt. Our essential affirmation is that *man cannot be guilty before God, but only before the gods.* Inasmuch as God has chosen to regard the whole fallen cosmos from the vantage point of its participation in Jesus Christ, according to Scripture, man *is* not guilty and cannot be if God chooses to take this guilt upon himself. That is our proposition. However much man may be idolatrous, his idolatry is only an attempted negation of what he truly *is* before God—a value negator whose negations are judged and negated by the forgiving remembrance of God.

Two penetrating biblical analogies grasp this understanding of imputed righteousness:

(1) It is as if mankind were standing before the judge in the End Time, deserving condemnation. But surprisingly, the judge himself is judged in our place! We are clothed in *his own* righteousness, enshrouded by his cloak, regarded *as if* we were covered by his imputed goodness! [11]

(2) Or, it is as if we were at a wedding. An unrighteous bride (a harlot) is being married to a fine, upstanding, respectable young bridegroom! The harlot (humanity) receives as a gift all the righteousness of the respectable groom (the messianic servant) *as if* it were her own. Likewise, before the source and end of

---

[10] My distinction between phenomenology and kerygma follows the general pattern of Bultmann's distinction between *Daseinsanalyse* and the kerygma. Cf. "Die Geschichtlichkeit des Daseins und der Glaube: Antwort an Gerhardt Kuhlmann," *Zeitschrift für Theologie und Kirche*, XI (1930), 339-64; "The New Testament and Mythology," *KM*; *Jesus Christ and Mythology* (Scribner's, 1958); also Schubert M. Ogden, "Bultmann's Project of Demythologization and the Problem of Theology and Philosophy," *The Journal of Religion*, XXXVII (1957), 156 ff.; Oden, *Radical Obedience* (Westminster Press, 1964), chs. 3 and 4.

[11] Ps. 132:9; Matt. 27; Mark 15; Eph. 6:10-17; Barth, *CD*, IV/1, 211 ff.

values, the creator and judge of history, our guilt is regarded *as if* it were absorbed and redeemed by the righteousness of the bridegroom, Christ.[12] The center of all classical theories of the atonement is: God himself takes our place, takes our guilt upon himself.

15.2 The New Ontological Status of Guilt Feelings. What status does my past value negation now have? What ontological reality does it possess before God, however I might happen to feel about it? Does my awareness of value negation now have any legitimate ground in being? It is wiped away, canceled out, X-ed off the ledger. One of the principal nuances of "forgiveness" in Greek is to X-out or to cross off a payment from the creditor's books.[13]

If so, *the psychological experience of demonic guilt feelings is now perceived to be rooted in an ontological impossibility.*[14] However much I may experience destructive guilt, before God it is impossible to *be* guilty. I may *feel* guilty before my gods, but I cannot *be* guilty before God. Insofar as I continue to feel demonic guilt, I am living out an illusion and embodying an absurdity.

In the light of the divine pardoning verdict, what can I now say about the ontological status of time past? Has the past really been changed? Have value negations actually been wiped out or obliterated from history? Or are they merely "not counted" against the negator? Are they remembered *as if* they had not been done? Does the memory of God affirmatively embrace the negated value, or finally obliterate it?

In one sense, the past has not changed; only our perception of it has changed. The past has always as a matter of fact been objectively received into the forgiving memory of God. The Christ event did not in that sense *change* the will of God, but rather it more clearly expressed his eternal will toward the totality of history. For the New Testament reads history both forward and back-

[12] Hos. 3:1–4:19; Matt. 25:1-13; Mark 2:18-22.
[13] *The Interpreter's Dictionary of the Bible* (Abingdon Press, 1962).
[14] For what follows I am deeply indebted to Karl Barth, *CD*, III.

ward from the Christ event. This is the meaning of the penetrating emphasis of the developing New Testament tradition on the preexistent *logos:* The Word of God exists before creation and time, but manifests itself once for all in time.[15] Thus it is in response to the kerygma that I grasp what the past has been for God from the beginning. Whereas I had been imagining that the past is composed of immutable value negations which could only be mourned, now all things are seen as embraced by the memory of God.

From this indicative there follows an imperative: Whatever God allows to be received into his memory, I am called freely, within the limits of my finitude, to receive in my memory. Anything that God affirms, I am free to affirm. Whatever God forgives, I can forgive. Thus we have the kernel of an ethic of self-affirmation based upon the analogy of faith.[16] The basis of one's affirmation of the past is the divine affirmation of it. That does not mean that the past has suddenly changed objectively or become "unpassed," but rather what has changed is my inadequate perception of the reality of the past.

15.3 The Temptation to License. Up to a certain point, this means I am being offered the freedom to negate values, to ignore certain responsibilities in favor of others, to deny many goods in order that the one situational good might be actualized. In a sense this is what the New Testament authorizes with its ringing affirmation that Christ is the end of the law, the end of self-destructive attitudes toward exalted duties and idealized requirements which prevent one from loving the neighbor where he is.[17] The Christian life is an embodiment of this *freedom to deny* certain good things in the service of receiving and creating other goods, and in that way directing oneself ever anew toward self-actualization and responsiveness to reality.

Responsive Christian freedom thus celebrates the negations

[15] Rom. 3:21 ff.; Eph. 2–4; Col. 2; Heb. 1–3.
[16] Barth, *CD*, I/1, 279 ff.; II/1, 223 ff.; Oden, *KC*, ch. 3.
[17] Thielicke, *Theological Ethics*, pp. 51 ff.; Paul Lehmann, *Ethics in a Christian Context* (Harper, 1963), Part I; Søren Kierkegaard, *Works of Love*, trans. David F. Swenson and Lillian M. Swenson (Princeton University Press, 1946).

of value as well as its affirmations. The mother who says no to her child's overdependency and yes to her own humanity and adulthood is not only free to say no but to celebrate that negation, however painful, as a part of a larger affirmation. The student whose responsible political activities have cost him study time may take a failure on a quiz without a disastrous scar to his whole self-understanding, freely affirming the failure as consistent with a broader self-understanding which regards neither the political process nor the academic mark as a final value by which other values are ultimately to be judged. The productive businessman whose only joy has been the creation of wealth finds himself freed under the forgiving word to value himself in spite of his occasional lack of productivity and learns to say an occasional no to his business in order to say another contextual yes to his family, civic order, friends, or to his own health.

Much supposed freedom, however, is nothing but a deeper entanglement in the guilt-creating process of idolatry, and finally a denial of genuine freedom. Genuine freedom means total organismic responsiveness to one's environment (which is to say the revelation of being in the now) with its inevitable consequences of value negation. Forgiveness functions so importantly as a liberating force in that process that it seems incredible that man can do without it.

But are we thus opening the door to lying, thievery, sexual license, and the indiscriminate subversion of human values, under the clever guise of divine forgiveness? Shall we sin that grace may abound (not a new question for Christian liberty)? How can we establish safeguards against the trampling of certain valued relationships or principles without exalting them to absolutes? Genuine freedom needs such safeguards and, in fact, fights hard to protect them. When freedom is turned into sheer irresponsible license in the name of self-actualization, it tends toward self-destructive anarchy. It becomes undisciplined and therefore unspontaneous, spurious freedom. The distinction between evangelical freedom and *antinomian* (irresponsible, anti-legal, anarchic-pseudofreedom) has been wrestled with for many theological generations, from Paul to Occam to Kierkegaard to Bultmann.

95

Minimally it must be said that genuine evangelical freedom exists amid covenant co-humanity with the neighbor and therefore exists in responsibility to him, and thus in grateful acknowledgment of the social and legal structures through which the neighbor's interests are protected. If the word of forgiveness becomes an invitation to libertarian irresponsibility so as to ignore and dehumanize the neighbor, then one has never understood himself to be grasped by the infinite forgiving love of God, since he himself does not in any significant way embody and mediate that love.[18]

With a strong emphasis upon self-affirmation, admittedly my argument stands in tension with a stronger tradition in Christian history which has regarded *self-denial* as the most responsible basis for a relation with the neighbor. There is a certain judicious wisdom in the mainstream tradition of self-denial which should not be overlooked, since it constantly warns against the temptation of self-affirmation to pride, self-idealization, and the neglect of the love of God and neighbor. Under the persuasive tutelage of recent behavioral sciences, especially psychotherapy and social psychology (as well as Scripture), however, I have taken the position (which seems to me the deeper intention of that mainstream) that the most open and accountable relation to the neighbor does not take place on the basis of self-negation or a reduction of self-esteem, but on the basis of a more profound self-affirmation rooted in the reality of God's own affirmation.

15.4 The Legitimate Renegotiation of Contracts. If the principal cause of demonic guilt is the idolatrizing process, with its self-deceptive distortions in awareness and exaggerations of value loss, then an antidote to idolatry would go a long way toward resolving demonic guilt. Of course something quite good always motivates idolatry, or at least something that contextually seems to be good. For the idolater has some cherished relationship, something deeply loved, viewed as an enduring value, which

---

[18] Rom. 6, 12, 13; Jas. 2–4; I John 3–4; Luther, "Treatise on Good Works," I, 173 ff.; Calvin, *Institutes*, Book II, pp. 208 ff.; Bultmann, *TNT*, pp. 327 ff., 428 ff.; Barth, *Community, State and Church* (Anchor Books; Doubleday, 1960), pp. 71 ff.

appears to be so necessary for self-fulfillment that all other po-tential values come to be judged by that one value, and all other relationships temporarily revolve around that one relationship.

The divine judgment and pardon relativizes all contextual values, however, and consequently relativizes demonic guilt by showing us the vulnerability of our gods and by reintroducing us to the basic fact of our finitude. This is profoundly healing. To the idealistic moralist this relativization of value may sound as if God were being viewed as the enemy of man's higher loyalties. There is some truth in that. Indeed, God may be against my highest finite loves and aspirations. But only the forgiveness of God frees me to celebrate even my value negations in the aware-ness that all created things are as grass, i.e., of relative value and subject to passing and death.

Idolatry is a subtle *transaction*[19] between my self and its cherished value, in which I tacitly agree to absolutize the relative good, *provided* it will render some sort of ultimate benefit. But suppose I learn that fulfillment is possible *without* that idol-atrized value? Would that not be a revolutionary assault upon guilt? What if I learn that this particular idolatrized value does *not* in fact render my life ultimately meaningful? This is precisely what the self learns in due time under the pedagogy of the judg-ment and forgiveness of God. With the unconditional pardon of God, the self is unexpectedly liberated to *renegotiate its contracts* with all values and gods, which previously had been considered unnegotiable. Under the power of the forgiving word it is learned that nothing in finite history is to be named God, and that there-fore certain idolatrous contracts with their guilt-creating tentacles can now justly be abrogated. One is free to shop the market of situational values and learn anew to buy, create, sell, and receive new value possibilities in newly emerging contexts.

But I have not yet reached to the most decisive phase of the revolution effected upon guilt by divine forgiveness. For through our idolatry *we* ourselves had hoped to be valued, or to find *our-selves* affirmable as persons! We had trusted our gods to deliver

[19] Eric Berne, *Transactional Analysis in Psychotherapy* (Grove Press, 1961), pp. 83 ff.

us into some genuine self-affirmation in which we ourselves would be actually accounted worthy and valuable.

Suppose, however, that I should find that I myself am valued just as myself, and not for the values I create or receive, and wholly apart from my gods! Suppose that I discover that I am in fact positively regarded, unconditionally loved, even in spite of the failure of these cherished values and absolutized relationships to render their promised benefits! That would indeed be a remarkably liberating force against the bondage of my idolatry. It would make my desperate quest for self-affirmation through idolatry quite absurd, outmoded, and simply no longer desirable because of its vulnerabilities. That is precisely what the New Testament alleges as having occurred in the salvation event.

15.5 Rethinking the Distinction Between Sin and Guilt. Sin is the missing of the mark of my authentic humanity. Sin is my failure to respond to reality and therefore irresponsibility (or disobedience) to the concrete self-disclosure of God. Guilt, on the other hand, is the *awareness* that I have been missing the mark which I have set for myself, that I have been failing to achieve the authenticity for which I strive.

In my sin I am guilty of not being who I am. Guilty before whom? Myself and my gods. I would be utterly guilty before God himself, if he had not chosen to forgive me, to take my place, to render a verdict of pardon for me. But upon that *if* hinges the force of the evangelical witness. For even and precisely amid our failures to actualize values we regard as ultimate, God himself, according to the New Testament, continues to perceive us *as if* we were clothed in his own righteousness. The Reformation formula, *simul peccator et justus*, means: I *am* a sinner, deserving condemnation for my idolatry; but from God's point of view, I am *at the same time* pardoned, regarded as if the charge against me were canceled! The final verdict is thus not one which I give myself or the one that may be given in the courts of law or gossip, but which God himself decides about my situation, how he regards and perceives me. Through God's own incomparable initiative, man's sin is not remembered against him, even though he may remember it against himself.

It might seem that the fifty-first psalm constitutes a major exegetical embarrassment to our whole line of argument, since it insists:

> For I know my transgressions,
>   and my sin is ever before me.
> *Against thee, thee only, have I sinned,*
>   and done that which is evil in thy sight. (vss. 3, 4)

Does not Scripture therefore witness against our assertion of the impossibility of guilt before God?

However challenging the text might at first seem to our argument, upon close inspection our formulation receives support even from this unexpected quarter, since: (1) Confession of sin in psalm 51 is already based upon the clear awareness that the judging God is none other than the covenant God of "steadfast love" (v. 1), who has already made himself known as "abundantly merciful" (v. 2). (2) "Against thee, thee only, have I sinned" means that in our idolatry we have indeed sinned against God. Our argument has no quarrel with that. Following the previous distinction between sin and guilt, it is precisely *in spite of* our sin against God that we are regarded by him as forgiven. The psalm does not say "against thee only am I guilty," but "against thee, thee only, have I *sinned*." Whether one is guilty before God is exclusively for God to judge. He has allegedly done so in the Christ event.

My sin in creating idols is admittedly a sin against God, and finally *only* against God. For ultimately I am accountable only to him and never finally to my gods. But this in no way subverts God's decision to view me as clothed in the righteousness of Christ, a righteousness which is imputed as sheer gift. God's verdict of forgiveness is rendered not upon the righteous, but precisely upon the sinner! For the well have no need of a physician, remarked Jesus ironically, but only the sick (Mark 2:17).

God's pardoning verdict is not merely an empty possibility

which we may or may not actualize, but is already in the most radical and universal sense an *actuality!* It is only on the basis of forgiveness being an actuality that it can truly become a possibility for us. In the Christ event the forgiving intention of reality is made known once for all as an established presence. Whether we hear it or not, it is rendered. Whether we order our lives in terms of it or not, it is the proper center of all our life ordering.

16. Anticipating Objections

16.1 The Wrath of God. Are we suggesting that the source and end of values simply condones everything in history, that there is no divine negation, that there exists in history a sentimental God who loves us despite all our stupidity and duplicity? That surely would be an invitation to irresponsibility.

God's judgment and wrath are directed not against the value negator himself, but the spurious gods which he worships, the values themselves which have become overvalued, or more accurately the idolatrous process by which certain good values themselves have become misvalued. God hates the gods. He is a jealous God.[20] God does not hate the finite values as such—they are his own gift and therefore good insofar as they are received as relative, finite, limited goods. The wrath of God is not directed against values or persons as such, but against the idolatrous self-assertiveness through which persons attempt to embody the stubborn illusion that they are not finite recipients of infinite love.

All talk about the wrath of God in the Bible intends to express the determination of God to undercut our gods, to slay our idolatries, to show the vulnerability of these exalted values.[21] Because God hates sin, he determines to call man back to his authentic being as covenant man. He wants man to be who he is. He hates for his covenant partner to be self-deceiving, unloving, unforgiving, and therefore irresponsive to reality itself. He grieves when man tries to affirm the ontologically impossible, to live absurdly as if he were not loved. The wrath of God is directed

[20] Exod. 20:5; Deut. 4:24; 6:15; Ps. 79:5.
[21] Job 19–21; Ps. 78; 88; 90; Isa. 51:17-22; Jer. 10; Ezek. 20.

against that illusion. The pardon of God is not sentimental romanticism or libertinism.

16.2 Real Guilt. Admittedly my discussion has focused primarily upon subjectively experienced guilt feelings instead of "real" guilt. Have I intentionally avoided objective judgments about actual offenses against socially accepted values? Already I have referred to the elaborate judicial process which shows the difficulty of assigning real guilt, in a public and legal sense. But is this all I have to say? Don't I have some modest judgment to render about whether a person can really be guilty or not? [22] Obviously I must ask in reply: Guilty before what? I answer: Before one's values, certainly. Before the gods, yes. Before God, no.

I am not arguing that there is no real guilt, but merely guilt feelings. Rather, all men are really guilty before their gods, and live constantly amid the tragic, illusive, self-deceptive, burden of that real guilt, which causes them to withdraw from human intimacy for fear of being perceived as value negators.

[22] This question cannot be adequately dealt with without reference to the contribution of O. Hobart Mowrer, who has emerged from the tradition of behaviorist psychology and learning theory with the astonishing conclusion that neurosis is the result of "real guilt," against Freudian views that guilt is merely a psychological function of the super-ego. In *The Crisis in Psychiatry and Religion*, Mowrer has confronted Protestant pastoral care as well as psychotherapy with a serious accusation of unmitigated irresponsibility for capitulating to the Freudian view that guilt is not real. Neurosis has been compounded. Psychoanalysis has increased our problems. Ministers are in part to blame for not fulfilling their historic function of providing some sort of constructive context for guilt-awareness, confession, and penance.

It is granted even by psychoanalytic therapists that guilt *can* cause certain personality disorders. Mowrer's question is whether all neurosis is *always* caused by real guilt over real sin. This is his importance. He argues that all psychotic behavior is an unconscious pursuit of punishment, to find some way of atoning for sin, if only through the disgrace often connected with being psychotic. The depressed are something like men serving time. He argues that the reason why electric shock treatment is partially successful is merely that it aids the painful work of expiation and gives the neurotic a feeling that he is paying for his sins. The only real sacrifice of most talk therapy is having to pay the bill, and that may be its greatest validity—as an act of penance.

Mowrer's importance for us lies in the fact that he has framed, from a behaviorist point of view, the problem of confession in an utterly new way. Under his terms the role of the therapeutic agent is essentially that of a prosecutor. At one point he quotes a hospitalized paranoic-schizophrenic who describes the most helpful form of therapy to him as a "Dick Tracy theory of therapy": going after the lawbreaker, finding him out, exposing his guilt. The prosecutor-detective-therapist ferrets out the

But there is one thing that is not finally possible for man: to negate the forgiveness of God, to escape the gracious covenant which circumscribes his existence, to relieve himself of the constraint of the friendly divine verdict. He cannot run away from that, because he cannot run away from himself. God continues to renew the covenant even when it is from our side broken or neglected. That is the story of Israel and, symbolically, of all humanity. When the people of Israel are disobedient, the judging covenant lord delivers them into captivity as an expression of his covenant love, in order to call them back into an awareness of their covenant freedom. From time to time the people indeed do actualize the covenant relation from their side in faith and obedience, but they remain a covenant people whether in idolatry, bondage, or faith. There is a sense in which, as the ancient fathers said, *grace is irresistible,* viz., the sense that it cannot from our side be destroyed, even though it can from our side be unreceived.

It could be seriously objected that it is possible to be loved

crime, above all *not* affirming him in his transgressions in a Rogerian fashion, but rejecting him, assuming that he is guilty and approaching him from the standpoint of "we are going to find out why." Therapy proceeds by digging away, discovering, and accusing the individual of his crime. The noncommunicative indifference of the psychotic is a deliberate attempt to prevent others from knowing his guilt. Psychosis is the cultivation of a lie. The psychotic learns to baffle his pursuers. Unpredictability is his stock in trade. His approximate goal is to avoid being understood. His ultimate goal is to avoid punishment. He is not a sick man, but a "crook" of "no mean thesbian ability." His basic norm: "Thou shalt not get caught."

Such a theory of therapy is, of course, precisely contrary to much of the Rogerian approach which I have been following, which would free the client to tell his lie by permissive empathy and unconditional positive regard. What interests me is the implied theology behind this understanding of therapy. Mowrer says he does not want to get into the "tedious" theological debate as to whether salvation is by grace or good works. That is the whole issue. When he states elsewhere (p. 102) that "for myself . . . I personally take my stand with the Apostle James and Dietrich Bonhoeffer as against the Apostle Paul and Martin Luther," he thinks he means that he has taken his stand for good works against justification by grace, but how little he understands that free grace is as central to Bonhoeffer as Luther, and good works as important for Paul as they were for James. Mowrer gives lip service to Bonhoeffer, but what Mowrer calls costly grace might ultimately be little more than costly moralism.

The essential theological failure of this view is that it develops a high doctrine of sin with a low Christology. In traditional Christian thought the most serious views of sin are possible only in relation to a serious view of God's taking responsibility for sin (Augustine, Calvin, Barth). There is in Mowrer no real concern for forgiveness, only moral right, confession, and restitution. At that level, however, he has much to contribute to Protestant pastoral care.

by another and reject this love by not receiving it. If this is so, then perhaps in our freedom we *can* say no to God's forgiving love, and thus finally destroy the covenant relationship. However plausible this may seem, we must quarrel even with the implication that one can destroy genuine love by rejecting or ignoring it. For it is possible for someone to value you and you not even know it. Even when the beloved refuses to acknowledge the existence of the lover, it still might in no sense change his determination to love. So it is, in our relation to the giver and destroyer of values, that our being unconditionally valued is not in any sense conditioned by our acceptance or even our understanding of it.

The most man can do against the truth of God is to propound a lie. The most man can do against the concreteness of God's deed is to propound an *abstraction* which alleges that he is somehow abstracted out of a covenant relationship of grace and responsibility.

16.3 Rationalization. Could it be that our entire proposal on the impossibility of guilt is itself a gigantic self-deception, merely a curious rationalization to curb the pain of conscience? Could it be that we are, as Feuerbach suggested long before Freud, merely projecting an unconditional forgiver merely because we *need* forgiveness? Could the whole matter be settled psychogenically without reference to any truth claims? Perhaps it is merely our economy of abundance, our permissive morality, our Western emphasis on self-determination, and in general "the recent deterioration of our moral fiber," which shapes this strange theological allegation so curious to our ears.

The Christian community is not saying that divine forgiveness exists because we need it, although we indeed do need it. Rather it is saying that we are encountered by divine forgiveness even amid our almost dogged, recalcitrant resistance to it, and amid all our persistent attempts at self-justification.

One might suppose that divine forgiveness might be gladly received and welcomed by guilt-burdened individuals, but actually it is extremely difficult to sell to persons who are convinced that any goodness they have must ultimately come as a result of

103

their own willing and doing, and certainly not as a gift. Although one might expect the guilty man gladly to receive the good news of forgiveness, experience shows how deeply he is resistant to it, and how persistently he insists upon accepting no other justification than his own.

As for linking forgiveness to the deterioration of social controls, it may be that we are just now coming to the point in cultural history where theology is being liberated to speak more freely of the deeper implication of forgiveness, without the power of moralism overwhelming it. It may be that the technology of abundance is finally freeing man to speak openly of the ontological impossibility of guilt, whereas before it was unthinkable because of its potentially disordering social consequences.

16.4 Universalism. Does our line of reasoning finally lead to the conclusion of a weak, sentimental, and overly optimistic idea of *universal salvation*, wherein God finally accepts all human lechery, avarice, pride, recalcitrance, evil, and insensitivity?

To answer, I make a sharp distinction between universal justification and limited salvation: God's pardoning verdict is declared and established for *all*, not some. It is unconditional, not contingent upon our response. And yet admittedly only *some* do in fact respond to it, answering it with their own will and behavior.

Salvation (from the Latin *salvus* or health, wholeness) differs from justification in that it involves not merely the bare fact of a divine juridical verdict, but also the human response to that verdict. Salvation is not actually realized by every man, although doubtless it is intended for all men. Only *some*, not all, actually hear and choose to be participants in the saving event, responding with their own being and doing. Only some concretely and awarely participate in the wholeness of God, and reflect that wholeness experientially. But the Word is spoken for all and the justifying deed is done for all. This is why I *reject the notion of "universal salvation"* (understanding salvation as the volitional participation of man in the saving deed of God), but at the same time thoroughly affirm the scriptural view of *universal justification,* which remembers that the divine pardon is addressed to all. Not all receive what is given to them. Not all hear that it is even possible to live under the forgiving verdict. Some hear and do not respond. But Christ died for all.

This question may be helpfully correlated with the distinction between the *indicative* and *imperative*: The *indicative* concerns what has occurred, the *imperative* concerns how we ought to respond to it. God pardons all. This indicative has embedded within it implicitly the imperative requirement that we reshape our lives in terms of what is there. The imperative is: Become who you are as one who is pardoned by God. Receive your inheritance! Be who you are as a forgiven man! It is in this way that the indicative is universally applicable, but the imperative places the burden upon the hearer to embody that universal verdict concretely. If forgiveness is essentially God's doing, it is not finally subject to man's undoing.

This does not mean, however, that "all men are saved," i.e., that all men are in fact made whole by God's grace through their conscious participation in it. For even and precisely amid the eucharistic community as well as in the world we know that we ourselves lack health, that we can only come to the Lord's Supper with a confession on our lips, and that even the most responsible man remains an unprofitable servant. But we live in a community which celebrates God's valuing us precisely amid our irresponsible value negations.

Thus the salient issue concerning universal salvation hinges upon whether we are viewing the covenant merely from the viewpoint of our decision about it or from the viewpoint of God's decision about us amid our decision or indecision about it. If we are perceiving the entire quandary of guilt strictly from the human, subjective, and experiential side, then it is obviously the case that there are tremendous human resources which are continually wasted, never to be situationally recovered. Abstracted from the divine pardoning verdict, the human past remains unalterably fixed in wretched bondage to value negation. The only reasonable attitude to adopt toward it is despair.

But if we are perceiving guilt not only from a subjective

105

stance but from the unique vantage point of God's own self-disclosure, then it is an entirely different matter. This is the deeper, ontological ground of human experiencing, from which the guilt-burdened individual can never succeed in escaping: the ontological impossibility of guilt before God.

chapter V

EXEGETICAL AND HISTORICAL ISSUES

In order to achieve textual concreteness in our conversation with the Bible, we are now going to focus specifically upon a single text which succinctly condenses most of the principal themes of the preceding discussion. Our path has led from phenomenology to theology, from experience to tradition. Far from arguing that we must now dig up some scripture to support an already established viewpoint, we are instead suggesting that Scripture and tradition themselves demand just the kind of analysis which we have proposed. It now remains to be shown just how the witness of Scripture and tradition appear relevant to our argument and how they can be translated into contemporary language without distortion of their essential message.

17. The Peril of Unreceived Pardon

17.1 The Parable of the Unmerciful Servant. This parable (Matt. 18) has the unique advantage of taking most seriously the very point which has thus far been the weakest link in our argument: the pivotal importance of *receiving* the pardon of God in such a way that it changes behavior and the possibility of annulling it through our unreceptiveness. Jesus is reported by Matthew as having told the parable in this way:

"The kingdom of Heaven, therefore, should be thought of in this way: There was once a king who decided to settle accounts with the men who served him. At the outset there appeared before him a man whose debt ran into millions. Since he had no means of paying, his master ordered him to be sold to meet the debt, with his wife, his children, and everything he had. The man fell prostrate at his master's feet. 'Be patient with me,' he said, 'and I will pay in full'; and the master was so moved with pity that he let the man go and remitted the debt. But no sooner had the man gone out than he met a fellow-servant who owed him a few pounds; and catching hold of him he gripped him by the throat and said, 'Pay me what you owe.' The man fell at his fellow-servant's feet, and begged him, 'Be patient with me, and I will pay you'; but he refused, and had him jailed until he should pay the debt. The other servants were deeply distressed when they saw what had happened, and they went to their master and told him the whole story. He accordingly sent for the man. 'You scoundrel!' he said to him; 'I remitted the whole of your debt when you appealed to me; were you not bound to show your fellow-servant the same pity as I showed to you?' And so angry was the master that he condemned the man to torture until he should pay the debt in full. And that is how my heavenly Father will deal with you, unless you each forgive your brother from your hearts." (Matt. 18:23-35 NEB.)

Eta Linnemann[1] correctly shows that, even as most of Jesus' parables have a single concise point, this parable also focuses sharply in the concluding rhetorical question: "Were you not bound to show your fellow-servant the same pity as I showed to you?" That question implicitly embodies a penetrating analogy: we are being called to forgive as we have been forgiven, love as we have been loved, relate to our neighbor as God himself has related himself to us. That is the analogy we shall explore, using this parable as our textual medium.

[1] *Gleichnisse Jesu* (Vandenhoeck & Ruprecht, 1962), pp. 115-16.

The basic story line may be demonstrated in two parallel columns of twelve moments:

1. Prologue: A king is settling his accounts with servants.

SCENE I	SCENE II
A Servant Pleads for Patience	*The Forgiven Servant Meets a Debtor*
2. One servant owes an immense debt. When the king demands payment, he cannot pay.	6. A fellow-servant owes that same servant a very small debt. When the servant demands payment, the fellow-servant cannot pay.
3. The king orders the servant sold, with wife and possessions, to pay part of the debt.	7. The forgiven servant insists, "Pay up!"
4. The servant pleads for patience and promises to pay in full.	8. The fellow-servant pleads for patience and promises to pay in full.
5. The king is moved to pity by the plea. Mercifully the king cancels the debt and sets the servant free.	9. The servant is unmoved by the plea. Unmercifully, the servant refuses and has his fellow-servant put into prison until he should repay the modest debt.

SCENE III

The Final Reckoning

10. A report comes to the king of the servant's lack of mercy.

11. He summons the servant, reprimands him.

12. He then metes out to him the same punishment which he had given his fellow-servant: that he be turned over to the jailers until he should repay his debt.

17.2 Scene One: A Servant Pleads for Patience. Let us suppose that we are looking at three brief scenes of a motion picture which moves very rapidly, and yet with certain definite moments, through twelve frames of glimpsed action:

Frame One: The prologue. The subject under discussion is the reign of God, which is compared to a king who has decided to settle his accounts. The setting: We are at the end of time. Anyone who owes anything is now being required to pay.

Frame Two: The scene now focuses on a certain servant who owes the king a fantastic sum (ten thousand talents would be one hundred million denarii, perhaps ten million dollars), a debt almost impossible to calculate and totally beyond the range of the debtor's resources.

There are numerous elements of surprise in this parable, the first of which is the sheer, fantastic quantity of the poor man's debt. Before hastening on, however, let us ask how the parable, through its lucid imagery, already reflects something we have systematically observed in our discussion of guilt: the immensity of man's accumulated memory of value negations. We are not trying to make an allegory of the parable, as if to say that servant is the symbol of humanity and his debt is the symbol of the fantastic indebtedness of all men to their gods and values which have been negated in the past. Instead, the parable with its own image-creating power is merely giving us a brief glimpse into one penetrating human scene: a servant owes a gargantuan debt he can never pay, which reminds us of the immensity of our own indebtedness as value negators.

Frame Three: In an instant, and with peremptory justice, the king orders him to be sold as a slave, with his wife and children and all his possessions, in order that something of value could be salvaged from the bad debt. Like a banker's cool examination of the value of a man's possessions in order to know whether he can loan him money, the question suddenly becomes "What are you worth?" The average value of a slave is from 500 to 2,000 denarii. He owes 100 million denarii.[2] Well, obviously everything he has and is cannot begin to pay his account. Our common human condition is reflected in this simple picture of a debtor unable

[2] Joachim Jeremias, *The Parables of Jesus*, trans. S. H. Hooke (Scribner's, 1955), pp. 146 ff.

to pay. Again we are not allegorizing but merely associating images which the parable itself elicits. In more systematic language, the end-time settlement is requiring that we pay up what we do not have, so we are being asked to pay with our very selves. In fact, our indebtedness brings suffering and slavery not only to us but to our loved ones as well. That is the radical reckoning to which we are being summoned.

Frame Four: The servant falls prostrated at his master's feet and implores: *"Be patient with me, and I will pay in full."* He is asking for *time* in order to make up the negated value, only time to perform the required duty (not for forgiveness—that never occurred to him). His only expectation from his master is one of strict legal correctness.

How our sympathies are drawn to this pitiable figure! He fears the judgment in which he is already inextricably caught. However inadequate his resources, he promises to repay in full. But it is the end-time. There is no time for patience. The account must be settled.

Frame Five: Moved with pity by the servant's plea, the king cancels the debt and sets the poor man free. With dramatic swiftness, in one bold single stroke, the king changes the whole objective situation. He renders an unimpeachable verdict of pardon, and the debt is suddenly wiped off the books! Unbelievably the man finds himself totally free and unburdened of all the penalties which the debt had incurred. All that was about to be liquidated is now instantly restored. This is the second dramatic twist in the narrative: The vast debt is simply and totally remitted.

Now perhaps it is becoming clear why we have chosen this parable to speak so pointedly of the ontological impossibility of guilt. For, again without allegorizing, a simple image is called before us: simple, swift, total cancellation of an immense indebtedness. Mark carefully: *If the debt is canceled, then it is impossible for one to be indebted!* It is the creditor who controls the debt. Likewise, if the giver of values pardons our wretched and intolerable value negations, then there is nothing that we can do to be guilty. One may (absurdly) continue to *feel* indebted, even though the debt is canceled, but as a matter of fact there *is* no

111

debt, since the debt is not finally in the hands of the debtor but of the creditor. Any feelings of continued indebtedness are simply groundless. So ends the first scene.

17.3 Scene Two: The Forgiven Servant Meets a Debtor. As the servant walks away, it is presumably the intention of the king that his mercy and forgiveness would nurture a like attitude of mercy and forgiveness toward others. But the third and central surprise of the parable now appears, and the premise of the whole story now becomes curiously ironic. For "no sooner had the man gone out than he met a fellow-servant who owed him a few pounds; and catching hold of him he gripped him by the throat and said, 'Pay me what you owe.' "

Frame Six: No sooner had the man gone out! One would expect that he would be so grateful to receive his very life back again that he would gladly give away all that he had, and certainly cancel the petty debts which others owed him. It is clear, however, that he never really understood what had happened to him, never really comprehended who he was as a free and pardoned man! He cannot respond to the forgiving reality that encounters him because he does not know he lives in it. He lives in his own abstract and absurd world of petty legalism.

Frame Seven: Seizing him by the throat he said, "Pay what you owe." Let us sharpen the contrast. What does the fellow-servant owe? One hundred denarii (NEB: "a few pounds"; Phillips: "a few shillings")! He himself had owed 100 million denarii but a few moments ago—more than the total value of all his possessions and he himself and his family sold in slavery! Let us not miss the irony of this absurd comparison. He is now demanding a paltry debt of one millionth the value of his own indebtedness. Yet so little does he understand the depth of what has just happened to him that he cannot be sensitive to the need of his neighbor even at this most elementary level.

Frame Eight: The fellow-servant falls prostrate at his feet and implores him: *"Be patient with me, and I will pay you."* That sounds familiar. In fact, it is precisely the same plea which he himself has just made a moment ago. Surely he will hear this

112

virtual echo of his own voice. The analogy is being strictly drawn: he is being called to mediate the same forgiveness to others that has been mediated to him. From here, events follow swiftly.

Frame Nine: He refused and went and put him in prison till he should pay the debt. He cuts off even the possibility of paying the debt. He does not offer to explore any other alternatives. His hardened, legalistic obstinacy contrasts sharply with the open readiness and nonrigidity of the king. His precipitous, dehumanizing, imprisoning action is just as abrupt and instantaneous as the king's radical liberating decision. With the wave of a hand a fellow-servant is now in impossible bondage, just as earlier with the wave of the king's hand the servant was in an instant free.

The imprisoning image is a particularly dramatic one to express the capacity of man to dehumanize and totally disvalue his neighbor. A prison is a place where there are only minimal value-creating possibilities. The imprisoned man is not only denied the ability to pay back the debt but is denied even the opportunity of showing his good intention to pay it. This is the most degrading and dehumanizing action we can take toward our fellowman: to cut him off from even the barest possibility of reconciliation, to refuse to share with him the reality of mercy and goodness which has been freely shared with us, to put a total and impenetrable barrier between us and our neighbor so that even the hope of recovery is denied.

Patience is a virtue which exists in time, which willingly allows time to pass while awaiting expected value actualizations. But the servant has no time. Like the king, he wants to settle his accounts. It is the end-time. The reign of God is a time like this. It calls for a radical decision for or against the neighbor.

17.4 Scene Three: The Final Reckoning.

Frame Ten: When his fellow-servants saw what had taken place, they were greatly distressed, and they went and reported to their lord all that had taken place. They did not go to accuse, but merely to report. They were distressed that such a great gift

113

was so poorly received that the spirit of the gift could not be mediated even in the slightest way to the fellow-servant.

Frame Eleven: The lord summoned the man and said: "*You wicked servant! I forgave you all that debt because you besought me; and should not you have had mercy on your fellow-servant, as I had mercy on you?*"

Does this mean that God's pardoning verdict, once given, is now withdrawn? Does it imply that divine forgiveness is conditional upon its human acceptance? Such is the common interpretation by writers such as Jeremias, who declares, "God will revoke the forgiveness of sin if you do not wholeheartedly share the forgiveness you have experienced." [3] If forgiveness is conditional, however, the whole case we have built for the ontological impossibility of guilt is undercut, since the gift of pardon would be contingent upon our receiving it. Although this is a typical reading of the parable, I think the parable itself says something quite different.

Frame Twelve: The king hands over the man to the torturers, until the debt is paid. The torturers are the demonic powers. This is a mythological way of saying that when genuine love cannot make its presence known in the life of a man, when he blocks himself off from the reality of forgiveness, then he finds himself by his own decision handed over to the destructive powers of guilt and despair. The judge then judges the debtor by the same standard he has applied to his fellow-debtor, so as to say, "If you have not learned to respond to mercy, then have a taste of your own medicine. Maybe you will learn through the pain of demonic guilt how important it is to mediate to others the love you have received."

This does not mean that the pardoning verdict is rescinded or revoked. It means that it has never been accepted and that its recipient has chosen to live under his previous circumstances of indebtedness. The man merely confirms the legalistic self-understanding he has had from the beginning. The parable shows that the insensitive servant is determined to be judged by his own

[3] *Ibid.*, p. 147.

EXEGETICAL AND HISTORICAL ISSUES

petty legalistic criteria instead of the renewing criterion of divine forgiveness.

The point of the parable is not that God changes his mind, but that the man whose mind is not changed by the pardoning verdict remains condemned by demonic guilt. Far from arguing that the forgiveness of God is conditional upon our reception of it, the parable argues that anyone who truly hears the word of forgiveness is going to mediate it concretely to his neighbor, and if he does not, he simply excludes himself from its benefits and condemns himself to the burden of demonic guilt. He fails to realize the ground upon which he stands. That is damnation and bondage.

Unmistakably this is a parable of the relation of law and gospel. Here is a man who thinks he exists strictly under the law. When he pleads for time, it is only a plea for time to fulfill the law. He is indeed guilty under the law, and if that is as far as he can see, naturally he needs time. But the truth is, he has no time. It is the end-time, the time for a final settling of accounts. Normal rules of business do not apply. But ironically, he misunderstands the situation in which he actually exists. He is being called by his situation to pardon as he is pardoned. But all this is impossible for him to assimilate into his legalistic self-understanding. So the moment he is met with the needs of a fellow-debtor who calls him to be who he is as a forgiven and forgiving man, only the law is credible to him; so he tragically places the same law upon his neighbor under which he understands himself to be placed, and this is his damnation. The king in effect says, "So be it—let him live under the law if he must, let him be judged by his own damning criteria for righteousness, by his own deeds! He has his reward!" But he has thereby chosen not to enter into the new age of the reign of God.

At last we are ready to return to the central initiating question which motivated Jesus to tell the parable: "Then Peter approached him with the question, 'Master, how many times can my brother wrong me and I must forgive him? Would seven times be enough?' 'No,' replied Jesus, 'not seven times, but seventy times seven! For the kingdom of Heaven is like a king who decided to settle his accounts.'" (Matt. 18:21-23 Phillips.) Although Linnemann has argued that the parable has no direct relationship to this saying which directly precedes it,[4] I view the whole parable as speaking forcefully to the basic issue of the need for radical human responsiveness to the forgiveness of God, which is precisely the concern of Peter's question.

The whole previous chapter in fact sets the context for this parable, for Jesus has just warned against "causing one of these little ones" to fall and has spoken of the shepherd "rejoicing over the one sheep gone astray," while leaving the ninety-nine. It is just such a little one, an unprotected, helpless neighbor, for whom the unmerciful servant is being asked to care in response to God's care.

Is the pardon revoked because of its being unreceived? That is to read far beyond what the parable actually says. It does not mention any verdict being rescinded. It does say that the king is angry that his gift is unreceived, and that the servant is delivered over to the tormentors. But it does not say the original verdict is changed. It merely says that until he pays his debt in some fashion (either under his own legalistic terms or in receipt of the lord's pardon), he will continue to be tormented. But he himself has insisted upon the mode by which the account is to be paid.

The final frame of the drama makes one simple, piercing point: "This is how my heavenly Father will treat you unless you each forgive your brother from your heart." And indeed it is so. If we fail to respond to the reality of forgiveness, this is what happens to us. If we insist upon living under the demonic grip of our idolatries, then we will have to suffer the torment they mete out. But the text says nothing to the effect that God only forgives us *if* we forgive others. It merely says, this is the demonic bondage which persists if we ignore the reality of the new age of divine forgiveness.

18. The Freedom to Confess

The surprise of this parable startles us only because we have lived beneath a turtle-like shell of protective moralism which

[4] *Gleichnisse Jesu*, p. 111.

has systematically dismissed the deeper realities of guilt and forgiveness. The view that guilt is universally human and embedded in the very process of decision surprises us only because our moralistic perfectionism has taught us to expect ourselves always to have clean hands. The affirmation that it is impossible to be guilty before God surprises us only because we have read the biblical witness with systematic blinders to the unconditional, universal scope of divine forgiveness and implicitly assumed that God's pardon is wholly contingent upon our acceptance of it.

One remaining task is to show the relevance of all this for the act of confession, public and private, in contemporary worship and pastoral care.

18.1 The Priority of Pardon to Penitence. Our next major proposal is that *God's forgiveness is logically and psychologically before rather than, as usually conceived, after repentance. An existential sense of being actually forgiven is the precondition of genuine penance and restitution.* We hypothesize that it is only amid a community of genuine acceptance where unconditional forgiveness is concretely mediated that persons find the freedom to put down their self-righteous defenses and freely enter into a responsible covenant relation with their neighbors.

Christian worship and pastoral care are shallow and innocuous without some overt confession of sin and explicit declaration of pardon. Protestantism is today being called to reexamine its neglect of both public and private confession. Interestingly enough, the strongest impetus for this reexamination is coming not from the emerging Protestant-Catholic dialogue, as one might expect, but more urgently from certain behavioristic psychotherapists such as Mowrer who view sin as the basis of neurosis. If what we have proposed about guilt and pardon is at all correct, then it must have important implications for Protestant worship and pastoral care.

18.2 The Pietistic Prohibition of the Freedom to Confess. Popular Protestant Christianity is largely a conflation of (1) a *moralistic pietism* which has its roots in seventeenth-century puri-

117

tanism and nineteenth-century frontier revivalism, in clandestine alliance with (2) a *liberal optimism* which has emerged out of the spirit of the eighteenth-century Enlightenment and nineteenth-century bourgeois evolutionary idealism.

Moralistic pietism views the church as a converted community surrounded by an evil world. Salvation is reduced to a moral reformation in which one ceases to be irresponsible to social mores and joins the moral forces in their fight against immorality. The church's task becomes that of getting as many of the good people into its fold as possible and separating itself as much as possible from the world hastening toward corruption. It must build a wall to protect itself from the incursions and stains of the secular environment. In this way Victorian morality has become indissolubly wedded with an introverted, subjectively oriented religious pietism so as to produce a strange picture of the church as a community consisting not of sinners whom God has pardoned but of the morally straitlaced who rejoice in their own righteousness. Under these terms the basic function of worship becomes self-congratulatory. Worship is our time to get together to exchange signals about how good we are and ought increasingly to become.

18.3 The Polemic of Pietistic Liberalism Against Confession. Although we often think of theological *liberalism* as opposed to pietism, it actually may be shown that liberal idealism fitted into this moralistic pattern very neatly. Although liberalism and pietism have always existed in a certain tension, there is one crucial point at which they harmoniously agree: *serious confession is unnecessary.* Nineteenth-century theological liberalism developed a polemic against confession on the basis of its optimistic view of man and progressive view of history. Thus these strange bedfellows, liberalism and pietism, joined forces literally to root out any semblance of confession of sin from the free-church tradition. The whole basis for public and private confession and absolution was splendidly outmoded. For *if* we are fundamentally the good community, and *if* history is inevitably on the upward road of progress, and *if* man's basic nature is on the side of goodness and

118

social harmony, then we really have nothing to confess and no reason for any unseemly and degrading acts of penitence. Admittedly, we do perhaps have a few scraps of bad feelings when we occasionally fail to live up to our ideals and moral norms, but no deep gulf is acknowledged between the sin of man and the holiness of God. Far from being miserable sinners, we think of ourselves as protectors and defenders of God and sturdy builders of his kingdom on earth (in real buildings and organizational charts and programming devices).

In any event, it is clear that our theological assumptions about the church have taken concrete institutional shape in our present form of church life, worship, and pastoral care. Anyone who imagines that theology has no effect on institutional life needs only read the history of the church in the last two centuries. I am not suggesting that the church of liberalized pietism is lacking a theology of worship. We have such a theology; we just do not know it, have not articulated it, and our pragmatic activistic tradition has not helped us to reflect critically upon it.

Under this image of the church there was no real freedom to confess, no room to acknowledge ourselves as guilty men who negate cherished values. That might be appropriate at a bar or a peace demonstration or an AA meeting, but, above all, *not* in the church! In this moralistic context the last thing I want my neighbor to know about me is that I am something of a semi-skilled liar who bears false witness against my neighbor in many subtle ways. I conceal this, even from myself, and the whole bent of liberal pietism not only encourages me but helps me conceal it!

Public and private confession of sin and announcement of pardon are explicit constitutive elements in all authentic Christian worship and implicit elements in every act of pastoral care. Regrettably, though, in American Protestant worship confession is often systematically structured out of the service. And in many services with some minimal act of confession there still is no overt declaration of pardon or word of assurance of forgiveness. We commonly imagine that we can praise God, preach his Word, and celebrate his presence without ever confessing our persistent and irretrievable value negations and without perceiving ever

119

anew his forgiving word. But the worship of God is less than serious if not grounded in the confession of our radical inadequacies to do the good, and without some announcement that we are valued by God amid our value negations.

18.4 The Liturgical Issue. Honest confession is not a condition for pardon. It is, rather, our way of becoming seriously aware of the pardon which is already there. Pardon announces what only honest confession is able to hear.

Whereas confession is typically regarded as a *condition of* forgiveness, confession is better understood as a *response to* forgiveness. Confession is not what makes forgiveness effectual, but rather an expression of our awareness of an already actual and fully effectual forgiveness. It will take some doing for us to unlearn what we have learned from several generations of moralistic preaching and worship: that we have to earn some goodness in order to qualify for God's forgiveness.

But do not the historic liturgies make forgiveness conditional? In the Anglican service of Holy Communion, e.g., the prayer of absolution promises forgiveness of sins "to all those who with hearty repentance and true faith turn unto him." [5] Does this mean that only those who repent are forgiven, *or* that those with hearty repentance and faith are truly aware of the forgiveness intended for all? I think the latter.

Bucer's Strasbourg Liturgy of 1539, a prototypical Reformed service, contains a more thoroughgoing Protestant act of absolution, derived almost wholly from Scripture: "This is a faithful saying, and worthy of all acceptation, that Christ Jesus came into the world to save sinners. Let everyone, with St. Paul, truly acknowledge this in his heart and believe in Christ. Thus, in his name, I proclaim unto you the forgiveness of all your sins." [6] The prayer of absolution in the Sunday Service of John Wesley, commended to the churches in America, does not in any sense imply a conditional concept of forgiveness: "O Lord, we beseech thee,

[5] *The Book of Common Prayer*, the Holy Communion.
[6] Bard Thompson, ed., *Liturgies of the Western Church* (Meridian Books; World, 1961), p. 170.

absolve thy people from their offenses; that, through thy bountiful goodness, we may be delivered from the bands of those sins, which by our frailty we have committed. Grant this, O heavenly Father, for Jesus Christ's sake, our blessed Lord and Savior." [7]

Certain New Testament statements, often used as liturgical words of assurance, seem to imply a conditional concept of forgiveness: "If we confess our sins, he is faithful and just, and will forgive our sins" (I John 1:9). Although frequently interpreted to mean that divine forgiveness will be rendered only upon receipt of confession, it seems to me to have this deeper intention: You will truly understand and receive the forgiveness of God which is *there* for all when you are moved by the forgiving word to be honest to God about your value negations. Confession is merely the proper subjective condition for receiving and actualizing forgiveness in our own experience. We have reason to believe this is its deeper intention since the same passage continues with the unconditional affirmation that Christ is "the remedy for the defilement of our sins, not our sins only but the sins of all the world" (I John 2:2 NEB).

18.5 The Exegetical Case for Unconditional Pardon. It might seem brazenly irresponsible to some that we have asserted (1) that it is impossible to be guilty before God, (2) that God's forgiveness is directed not just to the penitent but to the whole of humanity, and (3) that the pardoning verdict is unconditional and irrevocable. For many of us have been nurtured by an opposite tradition of biblical interpretation which has insisted that (1) guilt is *always* before God, (2) forgiveness is available *only* to those who repent, and (3) the verdict of pardon is *conditional* strictly upon our faithful obedient response to it.

The clearest statement of cosmic pardon is in the first letter of John: "We have an advocate with the Father, Jesus Christ the righteous; and he is the expiation for our sins, and not for ours only but also for the sins of the whole world" (I John 2:1-2). An advocate is one who pleads the case of another. God himself ad-

[7] *Ibid.*, p. 418.

vocates our cause! "Ours only" means: We who have fellowship in him, who have heard the Word of life (v. 1), who proclaim eternal life (v. 2), who walk no longer in darkness (v. 6). The messianic judge and expiator is declared to be the guilt-bearer not for our sins only, but for the sins of the whole cosmos.

Nowhere is the comprehensive universalism of the pardoning verdict more clearly seen than in Paul's letter to Rome, where it is first made painfully clear that "*all* men, both Jews and Greeks, are under the power of sin" (3:10). Paul then clarifies the new stance of all (not some) humanity before God: "But now, quite independently of the law, God's justice has been brought to light. The Law and the prophets both bear witness to it: it is God's way of righting wrong. . . . For *all* alike have sinned, and are deprived of the divine splendour, and *all are justified* by God's free grace alone, through his act of liberation in the person of Christ Jesus. For God designed him to be the means of expiating sin by his sacrificial death, *effective through faith*" (3:21-25 NEB, italics mine). Far from saying that the veracity of God's deed depends upon our poor and tenuous acceptance, this passage boldly presumes that God's justifying deed is given to all alike, without distinction, and that it becomes effective and actualized by those who appropriate it in faith.

Summarizing the scope of God's reconciling action, in his letter to Corinth, Paul writes: "All this is from God, who through Christ reconciled us to himself and gave us the ministry of reconciliation": that is, God was in Christ reconciling the world (*kosmos*) to himself, not counting their trespasses against them, and entrusting to us the message (*kerygma*) of reconciliation (II Cor. 5:18-19). *Kosmos* means precisely that whole order of creation which exists in enmity with God.

In the same passage Paul expresses the *pantos* theme in this analogical image: "We are convinced that one has died for all; therefore all have died" (II Cor. 5:14). "From now on, . . . we regard no one from a human point of view," (v. 16) since all humanity is perceived as included in the reconciling event. Then he integrates indicative and imperative with this penetrating sentence: "And he died for all, that those who live might live no longer for themselves but for him who for their sake died and was raised" (v. 15). The same indicative/imperative occurs again forcefully, at the end of the same passage: "You are reconciled;/ therefore be reconciled." Be who you are!

Elsewhere Paul asks of those who had broken the covenant: "What if some were unfaithful? Does their faithlessness nullify the faithfulness of God? By no means! Let God be true though every man be false" (Rom. 3:3-4).

18.6 Protestant Dialogue with the Sacrament of Penance.

Private confessional in the Roman Catholic tradition consists essentially in three parts: (1) repentance, or genuine sorrow for sin, (2) an act of absolution, or priestly declaration of God's pardon, and (3) penance, or restitution, involving some concrete satisfaction in which the penitent tries to make amends for his sin. Any Protestant review of the question of confession must stand in realistic, creative interaction with the Roman Catholic sacrament of penance.[8]

All three elements of Catholic penance should in revised form find their way into a renewed Protestant interpretation of confession. If any of the three acts (repentance, pardon, and restitution) are omitted, surely it would constitute a serious dilution. However appreciative we may be of the essential movement of Catholic penance, certain questions need to be raised in each of its three phases:

(1) Both the psychoanalytic view of repression, as well as the Protestant assessment of the self-deceptiveness of man, have taught us that man is never quite fully aware of the depth and complexity of his sin, and that the most pernicious dimension of man's sin lies beneath the surface of his awareness. Thus the penitential assumption that man can indeed confess *all* his sin comes seriously under question. A Protestant reassessment of pri-

[8] Bernard Häring, *The Law of Christ*, trans. Edwin G. Kaiser (Newman Press, 1961); Dominicus M. Prümmer, *Handbook of Moral Theology*, trans. Gerald W. Shelton (P. J. Kenedy & Son, 1957).

vate confession, therefore, should acknowledge finally the inability of the self to be perfectly self-revealed, or completely to know the full depth and range of the human predicament, since the hallmark of man's sin is his illusion that he does not live under its power.

(2) Over against a rather constricted priestly act of absolution, Protestant worship is being called by its tradition to explore the question of the liturgical announcement of pardon by the whole church. The question of absolutism must be reconsidered in relation to the rethinking of the ministry of the laity. What does the doctrine of the priesthood of the whole people of God amid their worldly vocations have to say about the act of absolution? I suspect that it would lead us much more in the direction of Bonhoeffer's "confession to a Christian brother." [9]

(3) Popular Catholic penitential practice tends to drift even unintentionally toward a legalism which assumes that one can in fact do penance, that one can in fact satisfy what was lost in one's sin. Strict emphasis on restitution, however important, subtly leads the penitent to assume that divine forgiveness is in the last analysis almost superflous, if in fact our own doing is what finally rights the wrong. Too easily is the act of penance, as any parish priest can tell you, trivialized in some symbolic act of pious devotion or minor philanthropy.

But if Catholic views need correctives in these directions, Protestant views even more so need correction in the opposite directions. Our views of confession are made much less serious by our neglect of any emphasis upon concrete acts of reparation or restitution for our inhumanities to man. Confession is cheap grace without concrete acts of restitution to the injured neighbor. Even though these may be symbolic, they should not be reduced merely to nonethical acts of religiosity or petty almsgiving. Penance needs to be rediscovered by a Protestant tradition too long mired in a sentimental view of God's forgiveness which lays no requirement for the ethical mediation of that grace to the neighbor.

[9] Dietrich Bonhoeffer, *Life Together*, trans. John W. Doberstein (Harper, 1954), pp. 110 ff.

19. The Rebirth of Memory

19.1 Socratic and Psychoanalytic Anamnesis. Memory plays a crucial role in the Socratic, and in general the Greek, search for *therapeia*. For it is by a process of remembrance (*anamnesis*) that one gives birth to the truth within himself which heals his alienation from reality. *Anamnesis* takes place by means of a dialogue in which the teacher puts questions to the learner in such a way that he will *remember* the truth somehow already implanted within the very structure of his human existence.

Thus the ancient Greek conception of *therapeia* as self-discovery through remembrance is the essential prototype and anticipation of the modern psychoanalytic therapy, which seeks to discover the authentic self through an exploration of memory. The psychoanalyst puts questions to the client in such a way that he will remember the truth already embedded within his past personal history. Through conversation they trace the curious pattern of past traumas, fixations, and resistances in order that the client may be freed from bondage to unreality. Modern psychotherapy thus operates broadly upon a Socratic pattern of discovery of truth. The truth is not handed to the client as a piece of advice or diagnosis, but rather the therapist simply acts as a *midwife* to help give birth to the buried memory of one's past personal history, and frees the individual for increased self-direction.[10]

How does the biblical view of remembrance correspond to the Socratic and psychoanalytic understanding of truth as remembrance? There is a sense in which Christian faith affirms that the truth is primordially written into the relationships in which we always already exist, seeking to make itself known through the very structure of our being, even prior to our search for it.[11] For the biblical witness understands the human self as existing *per definitionem* in covenant with God. The human self is fittingly defined only as creature of the Creator, as recipient of divine judgment and grace. If selfhood *is* thus a relation to God, then authenticity

[10] Oden, *KC*, pp. 35 ff.
[11] Ps. 24; Col. 1–3; Heb. 1.

does not exist autonomously or individualistically *within* the self, but concretely within a set of *relationships* in which the self always already exists. In that prealienated sense, the truth is already given to the self. It is this truth that sin disrupts.[12]

What occurs in the redemptive action of God is the *rediscovery* of that which is implicit in human selfhood from the beginning, that human selfhood is derived from, shares in, and flows toward the life of God. The Christian kerygma addresses the unaware and incongruent man with the announcement of the self-disclosure of the ground upon which he already stands. Christian proclamation calls man to remember who he is, and therefore *be* who he is as one who already stands in covenant with God and neighbor. This scriptural affirmation (Col. 1:15-29; Rom. 1:20; 5:12-21; Mark 10:15) corresponds to our phenomenological description of innocence.

19.2 The Nowness of Truth. A corrective must now be applied, however, to the unqualified assumption that truth is buried within the self. For the self under the condition of estrangement exists in radical self-distortion. The self is busily involved in the predicament of trying to "unbe" itself, to run away from its own authentic existence. What is needed is a totally new birth of memory not now available to the estranged man.

Let us *suppose* along with Kierkegaard that *the truth is disclosed afresh in every new situation.*[13] What would that do to our concept of memory and *therapeia*? If this were the case, then the truth of this moment could be known only now. It could never be anticipated. It could never be remembered or traditioned, since it is uniquely embodied in the now. If that should be the case, then searching for the truth of the new through memory is going to be wasted time, is it not? For if the now is the exclusive boundary of the self-disclosure of the truth, then the past is going to exist constantly *in error!* The past indeed had its truth in its now-passed moment, but its truth is now past and

[12] Oden, *KC*, ch. 2.
[13] Søren Kierkegaard, *Philosophical Fragments*, trans. David F. Swenson (Princeton University Press, 1936), pp. 29 ff.

therefore in error in relation to the truth which is now. Anamnesis, whether Socratic or psychoanalytic, is thus from an existential point of view the systematic pursuit of error. Awareness of now is openness to the truth, a viewpoint which is being therapeutically developed by existential psychotherapy. *Philosophical Fragments* is not only the beginning of an existentialist view of time, but the end of a scholastic, static, abstract, propositional, unprocessive view of revelation.

How do we respond to this curious Kierkegaardian supposition? It brings a rich reaffirmation of the biblical faith in the living God who reveals himself so uniquely and singularly in the now that one cannot simply apply abstract criteria from the past to the occurring word of God. The now stands in judgment of all our criteria. It calls all our standards of value into question and summons us to decision in responsive love for the neighbor. Kierkegaard's revelatory moment, however, may be easily tempted toward religious fanaticism and introverted subjectivism. However true it may be that God addresses men in the present, this cannot mean that the present is cut off from continuity with the past or that it exists without a durable extensional sequence of time.

We are being called today to reaffirm the importance of *traditioning* the Christian message through time, so as to freight its concrete address *to* and not merely *through* the moment, without denying the uniqueness of the moment's address. Tradition is not merely archaism, but it itself can become the means of freshly awakening the self to the present moment as bearer of the demand of God.[14]

It is only in this context of the dialectic between tradition and renewal that we are now ready to propose that the Christian forgiveness is indeed a new birth of memory. It is only when the past is itself regarded as reconstituted that a genuinely new memory is possible. The pardoning verdict of God does precisely that. It frees the human memory to view the past and all its tragic value negations as embraced by the memory of God! Out of this indicative proceeds an imperative which summons man to em-

[14] World Council of Churches, *The Old and the New in the Church* . . . *Tradition and Traditions*; Oden, *Radical Obedience*, pp. 129 ff.

brace his own value negations as having been embraced by God.

If physical birth is the beginning of memory and indeed an event in which all things are made new, then we can say that the reception of forgiveness is very much like a new birth of memory. The renewed memory is now freed to explore the entire range of the personal and cosmic past, to receive it without demoralization or fear, in the confidence that it is taken up in its totality into the gracious will of God. The new birth of memory under the address of divine forgiveness, therefore, is an ever recurring new birth, a natal openness to every emerging now. To imagine ourselves without a past is to imagine being born again.

Man's memory exists in the context of the memory of God. Aware or unaware, all our remembering is a fragmented, broken, partial dimension of the perfect and total cosmic remembering of God. What remains as a negation of value in our past is received affirmatively into the memory of God. Thus the profoundest dimension of human memory is to be understood under the analogy of faith: the incompleteness of our remembering exists within the completeness of God's own pardoning memory of the cosmic totality.

part two

the threat of the future

chapter VI

THE STRUCTURE OF ANXIETY

20. Framing the Question

20.1 **The Vulnerability of Freedom.** Every man exists in a relation to the future. To imagine myself without a future is to imagine the situation of death.

The future can come to tyrannize over consciousness, looming as a threat to man's fragile being and to the values which bestow meaning upon his existence. Whereas my past is partially knowable, since it has already occurred, my future is opaque, enigmatic, and uncertain, until it ceases being the future by entering the present. But since human existence is a deciding existence, it is an existence bound up in a lively relation with futurity. Finite freedom faces awesome possibility, aware of its vulnerability to the defeat and frustration of its highest values.

Our question: What is the essential predicament of man as he meets the future? Although that predicament may take many varied contextual forms, does it exhibit a recurrent structure?

If I reveal the way in which I existentially experience anxiety, it is in the hope that this may serve as a heuristic device by which others may understand the structure of their own experience of anxiety. Although it sounds curiously abstract to speak of the "essential structure" of anxiety, I have found that it is precisely in the midst of the concrete situational experiencing of anxiety that its formal structure is most clearly revealed. My quest for the structure of anxiety may be correctly understood as a simple phenomenological inquiry, in the sense of an attempt to describe the essential structure of the experiencing consciousness without alien presuppositions being imposed upon the phenomenon itself.

20.2 Toward a Calculus of the Guilt-Anxiety Analogy. I have already suggested (1.1, 6.1) that guilt and anxiety function in exactly opposite temporal directions, but formally analogous ways. Guilt is directed toward the past, as anxiety is directed toward the future. This initiating observation, which has motivated our entire inquiry, now invites us to explore its implications for a revised theory of anxiety. A curious analogical calculus is in ferment in our entire phenomenological effort. Calculus in the broad sense refers to any process of reasoning by the use of symbolic analogies. I am attempting to correlate a very complex constellation of analogies which appear in the structure of awareness. As I have examined the structure of my own consciousness, these analogies have appeared with amazing consistency. As I have sought to condense the essential analogies into diagrammatic formulas, this process itself has yielded potentially new analogies. Some of these diagrammatic equations appear in our discussion, visually expressing parallel functions. Since the clue to the entire analogical process depends upon the defensibility of the analogy between guilt and anxiety, we will devote special attention to clarifying it, leaving it to the reader's curiosity to explore other potential analogies which lie latent on every hand throughout the whole structure of awareness.

The deeper we penetrate these analogical patterns, however, the less explicit detail we need to give them. Certainly I do not need to repeat much that I have already developed in Part One. Our discussion of anxiety can be more condensed than our discussion of guilt could have been, since the analogical process will apply throughout. Almost everything I shall have to say about the structure of anxiety has appeared in a dialectically opposite fashion in the structure of guilt.

20.3 Limitations of Current Literature on Anxiety. Since Rollo May's excellent study of *The Meaning of Anxiety* has already provided a perceptive, critical summary of historical and contemporary interpretations of anxiety,[1] I will attempt no such effort here. But I would be remiss to fail to acknowledge that this subject has occupied a great variety of commentators,[2] especially in the last four (post-Freudian) decades, and in a deeper sense during the whole span of Western history. Why then do I presume to write something more? Significant as the available literature might be, it seems woefully incomplete at several points:

(a) Most regrettably, it has neglected exploring the dialectical parallelism of guilt and anxiety. One could read exhaustively in the current literature on anxiety and come away never imagining that anxiety has its direct ontological and logical analogue in guilt. So elemental is this observation to the understanding of the essential dynamics of anxiety that one would imagine that by now it would have been comprehensively developed and criticized. Lamentably, such is not the case.

(b) Far too little attention has been given, especially in psychotherapeutic literature, to the ontology of anxiety, i.e., to the relationship of anxiety to the very structure of man's being and of being itself, and in particular to the structure of temporal awareness. The structure of anxiety is essentially shaped by the very character of human existence in time. It is an inevitable consequent of man's dialogue with possibility.

I do not hesitate to acknowledge my continuing indebted-

---

[1] (Ronald Press, 1950), pp. 17-190, hereafter MA.

[2] *Ibid.*; Charles R. Stinnette, Jr., *Anxiety and Faith* (Seabury Press, 1955); K. Horney, *The Neurotic Personality of Our Time* (W. W. Norton, 1937); Erich Fromm, *Escape from Freedom* (Farrar & Rinehart, 1941); O. H. Mowrer, *Learning Theory and Personality Dynamics* (Ronald Press, 1950), pp. 531-61; Sigmund Freud, *The Problem of Anxiety*, trans. Henry A. Bunker (W. W. Norton, 1936); W. H. Auden, *The Age of Anxiety* (Random House, 1947); Reinhold Niebuhr, NDM; Erik H. Erikson, CS, pp. 403 ff.

ness to Heidegger in this connection, whose discussion of the relation of anxiety to being and time is profoundly worthy of any
reader's further exploration.[3] Heidegger's rich ontological reflection on anxiety was written in 1926, however; and despite the four
intervening decades, we have not seen his reflection being significantly integrated into a psychotherapeutic theory of anxiety except among a very small group of therapists, and even among
them very little has been changed about the actual treatment of
neurotic anxiety.[4] After a year of study in Germany on the influence of Heidegger upon current psychotherapy, I concluded
that his influence has remained largely at the general level of an
allgemeine Anthropologie, and that regrettably little has been
achieved in the way of revising therapeutic procedures in the
light of his reinterpretation of the ontological roots of anxiety.

(c) This points up another widespread inadequacy in the
current literature on anxiety: like most other subjects which are
being pursued in the context of the increasing academic speciali-
zation of the "multiversity," anxiety has not been adequately
studied as an interdisciplinary question. The behavioral scientists
have studied it with their empirical tools, the philosophers have
ontologized it, the poets have imaged it, the historians have chron-
icled it, the psychotherapists have treated it, but what has not
happened is a perceptive interdisciplinary integration of multiple viewpoints.

It is worth noting, in this connection, that theology, more
than any other academic discipline, has recently matured as a
general science of man more capable of broader interdisciplinary
dialogue than many other approaches from which we have a right
to expect integral interpretation. Unfortunately, this may be because theology has not been sure of exactly what it was supposed
to be dealing with, and thus has become a general borrower from
almost anybody who has anything important to say. This has both
its limitations and possibilities. In any case, it is among the theo-

---

[3] Heidegger, *BT*, 225 ff.
[4] Medard Boss, *Psychoanalysis and Daseinsanalysis,* trans. Ludwig B. Lefebre
(Basic Books, 1963), Rollo May *et al.,* eds., *Existence: A New Dimension in Psychiatry and Psychology* (Basic Books, 1958); R. D. Laing, *The Divided Self* (Pen-
quin Books, 1965).

logians of the last generation, principally Tillich and Niebuhr, that the most perceptive interdisciplinary integrations have been achieved with respect to a general theory of anxiety.[5]

21. The Futurity of Awareness

21.1 The Abyss of Possibility. It is ironic that the future is filled with empty possibilities: its fullness is precisely its emptiness. To gaze upon the future is to gaze upon an abyss of possibility, totally void of any actualized being.

The best single word to describe the future is *nothing*. Nothing has ever happened in the future. For the future is precisely that expected range of time in which nothing has yet happened. It is just open—filled with the nothingness of possibility.

Until it ceases being the future by becoming now, the future is enigma. I can probe it with my imaginings, hopes, expectations, anticipations, prophecies, predictions, extrapolations; but until it becomes now, it remains an inexorable question mark. I try to guess it, second-guess it, project my nows into it, bind it to predictability; but it remains relentlessly, stubbornly itself, which means as yet empty, mysterious possibility. Whenever I think I have it secured, I am living under the greatest of illusions.

Properly speaking, my future does not exist. It only may exist. Only now exists. The future is as yet empty of any actuality. The future is always receding, retreating, retiring into the not-yet. That is just what it is: not yet.

However desperately I may try to close myself off from it, I am invariably turned toward the future. I do not just *have* certain possibilities, I *am* a relation to possibility. The futurity of awareness is elemental to the human condition.

I not only exist in a relation to the future, but in a very lively, intensive relation with the future. I play games with it, pretend I own it, or some part of it. Sometimes I take this game with great seriousness. Comically, I come to assume that the future is *mine*

[5] Paul Tillich, *The Courage to Be* (Yale University Press, 1952), c. 2; Reinhold Niebuhr, *NDM*, 182 ff.

to control and determine. But this is just a game. For life confronts me inescapably with the concrete here and now in which the fantasy of this game keeps on becoming clear. I am repeatedly forced by life into the awareness that certain hopes and wishes I had for the future remain forever unactualized. What I thought was mine turned out to be not mine, and other events I had least of all expected turned out to be fulfilled. When I play the God game toward the future, I find that I am always vulnerable to shocking disappointment, since I am not God, and the future is not mine.

The comprehensive phrase, "the future," is our way of symbolizing not only the events which are to come, but all *possible* events which might come into being. "My future" is quite different from the cosmic future. It is only that small part of the total future in which I may participate directly. It is that arena of time in which I will be given opportunity to share with my freedom in shaping the destiny of the total cosmic future to which I am in some sense accountable.

The essential character of the future is best understood by direct contrast with the past. If I experience the past as immutably fixed, determined, actualized being, then I experience the future as that open, undetermined, as yet completely unactualized abyss of possibilities. If the past is irretrievably filled with actualized being, the future is as yet void of actualized being. Ironically, however, it is precisely the empty, unfilled, undetermined quality of the future that places its most powerful demand upon responsibility and decision in the now. Although the future is utterly powerless in the sense that it is sheer empty possibility, this is precisely its power. It can loom before my consciousness as a profound threat, since I can imagine that it will be filled with the demise of my vulnerable values and gods. If the future were accessible and known, it would exert far less magnetic power to attract the imaginative awareness than it does as an uncertain, enigmatic, unknown question mark before me.

21.2 Pre-Imaging the Future. To say that the future is impenetrable does not imply that I can escape a vital existential

136

relationship to it. Even though possibility is empty, it is precisely toward its emptiness that human awareness lunges. The future impinges constantly upon awareness through what might be called the anticipative imagination. The future is visitable, not actually but imaginatively, through the function of anticipative expectation.

However important the future may be to us, our only access to it is through the precarious route of imagination. The anticipative imagination is to the future what the retrospective memory is to the past:

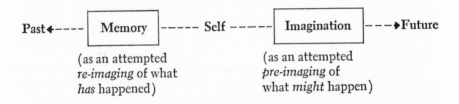

Imagination comes from the term *image*. The Latin *imago* refers to a picture, a likeness, a mask, or an imitation of something. Imagination is the act of forming mental pictures of possibilities which are not present to the senses. In a broad sense, memory is therefore a form of imagination, but it is distinguished from the anticipative imagination by the fact that it attempts to *re-image* what is past, whereas the anticipative imagination attempts to *pre-image* that which potentially might occur. When I use the term *imagination*, I am essentially referring to the anticipative imagination, as the dialectical analogue of the retrospective memory.

21.3 The Precarious Access to the Future. The imaginative capacity of man is subject to many curious and tragic distortions. To say that I pre-image the future does not imply that I image it accurately or objectively, since I am always viewing it from the constantly changing, uniquely limited perspective of the fluxing present. Every potential future event is, strictly speaking, merely an imagined event, and every imagined event is constantly being

137

reconstrued in the light of the always new situation in which one actually exists. However fragile it may be, imagination remains my only access to the vast ranges of possibility which are so crucial to my well-being. Imagination serves the immensely meaningful function of helping me grapple with and prepare for possibility, to condition attitudes for anticipated events.

The human organism has a much more complex and deliberate relation to the future than does animal creation. As the sciences of prediction have improved with evoluting history, man has become capable of more accurately pre-imaging the possibilities of the not-yet. Through the improvement of the science of statistics and the calculation of probabilities, man is much more able to project reasonably reliable predictions into the far distant future. Even ten million years from now, some things probably will remain unchanged; e.g., the Pacific Ocean will still remain on our planet in some form. Our rational and imaginative capacity enables us to "look into the future" with a certain tamed confidence. But in itself the future remains stubbornly impregnable. Even the most allegedly secure knowledge of the future is vulnerable to doubt because the future simply has not happened, and until it does, it always remains unknown. Prediction is always merely a matter of fragile probabilities. Although we have all come to expect that midnight will come tonight, no one can offer any satisfactory *proof* today that it indeed will certainly arrive. It is merely a matter of conditioning our expectation. We build our lives around such faithful expectations.

However serviceable this highly complex, sensitive, imaginative apparatus is to us, it nevertheless can become terribly upset and distorted. In fact, the imaginative capacity can become so distorted and imbalanced as to render completely inert the whole bodily organism, or under other circumstances move it to bizarre and absurd behavior. It is this dysfunctional encounter with possibility that I am now concerned to understand.

21.4 The Contextual Value Orientation of the Imagination. My imaginative function is closely related to my special value orientation. The imagination does not function without some sort of presupposed hierarchy of values, even though this may be vague or inarticulate. Thus, even as I enter the edge of the arena of the question of anxiety, I am already deeply involved in basic ethical and religious questions: What is good, what is supremely valued, what renders life significant? The particular time and place of my pre-imaging of the future is always a value-actualizing context which shapes the perceived future and even determines what is imaginable. If imagination is deeply bound up in my desire, my *eros*, in what I worship and adore, in what makes life bearable or meaningful in a particular time and place, then I cannot explore the imagination without exploring fundamental moral and existential questions: Who am I? What is my center of value by which I judge other values to be valuable?

Every moment of my existence is a complex constellation of dual value experiencing: receiving values and creating values. You do not have to be consciously aware of values in order to presuppose them importantly. You are reading this page with the help of some sort of light. If the source of that light were cut off and you were plunged in total darkness, you would suddenly become keenly aware of the immense importance of an ordinary value which you now take wholly for granted. Seriously to imagine a situation in which there is only limited light available is indeed to imagine a profoundly ominous situation.

I never confront any imagined future without my special value orientation, my understanding of who I am, my assumptions about authentic self-actualization. Conscience is the accumulation of internalized, stored concepts of value. While conscience does indeed have a judging function as it reflects backward toward past time, it also has an imaginative function which motivates and prods the self toward future value actualization. If certain goods are indeed worthwhile, if this is who I am, if my self-image is at stake, then I must try to manipulate various determinable aspects of the future in order that the values I prize may actually come into being and not be threatened with destruction.

The complexity and subtlety of the special value constellations impinging upon any given decision thus depend upon my presupposed value orientation and the unique situation which I confront. My valuing process is highly contextual, even changing from moment to moment. I weigh the situation and its possibilities in the light of current perceived values. I select one constellation of values at the price of negating others. Choice demands negation.

Accordingly, there is always a tragic dimension in my imaginative movement toward possibility. For I can envision all sorts of enticing possibilities for value actualization which can never be realized. The anticipative imagination can produce many more pre-images of self-fulfillment than can possibly be actualized. The artist can envision potentially great images which will never be put to canvas. The architect can sketch many imaginative structures which there is no time or money to construct. The poet is sometimes overwhelmed with incisive images which will never find their way to disciplined poetic expression. Many envisioned goods are never able to be pressed into the narrow, passing boundaries of the now, which is the only moment in time when anything ever happens.

21.5 The Legislative Analogy. The most illuminating analogy I have found to express the complexity of this imaginative movement toward possibility is the analogy between human decision and the legislative process. The imaginative legislator studies the problems of his society with a view toward conceiving new ways of doing things, new means of implementing justice, better laws, better forms of value actualization. If all the present statutes were wholly adequate, we would not need a legislature, but only an executive and a judiciary. But new situations call for a constant review of current legislation. The complexity of the legislative process is analogous to the complexity of all decision making.

The serious legislator allows his imagination to explore the range of possibilities for future social value actualization. He then asks how these possibilities might be written into law. He narrows the alternatives down to the more promising feasible possibilities. When he actually begins writing the proposed law, he selects language that will be understandable, legally defensible, and that will be agreeable to various groups in his constituency. Finally he has the task of persuading his colleagues that the proposed legislation is good enough to write into law. The individual decision maker is something like that complex legislative organism: exploring possibilities, limiting them for feasibility, and finally prescribing a rule of action.

Merely to pass a law, however, does not mean that it will be enforced, and therein lies an essential difference between the legislative process and executive enforcement. If the legislature is concerned essentially with the exploration of possibility with a view toward the redirection of social functioning through law, the executive is concerned to bring that enacted rule into being in an actual social context. Admittedly the legislator is also indirectly concerned with enforcement in that he would never wish to write a law which could not be enforced, but essentially the task of implementing the law belongs to the executive branch. Nothing shows the complexity and contextuality of imaginative decision better, however, than the process of developing imaginative legislation.

22. Potential Threats to Necessary Values

Having discussed the preconditions of anxiety in the temporality of awareness, I am now ready to deal with the emergence of anxiety itself. Nothing that I have said thus far about imagination and possibility hints toward any profound predicament, but as I will show, the very structure of man's relation to the future invites certain forms of miserably dysfunctional behavior.

22.1 The Predicament of Man in His Encounter with Possibility. Man's essential problem amid his conflict with the abyss of possibility is captured in the dynamics of a single term: *anxiety*. What do we mean by anxiety? We are searching for a structure of anxiety which admits of no exceptions.

We define anxiety *as the response of the self to some envisioned future possibility which is symbolized as a threat to some value regarded as necessary for one's existence.* Put more sparely, anxiety is the awareness of potential threats to one's essential values:

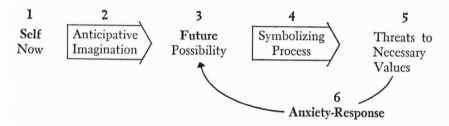

This means: The self (1) thrusts itself toward the future, exploring the abyss of possibility with the (2) anticipative imagination. All my moments are moments in relation with my special future (that particular future which I meet uniquely now), just as they are in a lively relation with my past. It belongs to human existence to be directed toward some (3) possibility through which I hope to actualize myself, through which I hope to receive or create certain values which I presuppose are good. But these values exist as yet only in the realm of the possible. They are glimpsed only by imagination. When some object of concern is perceived as threatened, the self relates to that possibility, thus symbolized (4), in the mode of dread. Anxiety is always preceded by this imaginary venturing into the threatening realm of possibility. When some possible event is imagined as (5) an actual threat to a necessary value, then even the bare subliminal awareness of that possibility will elicit vague, diffuse, and undifferentiated (6) anxiety, the source of which is not even clearly identified by the experiencing self.

A hospitalized actor, age fifty-one, formerly a very active man, has suffered a stroke. He has always thought of himself as a productive person and valued his capacity for hard work. His aging parents long nurtured in him the faith that if he worked hard then he would be a happy and self-fulfilled person. He is now flat on his back, overwhelmed by demoralizing thoughts that he might possibly be paralyzed for the remainder of his life. He tries to assess his future in the light of this astonishing new, awesome limitation. As his enlivened imagination surveys the future, every angle of its horizon looms as an anxiety-creating threat, since its every feature is a limitation on the central value he regards as necessary for his self-fulfillment. Since his vocation depends upon his health, when it is impaired, he stands before the total future as it were ominous in the most basic sense.

A child is being readied for his first day of school. He has experienced the security and ritual of a protected home environment for six years. His mother is the most significant person in his existence, since she represents and embodies to him comfort, support, and protection in a potentially threatening world. As he enters the high steps and massive doors of the public school, he immediately senses that he is in a different world of unfamiliar patterns where his mother's support will not be directly present. In an instant his imagination explores a variety of possibilities which to him symbolize awesome threats to familiar security patterns. Understandably he responds to this perceived threat in the mode of dread, until he learns that there are resources for support, trust, and the awakening of freedom in the new environment.

22.2 Contextual Values and Situational Anxiety. That which makes a person anxious depends entirely upon what he values. One child may delight in a Frankenstein movie which absolutely terrorizes another child. A letter from the draft board may cue off severe anxieties for one young man, whereas for another it is accepted stoically and without emotion. A speech before a large political rally may inspire the candidate to confidence and optimism; whereas, if the janitor who cleans up afterward were asked to say a few words to the multitude, he would be terrified. The content of anxiety depends entirely upon the situational values which one perceives to be under threat.

By carefully scrutinizing my anxiety and the situations under which it occurs, I can always learn something significant about what I am valuing and therefore who I am. However uncertain may be the source of anxiety, one thing is certain: Some perceived hidden *good* is always at stake in any anxiety-creating situation,

143

something that I regard as worth protecting. Clearly to identify that value is a major step in the process of dealing constructively with anxiety.

22.3 Anxiety as the Analogue of Guilt. I have defined guilt as the memory of some past action which is inconsistent with the present self-image. Anxiety is analogously defined as the imagination of some potential action which is inconsistent with the present self-image. When my self-image is idealized, exaggerated, and neurotically distorted, then I must all the more desperately attempt to protect that self-idealization from potential threat.

If guilt is described as the awareness of irresponsible (*unresponsive*) value negation, anxiety must be understood as an *overresponsiveness* to potential threats to values associated with the self-image. While guilt points to some former lack of sensitivity to a past situation of value loss, anxiety oppositely and analogously points to an overalertness, an exaggerated sensitivity to future situations of potential value threat. Thus in multiple modes we can describe anxiety as the dialectical opposite of guilt, with an analogous structure and parallel dynamics.

Like guilt, anxiety has an extremely personal character. I am aware that not merely certain generalized, abstract values are being threatened, but *my* values, the cherished relationships which I associate with my very self-definition. The mere pre-imaging of the possibility of their being undermined may throw me into a horrifying awareness of my own vulnerability through them.

If anxiety is a response to the anticipation of possibility, then it cannot be directed toward the past. One cannot anticipate what is past. It is impossible to be anxious over that which does not lie in the realm of possibility. The past has been irretrievably removed from the range of possibility. If so, it is an infinitely comforting thought that it is impossible to be anxious toward anything that is past (except in the limited sense that what is past has future consequences about which one may be anxious). Anxiety thus has its ontological limit in the now. It cannot penetrate into the past. Persons crippled by neurotic anxiety have a right to

144

understand the ontological limits of the anxiety under which they suffer.

22.4 Images of Anxiety. Every language has words that refer to the awareness of potential threats to essential values. In the Greek, Latin, and Germanic languages[6] we find many words whose derivatives are readily recognizable in English, such as *phobos, Angst, timor, terror, anxietas,* etc. Several images recur.

Etymologically, anxiety is closely related to the image of being in a *tight situation,* under constriction, pressed into narrow, limiting circumstances. The Latin *anxietas* connotes the experience of being placed in a cramped, limited environment.

Anxiety is related etymologically to the image of *fleeing.* The Greek *phobos* projects the image of desperate flight from danger. In the language of this discussion, as the self stands before the abyss of possibility and experiences the force of its threat, the understandable response is like desperately running away from potential destruction.

Anxiety is related to the image of trembling, a familiar physical response to the threat of possibility, as reflected in both the Greek *tromos* and the Latin *tremor.* When I feel the potentially destructive power of possibility, it is profoundly shaking. It is fitting that our age be called an "age of anxiety," since the shaking of the foundations which has occurred in our time is not only externally present in social, economic, and cultural history, but also internally experienced by most men of the twentieth century.

Finally, in many languages, to be anxious is *to care.* The Greek *merimna,* the Latin *cura,* and the German *Sorge* all connote this suggestive image of concern. When one cares for another, he is *concerned* over potential threats to that person. Even in the medical image of caring, treating, healing, there is the connotation of anxious concern for the welfare of one in danger. This image is especially penetrating in relation to our thesis that anxiety is

[6] William F. Arndt and F. W. Gingrich, A *Greek-English Lexicon of the New Testament* (University of Chicago Press, 1957); OED, I, 378; Charlton T. Lewis and Charles Short, A *Latin Dictionary* (Oxford University Press, 1958).

always fundamentally bound up in one's value system. One is anxious over that which one really cares.

22.5 Paradigmatic Anxiety. Paradigmatic anxiety occurs when some minor, otherwise insignificant event becomes broadly symbolic of one's total situation of finitude and vulnerability. Linus is the character in the "Peanuts" comic strip whose security is symbolized by a blanket. If the blanket is lost, snatched away by the dog, or if it has to go in the wash, he instantly pre-images his total vulnerability. The blanket is thus the paradigm, or model, the symbolic focusing of his whole human condition as being under threat.

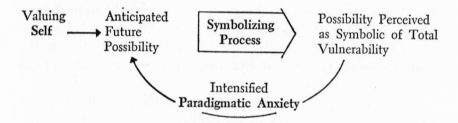

It does not require a dramatic image to cue off paradigmatic anxiety. Even an innocuous event can flash an urgent message in which the tender wound of finitude is laid bare. To one with an exaggerated, idealized self-image, the smallest touch or the slightest glance can be instantly telescoped into paradigmatic anxiety: a misplaced key, a telephone ring at night, an ominous headline, an overbearing handshake, a toothless grin—whatever is capable of pointing to the radical vulnerability of the self can elicit paradigmatic anxiety.

A certain young man has always pictured himself as an "A-student." Any threat to his self-image is instantly escalated into paradigmatic anxiety. He is convinced that the future holds nothing for him if he does not fulfill his scholarly self-expectations. His parents have always put a high premium upon academic achievement. He has grown up not merely wanting, but needing to be a good student in order to secure a means of valuing himself. Now confronting an exam he suddenly feels his entire self-image at stake. Although he reassures himself that he is prepared, his imagination wanders unbridled into numerous dreadful possibilities. He pre-images a catastrophe which ruins his whole career.

Characteristically the anxiety-possessed awareness tends to reach out for the worst, most deplorable possibilities. It is extremely clever in searching out the most threatening conceivable possibilities and examining them in horrid detail. Of course the quiz has not yet occurred, but its presence in his imagination is overwhelmingly real. His moment of paradigmatic anxiety may be the instant his roommate asks him how his preparation is coming, or a mere glance at the building where the test is to be given, or the smell of chalk or mimeograph paper.

A certain minister is horrified at the thought of being called to officiate at funerals. His parents successfully taught him to repress all strong feelings. One thing to "be a man" meant was not to weep. The possibility of ministering to the bereaved fills him with an acute sense of dread, since he is eminently afraid of being seized with uncontrollable emotion and weeping. Death is understandably threatening to all men. But to him the mere possibility of having to perform funeral functions plunges him into anguish of spirit. They remind him of his own vulnerability to death. Since he values life, friendship, and intimate family ties, and since he sees them broken asunder by death, he expects that it will be very difficult for him to stem the tide of emotion. Despite natural gifts for the ministry, he finds it very difficult to maintain his vocational commitment. His moment of paradigmatic anxiety is the sound of a distant ambulance, the smell of the hospital corridor, a bouquet of flowers, or the hoarse whisper of an aging voice, when the image of the dreaded possibility suddenly floods his consciousness.

23. The Idolatrous Intensification of Anxiety

Our next task is to show how the anxiety-creating process escalates into self-destructive behavior. Again our hinge concept

147

is the notion of idolatry, borrowed from the Judeo-Christian tradition.

23.1 The Demonic Reinforcement of Anxiety. Our previous attempt to demythologize the language of idolatry into value language acceptable to a contemporary world view (9.1) now must be applied to the dynamics of anxiety. We have defined a god as a center of value by which all other values are judged to be valuable. Idolatry is the adoration of some constellation of limited, historical, contextual values, so as to regard them as the source of absolute, unconditional, and final significance and value.

Our essential equation on the intensification of anxiety: *To the extent that limited values are elevated to ultimacy, we reinforce and increase the power of anxiety.*

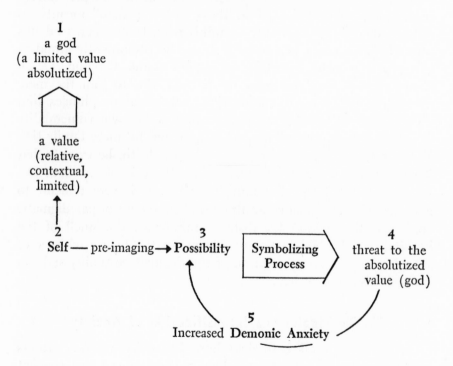

148

THE STRUCTURE OF ANXIETY

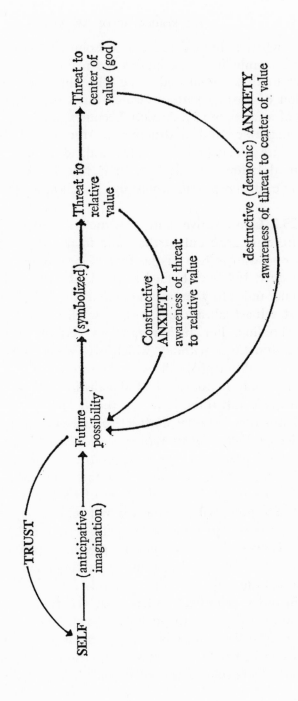

Thus, when a limited value is absolutized (1), and when the self (2) symbolically pre-images the realm of possibility (3) as a threat to that absolutized value (4), the response is an intensification of anxiety patterns which increasingly plunge below the level of awareness (5). Anxiety becomes self-deceptive, tyrannical, unmanageable, and destructive to the extent that contextual values are idolatrized. Thus the individual most deeply bound up in idolatrous self-idealization is the one most vulnerable to demonic anxieties and, ironically, least aware of their source.

23.2 Constructive and Destructive Anxiety. Both anxiety and freedom arise out of the same imaginative capacity in man. Only one who is free in the face of possibility has the capacity for anxiety. If I have tended to speak of anxiety always as disruptive and unhealthy or assumed that it is a deteriorating force against self-actualization, I wish now clearly to correct that misunderstanding. For anxiety provides certain corrective and protective functions without which we would find ourselves unprepared to deal realistically with the future.

It is only in the light of the distinction between idolatrous and realistic valuation, however, that I am now ready to sharpen the distinction between destructive and constructive anxiety: *To the degree that relative values are idolatrized, they increasingly exert a self-destructive force upon the anxious consciousness.*

I intend vigorously to affirm this constructive and normal function of anxiety: its exploration of the abyss of possibility, its search for potential options for self-fulfillment, its function of alerting the self to potential threats. It is this healthy, constructive anxiety which puts constant pressure upon the self for improving its value actualization. Even though it causes a certain consternation and inner division, this is precisely what is necessary in order to protect and nurture the value system. This brilliant human capacity to pre-image possibilities only becomes sick when man seeks spuriously to lay claim to the future as if it were his own, when man reserves some portion of the future for himself and plants some image of himself firmly in the future which, if he does not actualize it, causes life to lose its meaning for him.

It is normal and healthy that I feel anxious over actual, realistic, contextual threats to relative values. But precisely to the extent that limited values are elevated to ultimacy, the anxiety-creating process begins to accelerate into demonic proportions, reinforced through repeated decisions, compulsively pursued. So what was intended to be a constructive force moving toward self-actualization becomes a compulsive, tyrannical monster which cripples effective action and terrorizes the whole arena of consciousness.

23.3 Maturity as Proportional Valuing. If constructive anxiety requires realistic value assessments, how does one proceed to make realistic judgments? That question of course is framed very abstractly. The fact is that realistic value judgments can only be made concretely and situationally. To attempt to answer that question seriously would be to divert our attention to the writing of an entirely different book. A formal or generalized answer to the question, however, would suggest that maturing self-actualization is the process of learning to assess competing claims proportionally in terms of their *actual* situational value.

It is not my purpose, however, to call for a general devaluation of all values as a preventive measure against anxiety. Indeed, that would be one strategy for reducing the intensity of anxiety which is already familiar in the history of asceticism. For if nothing is at stake in the future, there is nothing to be anxious over. Reduce what you care about, and you will reduce the intensity of your care. But this curious stratagem stands in a certain historic tension with the Judeo-Christian assumption that creation is good and therefore finite goods are to be valued, prized, received as genuinely worthy of human care. But this, of course, is built upon the broader assumption that no created good is to be absolutized as a final source of value. No thing, no human relationship, no social structure, no idea, nothing in fact in the created order is finally capable of deification. Finitude and creaturely goods are to be valued for just what they are, viz., limited, relative, contextual values.

151

23.4 The Distinction Between Fear and Anxiety. Fear is directed toward an object. Anxiety is directed toward a possibility, which because of its ontological status as "mere possibility" is never an object. A possibility is empty; which is to say, it does not have objectivity, except in that peculiar form of objectivity known only to the imagination.

In fear, I feel threatened by something which can be presently and concretely envisioned as an object. But when I am apprehensive over an objectless possibility, I am experiencing not fear but anxiety. When I drive at night, I sometimes become very apprehensive about meeting the headlights of an approaching car suddenly atop a hill. As long as there is no object moving toward me in a menacing fashion, I experience anxiety which involves a possibility without object. But should I actually encounter a car out of control and headed directly toward my lane as I top the hill, I experience fear, which is directed toward an identifiable object, which actually is a good deal more manageable than anxiety, since one is dealing with something instead of nothing.

Since anxiety attacks the foundation of the security system itself, the individual cannot "stand outside" the source of the threat. He cannot objectify the threat, and he cannot separate himself from it. This is why anxiety is so much more difficult to understand and alleviate than fear. The individual feels overwhelmed, but uncertain about what it is that overwhelms him. It is for this reason that anxiety tends to be experienced as a feeling of undifferentiated apprehension, as if the threat were sourceless. It is understandable that the anxious man has a strong tendency to transform vague anxiety feelings into the definite fear of some identifiable object. But of course this compounds the self-deception. Although fear is uncomfortable, it is at least experienced in reference to something that can be located in time and space. An adjustment can be made to something outside oneself. But the adjustment necessary in the case of anxiety is much more difficult, since I cannot stand outside of the source of the threat, since it is the foundation, the valuational basis of the self which is itself under threat. One *has* fear, but one *is* anxious.[7]

[7] May, MA, p. 192.

23.5 The Self-deceptive Stratagem of Idolatrous Anxiety. A consistent feature of chronic anxiety is its tendency to conceal its trail, making the source of the threat increasingly difficult to identify to the one experiencing it. Psychoanalysis has contributed a great deal to our understanding of the unconscious operations of anxiety below the level of awareness, although it is not my purpose here to repeat these findings. I have already mentioned the tendency of paradigmatic anxiety to telescope minor symbolic relationships into a comprehensive perception of one's total vulnerability. Closely related to this paradigmatic, exaggerative tendency is the whole complex dynamic of self-deception through which the self then attempts to conceal from itself the vulnerability which it actually intuits deeply, but the source of which it does not know.

Anxiety has been likened to an alarm bell warning of some vague, undifferentiated danger. Anxiety becomes neurotic when certain symptoms or sicknesses are created in order to avoid the already repressed and therefore unidentified danger which originally sounded the alarm.[8] Symptom formation is comparable to hearing the alarm and then putting in earplugs to avoid hearing it, or perhaps saying to oneself that it is really just the telephone ringing, or maybe sounding off another alarm so loud that the first alarm cannot be heard. The penalty, of course, is that by avoiding whatever elicited the original alarm, one has increased his vulnerability to the threat it signaled.

It is in this way that neurotic anxiety mechanisms tend to become complicated through repressive stratagems. We do not know *why* we are uneasy and defensive and hostile; we only know *that* we are threatened by situations which should not be objectively threatening. We may even acknowledge that the actual event or symbol that cues off our paradigmatic anxiety may be silly or bizarre, but we are anxious nevertheless.

The Judeo-Christian interpretation of man has always been aware of his tragic tendency to self-deception. The hallmark of man's predicament accordingly is that he does not really think

[8] Seward Hiltner and Karl Menninger, eds., *Constructive Aspects of Anxiety* (Abingdon Press, 1963), chs. 1 and 2.

he is in a predicament. So in the deeper sense the predicament of anxiety is that the anxious man is prevented by his anxiety from fully perceiving himself as anxious. It is nothing other than his own self-deceptiveness that convinces man that he can overcome his self-deceptiveness.

Since anxiety strikes at the security system of the self, rather than something apart from the self, it is extremely difficult to deal with objectively. Psychotherapists know that "mounting anxiety reduces self-awareness." [9] Thus the more threatened are one's idolatries at a deep level of subception, the less one is able to understand just what it is that is threatening him. In proportion to the increase in anxiety, our awareness of the dynamics of it become muted and confused.

23.6 Axiotherapy for Intensive Anxiety. The most intense anxiety-creating situations nevertheless present hidden opportunities for learning about oneself. Anxiety is attempting to perform a constructive function for the self. The opportunity to discover what values are at stake in any anxiety-creating situation, and which are being idolatrized, is the unique gift and promise of anxiety. This gift, ironically, is nowhere more richly given than in the most acute situations where anxiety is experienced.

I do not presume to propose any sort of general therapy for acute anxiety which might supplant or modify present effective psychotherapeutic practices. Note that I say "effective," since without question many current psychotherapeutic practices are not proving very effective. This proposal should be regarded as a respectful addendum to what is being now attempted and done in psychotherapy. What I essentially propose to add is a more deliberate value analysis, or review of the value orientation presupposed in the acutely anxious, to discover which central values have been idolatrized unrealistically so as to intensify the anxiety patterns.

An axiotherapy, or better an axiotherapeutic addendum to psychotherapy, would not be assigned the task of providing a

[9] May, MA, pp. 237 ff.

revised structure of values for the acutely anxious, but rather to help him understand the values which are already at stake in his anxiety so he would then be freed to choose whether they are in fact worth it to him, or in what sense they might be more proportionally valued so as to reduce the level of anxiety. The opportunity given in acute anxiety, however, is not merely to reduce the anxiety, but more so to learn about oneself as a human being, to discover oneself through the discovery of one's center of values.

It is in this way that effective psychotherapy bears a close, though often unacknowledged, kinship to ethics, since to ethics belongs the much more deliberate study of good, values, goals, and obligations, the abortive pursuit of which has caused the symptoms which the therapist is asked to heal. If properly developed, an axiotherapy would stand at the unexplored interdisciplinary juncture between ethical analysis and the medical arts.

23.7 Anxiety as Inevitable but Not Necessary. Anxiety is a correlate of freedom. How could we possibly be free without projecting ourselves toward future alternative possibilities? The most elemental characteristic of freedom is to experience the capacity to determine oneself toward one option while rejecting other options. Anytime one has values at stake in the future, one is vulnerable to certain anxieties. If we are to be free men, we shall be anxious men. Only on the basis of the denial of human freedom is the complete denial of anxiety possible.

The tougher question is whether demonic, self-destructive, and idolatrous forms of anxiety are indeed inevitable and universal. Again, as in our discussion of guilt (10.4), we must walk the razor's edge. In the Judeo-Christian tradition we must first make it clear that idolatry, and therefore demonic anxiety, is not necessitated by the very structure of man's creation. It is indeed a derived implication of his freedom, but not structured into his creation as such. Although man may choose inevitably to determine himself idolatrously toward inauthenticity, he is not by nature condemned to demonic anxiety. That would be an unthinkable scandal to any Christian doctrine of creation.

Nevertheless, to my own knowledge, among the persons I

155

have come to know well, I do not know any who are fully freed, or ever have been, from destructive forms of anxiety. I am not suggesting that every man in every moment is bound to demonic anxiety, but that so far as I know it seems inevitable that from time to time, due to the vulnerability of his own freedom, man in fact always becomes trapped in idolatrous anxieties. Again I do not mean that man is necessitated or predetermined to anxiety, but quite oppositely that he inevitably determines himself toward anxiety. When I say he freely chooses inauthenticity, I do not mean that idolatrous anxiety is a genuine expression of man's authentic freedom, but quite oppositely it is a denial of his authentic freedom.[10] Nevertheless, such a tragic denial seems universally present in the human situation. So if idolatrous anxiety appears everywhere in human history, this only sadly witnesses to the absurd and tragic capacity of man's freedom to determine himself toward unfreedom. It is in this way that I seek to affirm the inevitability and universality of anxiety without denying either the freedom of man or the goodness of creation.

I do not here speak of man, however, as an isolated individual, but as one who participates in a socio-cultural, historical environment which is always already distorted by tragic idolatries. Expressed mythologically, the man of whom we speak is already a participant in "Adam," the total human environment which exists, through its self-chosen idolatry, in absurd enmity against God.

23.8 Anxious Care in the New Testament. The Greek verb *merimnao* is used in the New Testament to refer to the attempt to reach into the future and secure it for oneself, the anxious concern one has over what might portend. Anxiety is the attempt to get into the future, control it, lay claim to it as if it were one's own; to possess the future, God's future.

Man's behavior, according to the New Testament witness, is fundamentally determined by what he *cares* for, what loyalties

---

[10] Heidegger, *BT*, pp. 312 ff.; Bultmann, *KM*, pp. 22-33.

THE STRUCTURE OF ANXIETY

are central to him. An individual's self-understanding is therefore profoundly revealed in the orientation of his concern (*merimna*). Riches can be deceitful, not because they are evil in themselves, but because they tend to invite us to accord them such ultimate worth as to forget the true center of value, God, the source and end of all creaturely values. So it is that man's anxieties over his daily bread, his national destiny, his religious identity, and his family ties are regarded in the New Testament as more profoundly symptomatic of his idolatries.

Anxiety and idolatry are linked by Jesus in these familiar words: "No one can serve two masters; for either he will hate the one and love the other, or he will be devoted to the one and despise the other. You cannot serve God and mammon. Therefore I tell you, do not be anxious about your life, what you shall eat or what you shall drink, nor about your body, what you shall put on. Is not life more than food, and the body more than clothing? Look at the birds of the air: they neither sow nor reap nor gather into barns, and yet your heavenly Father feeds them. Are you not of more value than they? And which of you by being anxious can add one cubit to his span of life?" (Matt. 6:24-27.) A certain value structure is here assumed: life is more valuable than food. The body is relatively more valuable than clothes. The human self is relatively more valuable than the birds. But in all this maze of contextual values, Jesus is calling for us to value ultimately only the Giver of the context. If anxiety absolutizes the relative value, its resolution must lie in some sort of de-absolutizing of our idolatries.

Even in the Bible, as in much of the literature of man, there is a comic aspect to much anxiety which is seen in our absurd attempts to get hold of the future, capture it, tame it, play like it really belongs to us. We play Napoleon, Superman, great lover, incessant do-gooder, and in every case our idealized self-image places us in situations of anxiety which objectively viewed are comic. The man who plays God to the future is always a comic figure—tragic too, of course, but never without his humorous and caricatured aspects. In fact, a good case can be made for the

157

argument that all comedy is based upon some idolatrous, and therefore absurd, response to reality.

Time makes our absolutes relative. That is always a bit funny from the outside, but tragic if experienced subjectively from within. In fact, comedy is the objectification of a tragic situation in which the vulnerability of our gods is unexpectedly illuminated.

chapter VII

THE NEONATE PROTOTYPE OF TRUST

In order to sharpen the dynamics of anxiety, we must see it in the light of its resolution in *trust:* openness to the future, confidence that one can move toward the future and lay hold of certain optable possibilities without fundamental threat to one's essential being.

In order to clarify the essential nature of trust and thus prepare the way for a theology of futurity, I will deal with it in developmental terms, first proposing that the prototypical condition of the self is trust in the neonate (newborn) situation, then clarifying the fall of the self into self-deceptive forms of anxiety, and finally asking how the recovery of trust is possible through effective psychotherapy and how this points implicitly to our subsequent theological discussion on the roots of trust in reality itself.

24. Primordial Trust and the Trauma of Birth

24.1 The Priority of Trust. The psychogenetic origins of trust may hark back to the foetal situation, in which the organism finds itself in a totally trustworthy environment. Everything is supplied: warmth, protection, food, comfort, security. Accordingly, the original situation of man is one of radical trust that his organism will be provided for. It is one of total lack of awareness of potential threats to value, and thus is radically free of anxiety. Trust is therefore chronologically and psychologically prior to distrust or anxiety. Whereas we must learn anxiety, trust in its most primitive and embryonic sense is not learned behavior, but given in and with the organism itself.

Stated in the form of a syllogism:

Premise I: If anxiety is the awareness of potential threats to values considered necessary for one's existence;

Premise II: if there is a stage of human development prior to the awareness of possibility and value assimilation in which no such awareness exists; then,

Conclusion: there is a primordial stage of human development clearly prior to anxiety.

Trust, in the sense of radical unawareness of threats to essential values, is unlearned, native, spontaneous behavior for the neonate; whereas anxiety emerges only after a lengthy and complex process of psycho-social development. Trust is therefore the primordial condition of the organism. Although this hypothesis has long been symbolized through the theological affirmation of the *imago dei* in man, it has been too long neglected by empirical observation. Nevertheless, it is amenable to purely phenomenological observation.

Something happens, however, in the life of everyone who is born, to shatter that primitive environment of total security, to which trust is the only appropriate response. That embryonic organism experiences itself as being pushed out of that warm environment! The environment ejects it! The muscles and the whole foetal arrangement push the embryo out into an open space!

As a newborn child I suddenly feel for the *first* time the immense openness of the world around me, a world which I cannot control—it is just there.[1] At this point I have no capacity for

[1] Although it may seem a bit awkward, I am now shifting the focus of this discussion to the first person "I," the "I" which refers to everyman, in order to achieve greater empathy and to invite the reader to rediscover this psychogenetic sequence experientially for himself. The core argument of this chapter follows the general pattern of Carl Rogers' essay, "Toward a Modern Approach to Values." (Cf. Oden, *KC*, ch. 3.)

symbolic imagination of future possibilities, and thus we cannot speak of anxiety, but only of traumatic surprise.

In contrast to the closed womb, I now experience the open world. In contrast with the warm, cushiony environment, now I touch things that are hard and resistant and experience cold for the first time. Whereas in the previous situation I was supplied with food automatically, now I do not have that supply anymore. I am cut off from it. It pushed me out! I have to find some way of getting food. I experience all this with intense immediacy. I am not concerned about the future, but only the immediate present. My feelings are completely in contact with my immediate experiencing.

Another indignity: I did not have to *do* anything in that previous foetal environment. I did not even have to breathe. The environment breathed for me! I was supplied oxygen and all my immediate needs through the uterine matrix and umbilical cord. Then when that immensely comfortable environment pushed me out unceremoniously, I suddenly found air in my lungs! I found that there was a mechanism already built into me to cause me to have to draw air into my lungs, and push it out.

All this fantastic newness, this frightening immensity of something completely unknown around me, experiencing my organism in a completely new way! My supply cut off—my problem is that I got born! The only thing I can do is scream, and I do that.

24.2 The Primitive Encounter with Possibility. If at first it seems like an affront to be cast out of one's protected situation, it soon appears that there are certain compensations. Whereas in the uterine situation I was cramped, now I can move, make noise, probe my environment. Previously the food was always the same, now I taste different things. I now find myself confronted by vast, infinitely enticing possibilities. I grow in an increasing sensitivity to what they can mean. Before I was pushed out, I knew nothing of possibility. I knew no future. Then, everything was now. But already I am learning that much is ahead. I am attracted by these possibilities. Their variety excites my imagination.

Yet still I remain in almost complete contact with my organismic valuing process. I feel no disjunction between what I feel and how I express myself. In that sense I am a healthy organism. I do not distort anything or deny it from my awareness. I may not like something I experience, but I do not pretend that I do like it. If I dislike it, I yell. If I like it, I laugh and thoroughly enjoy myself.

One of the big compensations in my new open situation is that I develop some significant relationships with some of these great hulking people around me, whom I did not know in my former situation. They actually care for me. They even want me to explore my freedom. They want to make me feel at home (right here, think of it, in this open, unprotected, cutoff, seemingly hostile, vast, unknown space)! That is just what they want to try to do: to help me to move out into that amazing world of possibility! They are trying to supply in this open situation much the same sort of resources I had in the foetal situation. They bring me food, protection, keep me surrounded with soft, comforting warmth. I have learned that I can even trust them in much the same way that I used to trust the comfortable womb before. These peculiar, very large creatures that surround me, strangely enough, are faithful to me. I respond to their trustworthiness with responsive trust in them. But their faith in me is beginning to give me confidence that maybe I can even move out into that unexplored territory and find new ways of doing what I have been doing all the time, which is to trust, remain open to my environment despite its threats. So as I grow up, this probing process continues. I become a first-rate explorer of this peculiar place called the world, learning all I can about it, because it looks like this is what I am stuck with.

25. The Fall into Distorted Symbolization

25.1 The Fracture of Awareness. Now I am going to try to describe to you what happened to elicit anxiety as I emerged out of this situation of primordial trust. Here I was, living with my feelings very immediately, expressing myself just as I felt. But then I experienced these enormous people around me as re-

162

quiring certain things of me. They wanted me to do certain things in order to gain their approval. I needed them very badly. After all, they were about all I had to rely upon in this frightening world. As my language capacity improved, they began to tell me that if I didn't do things the way they wanted me to, they would yell things at me. They made it quite clear that they would not give me comfort if I did not see things their way. The gargantuan issue arose as to where the B.M.'s had to be put. The whole conflict really jolted my experiencing process. They made me feel as if I should not have some of the feelings that I really did have. The forced me to cut out of my awareness certain feelings which, as a matter of fact, I really did feel.

This caused a painful split, somehow, in my personality. Finally I just gave up and decided to do it their way. I decided I would play like I did not feel the way I really felt. That is what they seemed to want. I would go ahead and play ball according to their rules, in order to gain their love, attention, and care. I would value what they value, instead of what I value. It all seemed to be a part of growing up, a part of the great exploration that loomed ahead.

That was just one early instance, among many that followed, in which I increasingly came to look toward them for what I should feel, instead of to my own experiencing process. Doubtless they were right about the need for learning to order my life in a way that would not cause them a lot of trouble, but in the process I came to distrust my own experiencing process. After much practice, and it took a long time, finally I convinced myself that their ideas and judgments were really mine anyway, and better than those false values I once held when I was just responding immediately to my experiencing organism.

25.2 The Loss of Congruence. After a long time, I finally found that it became very difficult to feel my real feelings. I lost touch with myself. Whatever I experienced I twisted around to fit into my firmly established structure of value borrowed from the parent world. I had to distort a lot, of course, in order to do

163

this, but I managed to reshape the facts to suit my system of beliefs and values.

How the establishment got so fouled up, I do not know, but I do know this: Somehow I had to learn its language, conform to its expectations, succeed in terms of its standards which were a far cry from the way I was really feeling. Not surprisingly, I often found myself basically divided within. What I intended most deeply, and felt most profoundly, I often had to clothe and disguise, even to myself, because it did not always fit into the rules that had been programmed into me.

The saddest part of this story is, however, that finally I learned to be on my guard against anything that threatened to make me look carefully at this whole elaborate system of deceptive rationalizing upon which I had begun by now to rely heavily. I did not want anybody to confront me with my own feelings. That would have been the most threatening thing anybody could have done. I learned to defend myself rather skillfully against any real self-disclosure to others, and especially to myself. I carefully erected barriers which would keep the overall structure intact.

Something kept telling me that if I were really being a healthy, full-functioning person, I would be symbolizing my new experiences accurately, not denying them to awareness. But when your life is valued by significant others only conditionally when you conform to their presupposed ideas of value, you learn to play the game their way, even if it means denying much of your experience to awareness. You in fact learn that you cannot value yourself except insofar as you fulfill their value expectations of you. So I increasingly lost touch with myself.

25.3 The Bondage of the Will. What I am trying to clarify is how compulsive anxiety developed in its prototypical pattern. When certain occasions threatened this whole elaborate structure or exposed it to unavoidable self-examination, I increasingly experienced the vague apprehension of subliminal anxiety. When experiences occurred which made it seem to me that I might have to rethink my idealized image of myself, or even when I became vaguely aware that an experience might cause such a revolutionary self-examination, then, even as that experience approached the edge of my consciousness, I began to feel deeply anxious, and sought to close it off from awareness. Consequently, now when I experience an event or a relationship in which my real feelings are trying to make themselves known to me, I tend to oversymbolize it as a threat to my whole order of living.

For if I should suddenly take my present experiencing seriously, and listen to its voice responsively, it might incite a tremendous revolution in self-image which would force me to deal with a flood of other incongruencies at many other points along the way, and I do not want to undergo that painful civil war. It seems that it might break me right in half.

I am trying to be very descriptive and specific about this process of experiencing anxiety, but the truth of the matter is that when I experience anxiety it is very vague and diffuse. I never know where it comes from. I only experience it somewhere out on the far edge of my consciousness. It comes from a very low, inarticulate level of awareness.

It is in this way that anxiety clangs an alarm signal inside which makes me cut certain experiences entirely out of awareness. It thus perpetuates the situation of the bondage of my will to distortions and inconsistencies within. Anxiety performs this very important function for my continued inauthenticity, cementing the bondage of my will to estrangement from myself. It keeps alerting me to any possible danger which might allow into my consciousness some challenge to my basic self-understanding. So anxiety is a relation to possibility, a particular relation to that possibility in which I sense my whole self-image to be under threat of rearrangement.

26. The Recovery of Trust

Now I wish briefly to raise the question: How is it possible, or is it even desirable, to get from here back to my original situation of primordial trust or something analogous to it? How is it possible to find myself again in that situation in which I was trusting my environment to provide a safe context for exploration of the vast range of possibilities of the frightening world, yet with a fundamental sense of openness to my own experiencing process? What is it that frees one to embrace oneself as an organismic valuing process, to receive oneself as a being in process, in movement toward possibility, embracing new possibilities without distortions in awareness?

26.1 Unconditional Trust. It can be argued, from both the theological and psychotherapeutic points of view, that liberation from anxiety occurs only through a relationship of unconditional trust in which I experience through another person the reality of unconditional trust. I experience a relation in which another is sufficiently capable of entering into my frame of reference so as to help me to see my distortions, bring them into awareness, and trust myself. I experience such a person as trustworthy, i.e., one to whom I feel free to entrust my very self and this whole dangerous process of self-scrutiny. I can learn to trust my own experience and venture imaginatively upon the enticing ocean of possibility, even allowing my idealized self-image slowly to crumble, because I no longer need to trust in it. Instead I can trust in my own concrete experiencing.

Such a healing relationship is only possible when one is confronted by another who is already in real contact with his real feelings, who has learned anew to experience himself just as immediately as he once experienced himself as a neonate. When I am in a direct relationship with such a congruent person, I suddenly see his openness and congruence as a possibility for myself.

How am I freed to trust? Is it because he has empathetically entered into my frame of reference and placed a mirror before me, so as to say, "This is how I hear you telling me you experience yourself"? Is it because his own feelings seem congruent with his experience, and his responses seem to be rooted in reality? Perhaps I can trust him only because he trusts his own organismic valuing process, and thus by analogy I can receive myself in a way which previously was quite impossible.

In any event, a necessary element of my learning to trust my experiencing is finding myself trusted by another. That does not mean that he trusts all my responses to be in line with his value system, but rather he trusts that when my responses are in line with my own deepest feelings, my behavior will be fitting, appropriate, responsible, and based in reality. Finding such a relationship permits a revolution in self-awareness.

I am speaking not of the *idea* of trust, but a concrete *relationship*, in which another person concretely mediates to me unconditional trust in my own organismic experiencing process. This is what frees me from the kind of idolatrous self-protection and denials to awareness which once intensified anxiety. I think I need not go into further detail here in pointing out that there is a whole theory of psychotherapy[2] that is based precisely upon this process which I have described as unconditional trust.

26.2 The Implicit Ontological Assumption of Therapeutic Trust. Now I am going to rechannel the issue a bit and talk more specifically about a theology of psychotherapeutic trust. There is a tacit ontological assumption underlying all effective psychotherapy that it is not merely the counselor who is the source of trust toward the client's organismic valuing process, but that the client is being met by a trust which is somehow rooted in reality itself and that the final reality which we confront in life is trustable.

It is not necessary for the therapist to be conceptually aware of that assumption in order to function effectively, but he must mediate trust operationally, relationally, nonverbally, if constructive change is to occur. The therapist himself is not the final cource of trust. He merely points to a trust which has its source beyond himself. He assumes that the future can be embraced, despite all seeming threats to one's essential self-affirmation. Throughout the therapeutic relation he is implicitly announcing that there is a source of trust in life itself, despite all human distrust and even despite the limitations of his own finite trustworthiness. If he were to die, that source of trustworthiness would remain. Even if all men were to die, that source of trustworthiness would remain. He is trying to say (nonverbally) through that

---

[2] Rogers, *PSS*, pp. 207 ff., *OBP*, passim.

relationship that the troubled person has no ontological need of being anxious; i.e., that there is no ground in being itself for his anxiety, that it is only a matter of his distrusting his own experiencing amid his self-idealization.

The therapeutic process assumes that there is no final threat in reality itself, and that it is always possible realistically to embrace one's own present experiencing however threatening it may seem and receive it into awareness. Although the good therapist may well understand that there may be perfectly meaningful reasons why an individual is experiencing anxious distortions in his awareness, he sees no ground in being itself, no ontological undergirding, for compulsive anxiety. He assumes that man does not know himself properly when he is neurotically anxious. This is doubtless a much broader, more profound ontological assumption than is ordinarily acknowledged by psychotherapy.

26.3 The Explicit Witness of the Kerygma. The last step in our argument concerns the worship and witness of the community of celebration. For it is precisely this implicit assumption of the faithfulness of reality toward us which is made explicit in the witness of the Christian community to God's self-disclosure in the Christ event. Christian worship celebrates and Christian preaching announces an event in which God has made known to us his faith in us.

We have been taught to think of faith as something we ought to have toward God. The biblical witness speaks of *faith in God as our response to the faithfulness of God.* Trust in God is our reply to the trustworthiness of God. The celebrating community points unapologetically, joyfully, to that event in which that faithfulness of God toward us is once for all dramatically made known.

If this is so, then the therapeutic agent (or anyone else) who mediates unconditional trust amid man's anxious distortions is performing a representative ministry implicitly communicating to the troubled person that his own experience is trustable, that he is free to embrace himself as a movement toward the future, that his trust and openness toward himself is rooted in reality

THE NEONATE PROTOTYPE OF TRUST

itself. Trust by whom or by what? That is not clear in the thera-peutic process as such. It is at least clear that the source of the trust is not merely in the interpersonal relationship; it is somehow in creation itself, or some principle in creation itself.[3]

All human forms of trust are conditional and limited. It is only in a limited way that the therapist can enter into the situa-tion of the other. It is only in a limited way that he can verbalize the client's feelings. It is only in a limited way that the client can receive into his own experience what he hears verbalized. It is only in a limited way that the therapist can trust his own organis-mic valuing process, since he is a finite and limited being, capable of only limited imagination and a limited verbal capacity. The final source of cosmic trust upon which that therapeutic function is resting, however, is a perfect and unconditional trust which according to the celebrating community is allegedly made known in an event in history. To this we now turn.

[3] Oden, KC, ch. 1.

chapter VIII

THE ONTOLOGICAL IMPOSSIBILITY
OF ANXIETY BEFORE GOD

Having viewed anxiety from the perspective of man's often distorted self-perception, we now turn to the attempt to understand anxiety from an entirely different point of view, namely, God's perception of man. It is precisely the audacity of theology to inquire into God's own encounter with and claim upon the future, and man's appropriate response to it. Theology differs from phenomenology in that it deals not merely with man's self-understanding but with God's understanding of man amid all the wretched dysfunction of human self-understanding.

27. The Vulnerability of the Language of Trust

27.1 **Reshaping the Question.** A covenant ontology (cf. 13.1) is distinguished from all other ontologies in that it inquires into man's being as he exists before God. A reappraisal of anxiety in the light of a covenant ontology would be a review of the being of man as he stands before God's future, as the promise of that future is laid bare according to the Judeo-Christian hope. Instead of asking how man experiences the future as an abyss of possibility (the phenomenological question), we are instead now asking a much more fundamental question involving what the future actually *is* before God, and therefore how man is being called to respond to the reality of God's future.

Although such a transition may seem abrupt, I wish to show how it is made necessary by the very logic of our previous analysis. We have now come to the edge of our phenomenological analysis only to find ourselves still burdened with the question of the ontological grounds upon which trust might proceed. The therapeutic process itself points to its ontological ground, but can only implicitly assume some unspecified resource of trust. It is in this way that a careful, purely phenomenological inquiry into anxiety itself calls for further theological inquiry. It asks whether futurity has revealed itself as trustworthy. An adequate phenomenology, therefore, implicitly awakens the question of revelation.

I am not here suggesting a method of correlation (Tillich) by which the existential situation of culture raises questions for theology to answer (thus inadvertently narrowing the range of the theological task to the boundaries of culture's often inauthentic questions about itself),[1] but rather a method of anaological reflection by which the deepest questions of culture are seen as already illuminated by analogy with the action of God, and in which the actual functioning of culture is seen already implicitly to presuppose in its own way the trustworthy God who is witnessed to explicitly in proclamation.

27.2 The Precariousness of the Theological Task. Admittedly the transition from phenomenology to theology plunges us into an avalanche of problems and potential misunderstandings which were not previously so harassing. Even readers who presumably have been nurtured in the Christian tradition (of course amid the accelerating process of secularization) will find the transition frustrating, for the simple reason that we know our own experience better than God's experience of us. And yet it is precisely God's own experience of the future and its revolutionary implica-

---

[1] Oden, *CTP*, ch. 4.

171

tion for human awareness that theology is assigned to attempt to clarify self-consistently and faithfully.

However audacious the Christian proclamation may seem, however many pitfalls it may reveal, it nevertheless proposes a reinterpretation of anxiety and trust which deserves the attention of every imaginative man. We are alleging as a consensus of the Judeo-Christian tradition that the reality of the future is understandable only in the light of God's own dealing with it, as made known in the history of the people of Israel.

I as much as anyone am aware of the vulnerability of such language to the charge of being merely an introverted monologue of a particular community of discourse. Admittedly, talk of God's action in the history of the people of Israel does take place chiefly within a special community which understands itself as charged with traditioning it, and even there it takes place with perplexing ambiguities, shameful inconsistencies, and regrettable misunderstandings. Why then do I persist, along with this community, in speaking of God's dealings with the future, God's perception of history, God's own claim upon the abyss of possibility? Why is such talk necessary? I answer: I am convinced, along with many historic and contemporary companions in the Judeo-Christian tradition, that the very reality of the future is not adequately understandable apart from God's own promise for it. If I did not have such a tenacious commitment at this point, I certainly would not waste my time being a theologian. I would stick to the much more obvious task of phenomenological analysis. So if others may view what follows as an innocuous Sunday school lesson, or prescientific mythological nonsense, or dubious subjectivism, from my own point of view we are only now entering into the real depth of the inquiry at hand, in relation to which the previous phenomenological analysis tends to become perhaps an interesting, but not decisive, prelude.

28. Belonging to One to Whom the Future Belongs

28.1 The Ontology of Trust. My central thesis may now be formulated: *It is impossible to be anxious before God if God* is understood as the one who has disclosed himself as trustworthy on the far side of the destruction of all our gods. No matter how absurdly I experience subjective anxiety over my gods, the future objectively belongs to God. He remains faithful to us despite our faithlessness toward him. That is the meaning of the covenant: The steadfast faithfulness of God toward man and toward future time is elemental to the human condition. I cannot exist in any other condition than as a recipient of the eternal trustworthiness of God, if God himself determines to be eternally trustworthy.

In the midst of all our anxiety-creating idolatries, the Judeo-Christian tradition remembers and celebrates the coming God to whose future man belongs. The unresolved question is: To what extent is God's future actually able to be acknowledged and received as my own authentic future? Put nonmythologically, how can I understand myself as *valued by the giver of values in the midst of all my threatened values?* Amid all potential threats to cherished relationships, how can I know that I am being valued precisely through the destruction of my highest values by the one who bestows all finite value and calls all finite values to nothingness? Only if that one makes himself known as trustworthy.

To entrust oneself to this negator of exaggerated values, this slayer of our gods, is to be freed and open to the future. This is a secularized way of talking about trust in the trustworthiness of God. For at the very point at which we are most deeply anxious about the death of our causes, the demise and twilight of our gods, we are being freed to be open to the future *without* our gods, i.e., as it is!

Anyone who has deeply experienced human existence knows that finite goods, however valuable, pass away, like flowers and grass. They wither and die. But there is a community of men who celebrate the fact that even in the midst of the death of these finite relationships we are being met by one who loves us and offers us a remarkable, limited, temporal share in his created order. This community of men does not merely remember the *idea* that the slayer of values is trustworthy, but rather an *event* in which he has made himself known as trustworthy. The code name which symbolizes the whole constellation of expectations,

173

meanings, and events through which this self-disclosure is clarified is Jesus Christ, which names a person and an event inextricably bound up with the history of Israel. To the community which lives out of that event, it is precisely amid its most intense consciousness of threats to finite values (nation, property, family, even life itself) that it is being freed courageously to affirm the abyss of possibility as God's gift, and therefore good.

From a certain point of view nothing is more absurd than the suggestion that even in the midst of my *death*, the final enemy of all my values, I can receive and affirm life. Although this is a seeming paradox, the gospel as a whole is paradoxical in the sense of going beyond our *doxa*, our common opinion about life.[2] For it is commonly held that value actualization ends with death. Christian celebration affirms the life which to be sure ends in death, but whose value actualization is only a fragmented mirror of the whole process of cosmic value actualization, in which for a time it is invited to participate. Life is an unearned given, to be received within the boundaries of death. Even its limitations may be celebrated as the gracious gift of the limiter, whose finite goods could not have been offered except under the conditions of limitation.[3] This remarkable Hebraic attitude toward God as value negator is dramatized by Job, who, having been denied all sorts of future value actualization (his wealth, his children, his friends, his health), stands before the destruction of his values and affirms, "The Lord gave, and the Lord has taken away; blessed be the name of the Lord" (Job 1:21).

28.2 The Absurd Illusion. If this is so, then insofar as we live toward the future as though it were not trustable on the far side of our gods, we are living under an illusion. To live as if the future were not in God's hands is to embody an absurdity. Subjectively, internally, psychologically, I may continue to experience intense anxiety over my gods. But my ontological condition, my being before God, the way I *am* from God's point of view, is as a finite

[2] Tillich, *Systematic Theology*, I (University of Chicago Press, 1953), 63 ff.
[3] Bultmann, *Essays Philosophical and Theological*, trans. James C. G. Greig (Macmillan, 1955), pp. 1-21.

creature living toward a future the purposes of which are already secured and to which I may entrust even my death.[4] To do so does not mean that I will get my stubborn way in the future, but that whatever awaits me in that empty nothing toward which my existence is being hurled is already knowable in the Christ event as trustworthy.

My essential affirmation is therefore that *man cannot be anxious before God but only before the gods*. This formulation places the psychological question of anxiety squarely within the context of the ontological question. Pursued to the depth of the covenant relation: even if man wanted to be anxious before God, he could not, since to know God appropriately is to know his trustworthiness and the promise of the future to which all men juridically belong, however much they may deny it with their own actions. Demonic anxiety has no ontological rootage, no ground upon which to stand in the created order. It is only the product of idolatrous imagination. Effective psychotherapy reveals this. A good therapist is the shepherd of being, witnessing to the trustability of being itself, not by mere words but through a living relationship.

28.3 Freedom to Face the Future. We are asking who man is, as one who exists before God, not merely how he feels about his existence. If he *is* freed for the future, he is therefore being called to *become who he is*, i.e., to become the free man, free to trust his present experiencing process, free to move toward the abyss of possibility in self-determining confidence. It is in this way that the New Testament promise of God's future is experienced as a profoundly liberating word. For if the trustworthiness of God frees us from reliance upon our gods, then it delivers us from demonic anxiety. If man actually *is* the recipient of unconditional trustworthiness, this frees him analogically to trust his own organismic experiencing, even amid profound threats to values.

It is precisely in response to the promise of the securing of God's purpose in as yet undetermined history that faith experi-

___
[4] Barth, *CD*, III/1; III/2, *passim*.

175

ences itself as most profoundly freed to direct itself freshly and openly toward the vast horizon of ever changing possibilities.[5] Man the valuer is now being freed to reject certain valued possibilities, to achieve only limited values, to negate his idealized self-image. He is free to choose some values and negate others, knowing that whatever he chooses will be received into the forgiving memory of God. He is free to stand before the future and say yes to this and no to that, confessing before God his inadequacy to embody all the goods possible and giving thanks for those that are possible.

29. Biblical Images of Trust

29.1 The Coming Reign of God. Jesus proclaimed: The reign of God is at hand. This means: God has robbed the future of its threat. He has asserted his own lordship over history. He has plundered the house of the strong man Anxiety. The future is in God's hands. God undercuts our anxieties by showing us that what finally makes life worth living is not under threat. What makes life worth living? Finally nothing less than the source and end of all finite values, the one whom the Christian community has learned to call father, even amid the destruction of our finite values.

The one who gives and finally slays all our values is not subject to value negation. That is a secularized way of expressing the proclamation of the nowness of God's reign. We can now rejoice that the one in whose hands the future exists has already asserted his lordship over time, and therefore over all the hazardous, threatening possibilities of the future.[6]

If so, then neurotic and self-destructive anxiety is undermined. The final reality is trustable. Man is freed for the future which God himself is bringing. Normal anxieties continue to be directed toward limited, contextual values, but the divisive power of demonic anxiety is undercut.

[5] Jürgen Moltmann, *The Theology of Hope* (Harper, 1967), pp. 139 ff.
[6] R. Bultmann, *TNT*, I, 4-15; W. G. Kümmel, *Promise and Fulfilment*, trans. Dorothea M. Barton (Allenson, 1957), ch. 1.

The world is therefore being offered a word of radical permission to receive the future without dread. The judgment of our gods continues, but the judgment is directed primarily against our gods and not against us. The final word is a word of grace.

29.2 Victory over the Demonic Powers. The crucial event in Christian memory which symbolizes trust on the far side of human finitude is cross-and-resurrection. The cross is a way of speaking about the worst that history can do to defeat the most promising form of value actualization (the promised messiah). The resurrection is a way of speaking about the trustworthiness of God's purpose which exists on the far side of hopeless crucifixion. On the basis of its memory of the resurrection, the earliest Christian community had an amazingly hopeful attitude of trust toward a most unpromising future. It looked with great expectation toward the fulfillment of God's purpose in a time of unparalleled persecution, suffering, conflict, and threats of all sorts. The early Christian community celebrated the total cosmic future *as if* the demonic forces were already defeated and *as if* history were already delivered into the hands of the one who had met them as trustworthy in the cross and resurrection.

After Jesus' death the proclaimer became the proclaimed, and was remembered as the one who ushered in the reign of God in history.[7] So the primitive Christian community understood itself as living in a historical context in which the reign of God had begun and would soon be consummated. The last battle has not been fought with the demonic forces, but the decisive battle has already been fought and won. The decisive victory is already in God's hands, and the proclaiming community now has the task of making known to all men that the victory has indeed already occurred. The early church understood itself as living in between the time in which the demonic powers had already been defeated and yet the final consummation of that victory was still being awaited.[8] Bitter skirmishes continue in an ambiguous history which has not yet heard the news.

[7] Bultmann, *TNT*, pp. 33 ff.
[8] Kümmel, *Promise and Fulfilment*, pp. 105 ff.

In terms of this understanding of history, what happens to demonic anxiety? Does it have any ground upon which to stand? The demonic forces are cast out of their fortress.[9] It is now absurd to regard them as having final sway over history. Although they still may be subjectively experienced, the demonic forces may be exorcized by the power of the Holy Spirit. They are now perceived to be rooted in an ontological impossibility. They have no ground upon which to stand in the new age of God's love. If we continue to choose idolatrous anxiety as a way of life, we choose that which is finally impossible, that which before God is impotent and defeated! Thus, according to the logic of the New Testament, it is absurd to continue to live *as if* we were under threat, merely because our gods are under threat.

Modern men may be loath to accept such a message, clothed as it is in primitive and mythological imagery. But the nub of the kerygma, so far as the future is concerned, in its bare demythologized form, is that man can be anxious before his gods, but not before God. Only one thing is not possible for me, and that is to flee who I am, to cease being the covenant partner of God who is confronted by God's future and God's promise. The story of the people of Israel is precisely the story of a people's attempt to flee itself, to escape the gracious covenant relationship, in the attempt to secure an idolatrous future. But the whole force of the biblical witness points to the God who is faithful to us despite our faithlessness toward him, whose future is actually offered to us even when we reject it.

29.3 The Gift of Freedom. That God secures our future does not mean, however, that human freedom is negated, but rather that it is enabled, liberated to be itself. Authentic human freedom is to determine ourselves as covenant partners with God, free for the future which belongs to him. Inauthentic human freedom is our spurious self-determination which moves us away from, rather than toward, our genuine humanity.

[9] Matt. 12:29; Mark 3:27.

It is worth carefully distinguishing that Christian celebration is not speaking merely of the *possibility* of God's claim upon the future, but of the actuality of that claim. That is, God's reign, God's determination to secure the future, is not merely a possibility which we may or may not actualize, depending upon our limited knowledge or weak inclinations, but instead is always already an *actuality* in the Christ event. It is not as if a potential new relation to the future had been conceptualized by Christian proclamation, but remained for man's ingenuity and volition to actualize.[10] Rather, the new future of man is already fully in effect through God's own verdict. The Christian hope is based upon the established actuality of God's lordship over the future, not merely its fragile possibility. Christian freedom for the future is therefore understood in the New Testament as a fully already given gift to be contextually received. But whether we receive it or not, it is nevertheless given. Whether or not we order our lives in terms of the reign of God, it has nevertheless begun and we live in the midst of it. The most that we can do against it is to choose to live under the illusion that we are still bound to now impotent demonic powers.

So the Christian witness does not merely speak of our human *hope* that the future *might* ultimately be taken into the purposes of God. Rather, it celebrates an event in which the future is already proleptically, anticipatively known to be taken objectively into the claim of God. For the New Testament proclamation, the future no less than the past is stamped with the image of the creator, who has met his estranged creation with redemption and reconciliation. This is why the Christian message does not speak first of all, or even principally, of *man's* hope for the future or man's stance before possibility, but instead fundamentally of *God's* objective claim upon the future and God's own determination to reclaim the far reaches of the abyss of possibility. Again the kerygma announces not the *idea* of the future being secured, or the *conception* of God's claim upon the future, but instead

[10] Barth, *CD*, II/2, 516 ff.; "The Gift of Freedom," *The Humanity of God* (John Knox Press, 1960), pp. 69 ff.

an *event* in which God's actual claim upon the future is once for all made known.

29.4 Anticipating Objections. Has the future really changed? Does Christian faith know of a future different from that which previously was known? Is the future in some sense reconstituted in the light of the eschatological divine claim upon it, or is it merely viewed in a different way?

The future itself has not changed, but faith's perception of it has radically changed. The future has always already as a matter of fact been taken up objectively into the promise of God. The Christ event does not change the will of God, but rather it more clearly expresses what his will toward the future has always been. If prior to faith we had been imagining that the future portends horrifying threats to values necessary for our existence, now it is possible to affirm even the potential negation of our values, since our values have been de-absolutized and thus de-terrorized.

Faith's analogical reasoning embraces the future in the confidence that God himself has embraced it. If God is open to the future, I can open myself to it. If God hopes in the promise of the future, I can hope in its promise. Faith reasons by analogy. God's freedom for the future enables authentic human freedom for the future.

Do I mean to imply, however, that the future will no longer threaten? Surely I am not seriously proposing that no conceivable possibility is evil. To regard all future possibilities as fundamentally or even obliquely good is hopelessly utopian. Yet how does our argument differ?

For the man of faith the future remains what it is: the abyss of possibility into which being has not yet entered. As such, it is and remains capable of threatening our lesser and higher values. All finite goods are hazarded as they encounter the future. In fact, we may go much further to insist that the future is the ultimate *enemy* of all finitude which would pretend to be more than finite. So we do not in any sense mean to be saying that the future will no longer threaten. What we do say, however, is that threats to finite values are no longer taken with ultimate seriousness, since these values have been de-absolutized and therefore de-terrorized. *The authentic man faces the future with an understandable and constructive anxiety over the limited values which he intends contextually to achieve, but without the idolatrous anxieties which cripple human eros.* The mature man learns to celebrate the context in which his values are threatened as well as those contexts in which his values are fulfilled. The student who is acutely anxious over an examination is being invited by being itself to learn to celebrate even this threatening context as a part of a larger affirmation of the learning process which makes his suffering not only bearable but meaningful. The businessman whose investment is jeopardized by a fluctuating market situation is being invited by being itself to learn to affirm even this threatening context as a part of the general, unpredictable arena of exchange of values which takes place in creation. The hospitalized patient who stares at the white ceiling and anxiously envisions his ominous future is being invited by being itself to learn what only the man facing death honestly can learn: that all his values come to naught in time, but that he can nevertheless in the courage of radical trust come to celebrate precisely those contexts in which his values come to naught.

Do I therefore open the door to a foolhardy attitude toward the future in which there is no sense of risk, no concern for the protection of significant values, but only a foolish and venturesome recklessness which calls itself courage? Surely that is not my intention. Hopefully the maturing self can learn to accept the invitation of being to value values appropriately, proportionally, which means contextually, relatively, and finitely; but this certainly does not mean that nothing is to be valued.

The opportunity we are being given by anxiety-creating situations is to learn to renegotiate our contracts with our gods. For when our anxieties press us most compulsively and demonically, it is just then that the chance is being given to examine which limited values we have absolutized into gods. From the viewpoint of our gods, these contracts are never open to renegotiation. But reality is always against the gods, and therefore continually on the side of renegotiation.

30. God's Faith in Us

It is only the trustworthiness of God which enables us to have trust in him. Expressed more pointedly: The heart of the biblical covenant is *not that we have faith in God, but that God has faith in us.* Much that we have learned in Protestant and Catholic moralism about our duty to have faith in God needs to be unlearned in the light of the biblical witness to God's steadfast faithfulness toward us.

30.1 How Is Trust Possible? The English word *trust* connotes assured anticipation, confident hope, reliance upon another's integrity. Trust is not possible without the trustworthiness of another. Trust in the future is possible and reasonable only if the future has proleptically made itself known as trustworthy.

Limited forms of human trust based upon solemnly entered contracts are elemental to the social nature of man. In the economic order, for example, trust appears as an indispensable word in credit relationships, implying a confidence in the ability and intention of a buyer to pay for goods supplied without present payment. Although trust is necessary to economic exchange, it sometimes is shown to be built upon the sand of man's tragic untrustworthiness.

Whereas every finite relationship remains subject to doubt as to its ultimate trustworthiness, the Judeo-Christian community witnesses to one relationship in which all men always already stand, in which an alleged unconditional trustworthiness is made known. In order to clarify the trustworthiness of God, the Judeo-Christian tradition tells a story, the history of the covenant of God with the people of Israel. In that story his steadfast faithfulness toward all men is dramatized in a way that invites men to trust him.

Paul develops the analogy most concisely as follows: "If we are faithless, he remains faithful—for he cannot deny himself" (II Tim. 2:13). What does that mean? God entrusts *himself* to us, puts himself in our hands, even though we are untrustworthy, even though we slay him! In the crucifixion, Jesus himself embodies the words of Job: "Though he slay me, yet will I trust in him." But the irony of God's action is compounded by the fact that he is entrusting himself to the worst that man can do. Such is the foolishness of the gospel.

God himself in the cross has given the example of radical openness to the future. We are being called not to do what Jesus did in fulfilling his messianic vocation, but to trust the same reality to which he unconditionally entrusted himself as we go about fulfilling our own special vocations.

30.2 Radical Trust. Radical trust in the trustworthiness of God is prototypically expressed in the Old Testament in the figure of Abraham, whom the Lord called, saying, "Go from your country and your kindred and your father's house to the land that I will show you. And I will make of you a great nation" (Gen. 12:1-2). Leave the security, the normal expectations and values which are presupposed in your familiar environment, and (pointing toward the endless desert) *go!* "So Abram went . . .," and was remembered by the Hebrews as the father of radical openness to the future. The supreme paradigm of Abraham's trust, however, is in the familiar story of the sacrifice of Isaac (Gen. 22, which should be read aloud by anyone wishing to receive the full impact of the narrative).

God instructs Abraham to take his only son, Isaac, to a certain mountain and offer him as a burnt offering. There is no question of Abraham's love for his son, but he trusts in the trustworthiness of God. "Abraham rose early in the morning, saddled his ass, and took . . . his son Isaac; and he cut the wood for the burnt offering." When he laid the wood of the burnt offering on Isaac and took his knife in hand, Isaac asked, "Behold, the fire and the wood; but where is the lamb for a burnt offering?" Abraham said, "God will provide." It was not until Abraham had raised the knife in his hand that a voice from heaven came to him, saying, " 'Do not lay your hand on the lad or do anything to him; for now I know that you fear God, seeing you have not withheld your son, your only son, from me.' And Abraham lifted up his eyes and looked, and behold, behind him was a ram, caught in a thicket by his horns; and Abraham went and took the ram, and offered it up as a burnt offering instead of his son." This is a typically Hebraic way of talking about radical readiness to trust in the trustworthiness of God. It was only when Abraham was ready to trust God even in the face of the loss of his dearest earthly relationship, his only heir, that God's promise to Israel through Abraham was reaffirmed, having been so severely tested. This is a story not merely about Abraham's faith in God, but about God's faithfulness toward Abraham which enabled his radical openness.

As historically sophisticated modern men, we must not become so concerned about the alleged facts of the case that we miss the parabolic impact of the story. We have no objective report of "facts," but only the memory of the people of Israel who wanted to make a certain point: The God who covenants with Israel is trustworthy even amid the most improbable circumstances of hopelessness. When finite values, such as human life or national destiny, are de-absolutized, the anxieties they engender are de-terrorized.

The future belongs to the one to whom the self belongs, the giver and ground of the self. If I belong, whether I know it or not, to that final reality to whom the future belongs, then my future is from a certain point of view already known, secured, warranted, even though from a contextual standpoint it looks as if my values are being slain.

part three

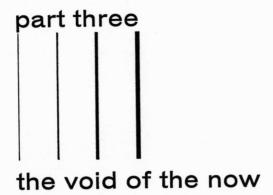

the void of the now

chapter IX

THE STRUCTURE OF BOREDOM

31. The Predicament of the Present

31.1 Inattentive Existence. Every man exists in a relation to the present. The only moment in which any man actually lives is now. He may pretend he lives in the past, or he may imagine himself in a possible future situation, but his vantage point while he is remembering or imagining is always the present.

Due to our anxiety over the future and our guilt over the past, we ignore and flee the present. Our lives are so bound up in living falsely toward the past and falsely toward the future that the momentous gift of the present is unreceived. We experience an inattentive, absentee existence, which disregards the promise of the now.

We are being called by being itself to receive each moment afresh as a new arena for value actualization. This is what our time should be filled with: receiving and creating contextual values. But instead we are *bored* with this now. Because of our preoccupation with the dead past and the possible future, our ears are dulled to the address of reality in the moment. Instead of experiencing the fullness of time in the present, as if now were eternity entering time, we feel on our hands the slow *emptiness* of time. Instead of understanding this moment as the only moment we actually ever live, we feel that this moment is perhaps the dullest, least interesting of all. It is only some past moment that we cherish, or only some future moment which we idealize as fulfilling for us.

So we play a game with time, pretending a glorious past and a promising future, but no present. Although it is a fantasy, we take the game with a certain absurd seriousness. In our romanticisms we dream of those good old days, and in our messianisms we dream of the great deliverances to come; but in the meantime we live as if the present had no being, or as if its being had no value. Real values and meanings lie behind us and before us in time, but certainly not now.

Like the characters in *Waiting for Godot*, we wait for something that is constantly meeting us. The one we wait for visits us every day, but we do not recognize him, since we cannot believe he could be so near.

31.2 Boredom as an Analogue of Guilt and Anxiety. As we explore the phenomenon of boredom, it appears to have an essential structure directly analogous to both guilt and anxiety. The following terms capture the essential parallelism of guilt, boredom, and anxiety:

Time:	PAST	PRESENT	FUTURE
Encountered through:	Memory (re-imaging actualized being)	Experience (encountering actualizing being)	Imagination (pre-imaging possible being)
Predicament:	GUILT (irresponsible negation of past value)	BOREDOM (disregarding unawareness of current value)	ANXIETY (overresponse to threats to potential values)

We do not assign to boredom a minor status in the order of human affections. We count it to be *the* essential form of the predicament of man in the present. Boredom is to the present what guilt is to the past. Boredom is to concrete experience what anxiety is to imagination.

A more detailed display of the parallelism of the structures of guilt, boredom, and anxiety may be seen in diagrammatic form: This diagram recapitulates the key terms of Parts I and II, showing their similarity to the key terms of Part III. Part I, the structure of guilt, is as follows: The self (1) looks retrospectively backward in time, through memory (2) to the past (3), symbolizing certain events or relationships as negations of values associated with the self-image (4). Guilt (5) is the awareness that one has negated values regarded as necessary for one's existence. To the degree to which those values are elevated to idolatries (6), the self is vulnerable to intensive, compulsive, demonic guilt (7). One is liberated from bondage to demonic guilt when he learns that he is affirmed by the giver of values amid his value negations, and on that basis is freed to affirm himself as forgiven (8).

Part II, the structure of anxiety, is as follows: The self (1) looks anticipatively forward in time, through imagination (2) to the future (3). When the future is symbolized as a threat to essential values (4), one experiences anxiety (5). Anxiety is the consciousness that values considered necessary for one's existence are under threat. To the degree to which one's finite values become god (6), one is vulnerable to demonic anxiety (7). One is liberated from bondage to demonic anxiety when he finds it possible to trust (8) in the trustworthiness of the abyss of possibility precisely amid the destruction of his gods.

Part III, the structure of boredom, analogously, is as follows: The self (1) relates to the now or present actuality in the mode of immediate experiencing (2). When that present (3) is symbolized as being devoid of values regarded as necessary for one's existence (4), one experiences boredom (5). Boredom is the awareness that the essential values through which one fulfills himself are not able to be actualized under these present circumstances. To the degree to which these limited values are elevated to absolutes which appear to be unactualizable (6), one is vulnerable to intensive, depressive, demonic boredom (7). When it

THE STRUCTURE OF BOREDOM

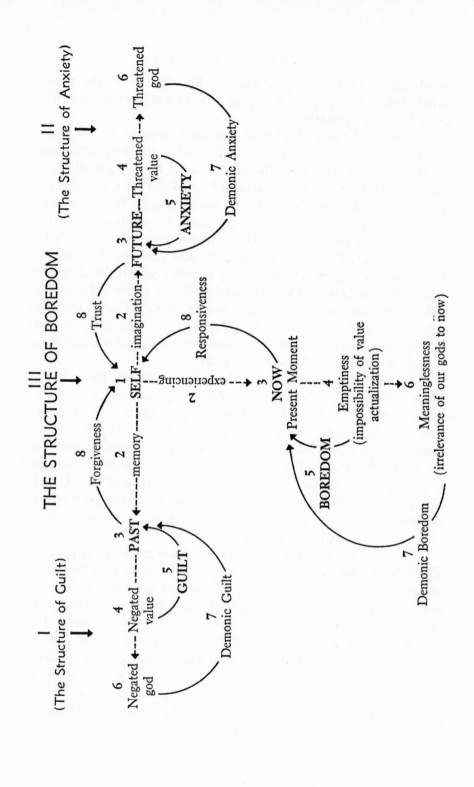

I (The Structure of Guilt)

II (The Structure of Anxiety)

III

8 — Trust
2 — imagination → FUTURE — Threatened value → Threatened god
3   4   6
5 — ANXIETY
7 — Demonic Anxiety

8 — Forgiveness
2 — memory → PAST
1 — SELF
3
4 — Negated value — GUILT
6 — Negated god
5 — GUILT
7 — Demonic Guilt

8 — Responsiveness
2 — experiencing → NOW — Present Moment
3
4 — Emptiness (impossibility of value actualization)
6 — Meaninglessness (irrelevance of our gods to now)
5 — BOREDOM
7 — Demonic Boredom

becomes clear to me that the gods I worship are irrelevant to the present moment, then I am easy prey to a nihilistic sense of emptiness and meaninglessness. The Judeo-Christian style of life affirmation in spite of the limitations of the present is a radical responsiveness to the now (8) as if it were indeed the gift and demand of God, a total listening to the now in the light of God's own self-disclosure and participation in contemporary history. It is this third structure that I will now try to clarify.

31.3 The Lacuna of Current Literature on Boredom. If previously we have commented on the inadequacies of the abundant literature on guilt and anxiety, it is not possible to do so in the case of boredom, since there exists no substantial fund of literature at all in this neglected area. Even the greatest contributions, such as Kierkegaard's pseudonymous literature,[1] are nevertheless tangential to our theme and do not provide us with a consistent phenomenology of the essential structure of boredom.

Although we have some excellent descriptive literary concretions of the life style of emptiness (Beckett, Williams, Ionesco, Albee, Salinger, Camus),[2] and although philosophy has explored the question of nothingness (Heidegger, Sartre, Bloch, Löwith, Kaufmann),[3] and although recent theology has concerned itself with questions of meaninglessness and responsibility in history (Tillich, Moltmann, Thielicke, Michalson),[4] and although psychotherapy has attempted treatment for various syndromes of

[1] Kierkegaard, *Either/Or* (2 vols.; Anchor Books; Doubleday, 1959); *Stages on Life's Way*, trans. Walter Lowrie (Princeton University Press, 1940); *Concluding Unscientific Postscript*, pp. 347 ff., 462 ff.

[2] Samuel Beckett, *Krapp's Last Tape and Other Dramatic Pieces* (Grove Press, 1960); Tennessee Williams, *Sweet Bird of Youth* (New Directions, 1959); Eugene Ionesco, *Four Plays*, trans. Donald M. Allen (Grove Press, 1958); Edward Albee, *The American Dream* and *The Zoo Story* (Signet Books; New American Library, 1960); J. D. Salinger, *Franny and Zooey* (Bantam Books, 1964); Albert Camus, *The Fall* and *Exile and the Kingdom* (Modern Library, 1957).

[3] Heidegger, *BT*, pp. 228 ff.; Sartre, *BN*; Ernst Bloch, *Das Prinzip Hoffnung* (Suhrkamp, 1959); Karl Löwith, *From Hegel to Nietzsche*, trans. David E. Green (Holt, Rinehart & Winston, 1964); W. Kaufmann, *The Faith of a Heretic* (Doubleday, 1961).

[4] Tillich, *The Courage to Be*, pp. 46 ff., 64 ff.; Moltmann, *Theology of Hope*; Thielicke, *Nihilism*, trans. John W. Doberstein (Harper, 1961); Carl Michalson, ed., *Christianity and the Existentialists* (Scribner's, 1956), pp. 1 ff., pp. 97 ff.

boredom and ennui (Horney, Binswanger, Frankl, van den Berg),[5] we have not yet seen any convincing integration of these resources, and certainly not any definitive statement of a purely phenomenological description of the structure of boredom. Much work remains to be done in building a basic literature on the predicament of man in the moment.

The times seem to call for such an effort, especially with the increase of leisure and the curious maladies of the society of abundance. The emerging generation is determined to live in the now. It is "the now generation," and we have yet to see what it will discover. Philosophically, the now is mostly unexplored territory, despite initial existentialist forays. The image of man toward which the emerging generation is struggling is increasingly open to the experiencing of the now, and increasingly liberated from certain forms of archaic traditionalism and, to some degree, messianism. Youth subculture is committed as never before to experimenting with the phenomenon of present existence.

32. The Gift of Reality

32.1 The Nowness of Experience. Consider the highly unique, absolutely unrepeatable, unsynonymous character of this moment. By the time I have a moment to reflect on it, it has already passed. All reflection is reflection after the fact, a second step away from immediate awareness of the experiencing now. Mark well the intensely mobile, processive, fluxing character of present time. We do not possess time, we are only recipients of it. It moves, and we either move with it or struggle vainly against it.

Does *now* mean this instant, this hour, this year, this century, or this epoch of history? We can and do use the term *now* in an extended sense, to refer to the "spacious present," the durable sequence in which many nows participate but together make up what is perceived as a single, complex, extended now. The fleeting

[5] Horney, NHG, pp. 259 ff.; Ludwig Binswanger, "The Case of Ellen West," *Existence*, pp. 191-365; Frankl, *The Doctor and The Soul*, pp. 121 ff., 239 ff.; J. H. van den Berg, *The Phenomenological Approach to Psychiatry* (London: Routledget Kegan, 1955).

192

instant might be symbolized by the snap of the finger, which has already ceased before the sound waves hit the ear. Even hearing and identifying the snap of fingers is a time-consuming process, existing in continuity with previous moments and presupposing a receiving organism which exists in durable time. The snap has meaning only as it is related to a whole set of events which make it interpretable as a snap. All human action has this character of belonging in a time continuum which lives out of a specific past toward an unspecific future. Whether now means an instant or an aeon, it is experienced as available, accessible, given, and objectively being met, in contrast to both the emptiness of the future and the irretrievability of the past. But however available and objectively given it may be, it nevertheless is experienced as in flux, a racing movement, a fleeting motion in which possibility is flooding into the present from the future, and disappearing into the past. What image might be used to express this torrent of movement? A rushing stream which erodes the structures of history, a cyclonic wind, a scythe which cuts down living organisms? Whatever images may be used, they must somehow capture active motion, since time is experienced as a movement in which infinitely complex possibilities are becoming first optable, then actual, actualized, and finally only remembered as having been actualized. Whether time is viewed as if the past is flooding into the future, or as if the future is pouring itself into the past, depends upon one's point of view, but in either case it is experienced as a highly complex processive movement which always must be responded to anew.[6]

32.2 Accessible Time. Since the future is inaccessible, and the past irretrievable, the only portion of time we experience as actually *given*, accessible to experiencing, is now. If the best word to describe the future is nothingness, or empty potentiality, perhaps the best description of present time is fullness, or immanent concreteness.

The nature of the present is best revealed by analogical con-

[6] Eugene T. Gendlin, *Experiencing and the Creation of Meaning* (The Free Press, 1962).

trast with the future and the past. The future is the only dimension of time which is filled with space. Nothing has ever happened in the future. Everything happens only in the present. While the past is immutable, the present lends itself to the redirection of being. While the future is impenetrable, enigmatic, the present is available for experience to explore.

Until it ceases being the present by becoming the past, the now is literally an explosive cosmic proliferation of happenings, a massive constellation of processive value actualizations. It is the unique time of the ripening of long-awaited potentialities, some of which have now come within the grasp of human volition. There is admittedly much that we can never know about any present moment, but this much we know: It is here and does not wait long for our response. It calls us to seize the opportunities it gives only once and then recalls. If we fail the opportunity of the now, it is absolutely irrecoverable.

Strictly speaking, only the present exists. The past has ceased to exist and the future does not yet exist. It is ironic that in contrast to the enormity of the envisionable future and the immense ranges of the historical past, the only speck of time bestowed to experience is that infinitely fleeting moment we call now. What do we actually possess of the past and future? Only their memory and imagination, which, to be quite candid, are nothing in reality except an image. The re-imaging of the past and the pre-imaging of the future are always one step away from the experienced concreteness of the present. The present is known by direct meeting, by sensual encounter: touching, hearing, tasting, seeing, smelling; while the past and future are known only through the precarious routes of memory and imagination.

32.3 The Self-Presentation of Reality. The great word for the now is *reality*. We are being called to be responsive to nothing more or nothing less than reality—that which is. Whereas imagination always has the tenuous character of venturing into possibility, and memory is always stalking the dead images of the past, immediate experiencing receives the great now gift of reality. That is all with which it has to work, and yet that is everything. Authenticity means responsibility. Responsibility means being responsive, sensitive to what is actually *given* in reality.

The form in which being meets me in the now, however, is always a highly channeled, specific form. As a finite being, I can only be in one place at one time. Optable possibilities meet me only under the limitations of the here and now. Therefore the concreteness of the demand of the moment is always given within a limited set of circumstances, never in some idealized, casebook situation. It is amid the unique interaction of the human organism and its real environment that responsibility takes place. This is why no one finally can tell another what his responsibility is. Only *he* can learn it in his specific time and place.

The tragic character of man's life in the present is seen in the fact that he is forced by time to leave behind many unactualized, envisioned values. Memory is strewn with unanswered calls, value negations, wasted opportunities, upon which guilt goes to work. Much that is offered goes unreceived. The now is the narrow boundary in which choices must be made.

33. The Idolatrous Intensification of Boredom

33.1 The Tyranny of the Present. To say that the present is an explosive proliferation of value actualizations, however, does not imply that I necessarily perceive it as such, or even share in it meaningfully. To say that I experience the now does not imply that I adequately or meaningfully experience it, or that I experience it without distortion.

The present, in fact, can come to exercise over me a vicious tyranny. It can become my enemy, the torturer and executioner of my dreams. I can so identify my well-being with some envisioned possibility or some remembered relationship that the restrictive conditions of this now become regarded as the crafty subverter of my self-fulfillment.

The essential predicament of man in the present is focused in the dynamics of a single term—boredom. Broadly defined, boredom is a form of awareness in which one symbolizes the present as emptied of potential or actual value actualization. Boredom perceives the present circumstances as objectively valueless and responds subjectively with inattentive passivity. When the now is symbolized as void of significant self-actualization, the understandable response is a sluggish, tedious sense of dullness.

One's special value orientation always shapes what is perceived as boring. A bored rancher watches his listless cattle, while he dreams of the wealth he will have when he sells his ranch and wishes for the day when he can attend a big league ball game. The wealthy stockbroker inattentively sits in a choice seat at a major league ball game, dreaming of the time he can buy a ranch and get away from the rat race. A bored student who loves to travel sits inertly through a dull lecture on the history of Greek civilization, wishing he could go Greek island hopping; while an impatient Greek youth puffs a tedious cigarette at the foot of the Acropolis, yearning for the day when he hopes to become eligible for a scholarship to an American university to sit in that same lecture hall. The particular value expectation of each would be fulfilled by the situation in which another exists amid abrasive, dull, passive boredom.

33.2 The Grind. The English word *boredom* has a very interesting history deriving from the verb "to bore," or to *make a hole* by boring.[7] The ancient Teutonic languages used the word *bore* to refer to the process of grinding or digging a hole in something that was previously filled and substantial. Something that has been bored is simply a cavity, an open space once full. Our ingenious English language has taken that descriptive image, which means making something empty, and used it to talk about our *feelings* at times when we feel that there is nothing to do, no significant option available to make our lives fulfilled.

Boring is a circular, monotonous, grinding image. If you bore a hole, you grind and grind. It is a repetitive, redundant, abrasive image. You are going around and around, digging deeper and deeper until finally you *make something empty!* This is a beautifully chosen image which speaks visually of the kinds of

[7] *OED.*, I, 1001 ff.

feelings we have when we are being ground by life, when certain relationships are experienced as abrasively eating away at us, making us feel hollow and empty inside.

Grinding is also a destructive image. It wears down something that once was tough and alive. It crushes into small fragments. It is a devastating image of pulverizing, reducing something to powder by friction. So when we experience the now as if it were a grind, we are experiencing something of ourselves being worn away by time—something inside being fragmented and destroyed by the abrasive character of the situation in which we exist.

So the image of boredom expresses a feeling we all have known well. A tiresome person who grinds away at us, makes us feel empty inside and wearies us, is contemptuously called a bore. We are made empty by him, and he continues to go on and on to dig his emptiness into us. That is how we feel in the presence of a real bore.

Similarly, our word *empty* comes from the Anglo-Saxon verb *empt*, to drain, to pour out, to exhaust. That is the way we sometimes experience relationships which have become drained of meaning, their value possibilities exhausted. The Latin word for this feeling is even more sharply focused: *inanitas*, which is the root of our word *inane*, a sense of worthlessness or emptiness. The French have a penetrating, untranslatable word which has entered into English usage: *ennui*, which is that empty, irritating experience of tediousness, weariness, dullness, lassitude, quietly grinding away at the self.

Being "empty-handed" is a penetrating word picture which appears in both the Old and New Testaments, expressing the image of not having anything in one's hands, owning nothing, and having nothing to do. It is the picture of the poor, the destitute, the outcast, the one who has no means or vocation. Empty-handedness is therefore a great curse in the Bible. The Covenant Code commands that "none shall appear before me empty-handed" (Exod. 23:15).

33.3 The Price of Absolutizing. The next crucial step in our argument: Our values from time to time become gods. Relative values become elevated to ultimate centers of value. Only the best and most cherished goods, things, and relationships are capable of becoming gods. Anything truly valuable, however, can become a center of value: education, golf, the company, the Playboy's playmate, votes, art, the game, the paycheck, etc. What happens to the emptied man under the influence of the idolatrizing process?

To the extent to which limited, contextual values have been exalted to idolatries, the destructive, grinding capacity of boredom is increased. When the present is emptied of limited contextual values, it is dull and inane enough; but when it is emptied of absolutized values, it is hopelessly absurd and meaningless. Boredom becomes cancerous, pathological, compulsive, self-destructive. The person whose existence is deeply and deceptively idolatrous tends to be most vulnerable to demonic, tragi-comic, demoralizing boredom. He lives in a context which he perceives as devoid of the values which he passionately regards as ultimate sources of meaning in his existence. Understandably he fastens his attention either totally upon the possibility of some new future deliverance from his present bondage, or perhaps upon the memory of former, better days, but certainly not upon now. Now is the least interesting of all moments. Thus idolatry intensifies the power of inattentive, slothful, indolent existence.

The gods (mere contextual values) are beguiling. They attract us to belief in their capacity to deliver us from the perceived meaninglessness of the now. We love our gods, because they promise genuine human fulfillment, and from time to time give us a foretaste of what it might be. Like Linus with his towel or Schroeder with his piano, we become attached to our gods. They become as much a part of us as our hands or teeth. To be without them is like losing something of ourselves. The threat of losing them makes us feel anxious, and the awareness that they are now unreachable invites boredom, emptiness, ennui.

33.4 Paradigmatic Boredom. Just as it is a part of the dynamics of anxiety systematically to select the worst possible situations to call to the attention of the imagination in order to ready the organism for possible danger, likewise it is a part of the dynamics of idolatrous boredom to exaggerate and oversymbolize the limitations of the present, selecting the worst, most stultifying images of emptiness and death to apply to the now. Boredom learns to project out from the subjective self toward the whole cosmic situation as if it were totally meaningless. This, of course, says more about the experiencing self than the nature of reality itself, but at least it reveals how intensely the void of value is being experienced.

Paradigmatic boredom is a symbolic focusing of the *whole* human condition as if everything were absolutely meaningless on the basis of one relatively empty experience. The small event escalates into a major defeat. I see myself as eternally unself-actualized, mirrored through a temporal event. Some otherwise insignificant relationship becomes sweepingly symbolic of my radical emptiness. A minor occurrence signals awareness of my whole persistent predicament of being forever unable to actualize the values I have absolutized. A falling leaf, a D on a quiz, a game lost, a friendship broken, instantly symbolizes my lostness from time, my caughtness in nonbeing. This sign easily becomes projected on a cosmic scale. The sailor on a six-month tour of duty, in love with a blonde in Peoria, may find that six-month tour looming in his consciousness as a symbol of the radical absurdity of life, the meaninglessness of the whole of human history. For six months he may in fact deal with the whole world as if it were in fact as meaningless as his internal situation is felt. No amount of preaching to him that life is meaningful will be convincing until he steps on the shore again and gets on the plane to Peoria. Only then may he discover that reality is not as meaningless as it once seemed.

33.5 Objective Emptiness. Are we implying that all situations are meaningful? Are not some partly meaningful situations plagued with accompanying nuances of meaninglessness? And are not some situations fundamentally quite meaningless, and therefore is not boredom a healthy and reasonable response?

There may indeed be a constructive or healthy form of boredom when one is placed in an obviously dull context in which virtually all desirable values are temporarily out of reach, to which the only credible response is boredom. Let us suppose that you must stand in a long line to obtain your automobile license tag. You find yourself trapped for forty-five minutes in a deadening situation of meaningless waiting. You could have spent those precious moments with one with whom you are in love, or in some kind of significant political activity, or reading an intriguing book—but no! You are now denied all those things. It is of little comfort to reflect rationally on the necessity of complex bureaucratic structures. What you feel inside is boredom. And yet, perhaps there are hidden potentialities even in that limiting situation which are indeed unique opportunities, for reflection, for interpersonal encounter, even for daydreaming. Letting the mind wander in daydreams may perform a very useful function of tranquilizing the organism during a time when other values are unactualizable. I wish to affirm a certain limited, constructive function of boredom, which adjusts its expectations to what it perceives to be the realistic limitations of the present.

Our distinction between constructive and destructive boredom again hinges upon the concept of idolatry. For to the degree that we have idolatrized limited values, then the whole experience of value limitation tends to become demonic, destructive, and demoralizing. When values are valued proportionally, however, in response to their contextual worth, then it is healthy to respond to the lack of value with disappointment, regret, or even lethargy and torpor. Lest it be misunderstood, I am not proposing that every moment should be an intense, activistic, aggressive orgy of value creation and value reception. The human organism needs the rhythm of passivity as well as activity, reflection as well as action, recreation as well as creation, sleep as well as work, preparation as well as execution. Authenticity is not sheer frantic productivity. But to the extent that idolatry goes to work on the absolutizing of limited values, the numbing dullness of the now situation which fails to actualize those values is increased to deadening proportions.

33.6 Axiotherapy for the Bored. The self-deceptive consequences of idolatry follow similarly for boredom as they have for
guilt and anxiety. Although we know much less about the self-
concealing, unconscious, symptomatic manifestations of demonic
boredom than we do of guilt and anxiety, we may safely hypothesize that compulsive boredom works in ways analogous to compulsive guilt and compulsive anxiety, so that we do not know
why we are bored but only that we are bored. The distinction
between fear (directed toward an object) and anxiety (directed
toward empty possibility) surely has its counterpart in the distinction between an objective dullness resulting from some visible
limiting situation, over against the more vague and diffuse feeling
of ennui, which identifies no objective source of discontent but
only subceives reality as blocking one from his centers of values.
Thus one responds in circumvented ways, the dynamics of which
he does not understand.[8]

As with anxiety and guilt, however, the thoroughly bored
individual often does not recognize himself as bored. Again the
deeper predicament of man is seen precisely in the fact that he is
unaware of the depth of his own predicament. Almost everyone
knows an utterly bored person who has convinced himself that
his life is full. This, of course, merely confounds the self-deception
of boredom.

I do not presume to propose any simple procedure for the
therapeutic reshaping of an empty life into a full and meaningful
one. In line with previous suggestions, however, I do suggest
what might be called an axiotherapeutic addendum to what is
now being tried in psychotherapy in the attempt at resensitizing
the compulsively bored.

There is a special opportunity being given in boredom to
discover who we are, what we value, what bestows meaning upon
our existence. Intensive boredom invites a profound review of
one's value system. It is precisely in the midst of the most deadening boredom that one is being invited to ask: What values are
now absent which would make my existence meaningful, inten-

---

[8] Tillich, *The Courage to Be,* pp. 46 ff., similarly distinguishes emptiness from
meaninglessness.

tional, fulfilled? By carefully scrutinizing our boredom, we can learn what we value and disvalue. Some value is yearned for in any boring situation.[9] Boredom is attempting to perform a constructive function for the self. The task of the therapist is to help boredom perform its constructive function of pointing the individual toward what he conceives to be more genuinely self-actualizing. The therapeutic agent is not assigned the task of providing a revised structure of values to one who experiences life as meaningless, but rather that of enabling him to understand the values which are already at stake in his boredom, in order that he might be freed to choose whether they are in fact worth what they are costing him.

33.7 Multiple Simultaneous Value Actualization. The style of life which contrasts itself to bored, depressive, anxious guilt, crippled by simultaneous value claims, might be called authenticity, or self-actualization, or perhaps more descriptively "multiple simultaneous value actualization." The astute, clever, intentional valuer learns to juggle various claims in such a way that one can be temporarily delayed in order that another may be fulfilled, or perhaps both may be fulfilled at the same time, or perhaps even several values be actualized at the same time. One who is capable of planning his time, ordering the sequence of his efforts, taking initiative at the right place and the right time, is one who embodies the process of multiple simultaneous value actualization. Value actualization becomes something like a game where timing is important. One learns to time his deed to the proper moment and to correlate it with other activities in such a way that one value is allowed to ripen while another is being actualized. Even the process of ripening is a part of the process of value actualization.

Patience may become a significant virtue as one strives for multiple simultaneous value actualization. For by patience one allows uncontrollable, nonvolitional processes to work. One allows time to intervene while hoped-for results are ripening for their

[9] Sebastian de Grazia, *Of Time, Work and Leisure* (The Twentieth Century Fund, 1962), p. 425.

unique moment of actualization. Patience is that virtue, or that excellent mode of behavior, that style of authenticity, by which one is willing *not to act,* in order to let other values take their course and ripen for anticipated fulfillment. Patience is grounded in promise. One is patient in hope that a promised good, a hoped-for value, will be fulfilled in due time. Throughout, however, we note the remarkably temporal character of virtue, the temporality of value, the contextuality of the good, emerging and disappearing in time, accessible only at certain unique moments in time. The brief nexus of fulfillment, however, belongs to a lengthy process of waiting, thinking, deciding, and persuading.

The concept of multiple simultaneous value actualization does not imply that there is no time for rest, since rest itself is simultaneous value actualization (the body recuperates, the unconscious plays a thousand games with available images, responsibility is relieved). Nor does it go against the concept of "purity of heart," the willing of one thing, since it acknowledges that any single moment is a unique occasion for a singular will, even though several values may be maturing while one deed is being done. Multiple simultaneous value actualization means listening to Mozart as I commute to work; having dinner with a friend (i.e., feeding my body and fulfilling needs for social companionship); bowling for entertainment and exercise; dressing for warmth, comfort, and aesthetic attractiveness. In each case multiple values are achieved. Like a computer analyzing complex problems of situational value, the astute valuer learns patiently to gear multiple values to develop simultaneously.

34. The Neonate Prototype of Responsiveness

A healthy relationship to unfolding reality would be an attentive existence in which the whole organism is sensitively and unselfconsciously attuned to the speech of the now.[10] Since the organismic responsiveness of the newborn child forms a prototypical pattern of a healthy relation to the present, we now turn

[10] Heidegger, *Essays in Metaphysics,* trans. Kurt F. Leidecker (Philosophical Library, 1960), pp. 26 ff.; Oden, *Radical Obedience,* pp. 94 ff.

to the developmental question of how that responsiveness first manifests itself, how it becomes distorted, and how it may be restored in effective psychotherapy.

34.1 Organismic Responsiveness. Our thesis is that the prototype of responsiveness is the neonate situation, prior to distortions in awareness which inhibit responsiveness. The original situation of man is therefore one in which boredom is totally absent. Responsiveness is chronologically, psychogenically, and logically prior to boredom in the developing self. Responsiveness is unlearned, natural, spontaneous behavior for the neonate; whereas boredom can only emerge after a complex learning process of conceptual value introjection in which primitive responsiveness becomes subverted.[11] Responsiveness, in contrast to boredom, is given in and with the organism in its most primitive developmental condition, a viewpoint long intuited by the Judeo-Christian tradition in mythological language and long neglected by deliberate empirical observation.

The digestion of nutrients is perhaps the most primitive form of respons-ability or responsiveness. The embryonic organism is asked to receive and ingest nutrients in preparation for future, unknown forms of response. Then the traumatic event of birth occurs, which totally transforms the environment to which one is called to respond. Although the organism is pushed out of the immediate, contiguous contact of the uterine situation into a strange new world, it readily learns to continue its living response to what is now occurring. The profoundest change is experienced when the umbilical cord is cut. The neonate soon learns that he is in fact a separate organism! A whole new apparatus for ingesting food must be experimented with. The prototypical form of neonate responsiveness is that of answering the gift of the mother's breast to receive the food, the oral excitement and comfort that accompany feeding time. What is asked is nothing more than that the child respond to what is offered, be a recipient, take pleasure in that relationship. All this occurs with intense im-

[11] Rogers, TMAV, pp. 162 ff.

204

mediacy. There is no thought in the neonate of whether he will get food next time, or how it felt the last time. There is simply the total, organismic responsiveness to the now.

The newborn organism is also being required to respond to its new atmospheric environment, by inhaling and exhaling. If for any reason the new organism cannot respond by the reception of oxygen, it simply means death. So respons-ability at this primordial level means survival.

The new environment involves space between persons, in contrast to the more restricted foetal style. This calls for increasing self-determination. As the child begins to explore this new arena for responsiveness, he begins to employ the full range of his sensory apparatus: tasting, touching, looking, hearing, smelling. Throughout this exploratory process, however, he remains intimately in touch with his own experience. There is no disjunction between how he feels and how he expresses his feelings.

34.2 The Fall into Unresponsiveness. If the self's primitive situation is active, receptive organismic responsiveness, how does that healthy situation come to deteriorate? How does man fall into emptiness and boredom? We can do no more than answer in the most sketchy way. As the dynamics of guilt and anxiety (12.3, 25.2) proliferate, the developing individual is increasingly distracted from the gifts and demands of presently experienced existence. As the imagination increasingly becomes preoccupied with future threats to value and the memory becomes increasingly preoccupied with past negations of value, both pull as centrifugal forces away from sensitive awareness of the now.

Furthermore, to the extent to which I have idolatrized limited values, I am vulnerable to intensified guilt and anxiety, and consequently to demonic boredom. If I am cut off from my gods in the now, there is nothing to do except to be bored. If nothing can now bring homage to my gods, the now is experienced as the most empty segment of time. Compulsive boredom tends to perpetuate the bondage of my will to my idolatrized self-image, since to face reality would require a recognition of the vulnerability of my gods. Boredom thus functions as an opiate

205

on behalf of continued inauthenticity by lulling the self to sleep in relation to present reality, while awakening the self only to its idealized self-image.

34.3 The Possibility of Reawakening. How is it possible to recover organismic responsiveness? How can one learn to listen in a fresh new way to the speech of being disclosing itself in time? What is it that frees one to be open to one's feelings and the claims of the neighbor? These questions are framed in the most urgent way by psychotherapy, but in a more general sense by the human situation itself.

To begin with, it seems evident that one is free to respond to a situation meaningfully only if it is actually meaningful. If it should turn out to be the case that reality is absurd (Camus),[12] then the only meanings possible are those we project onto reality by the strength of our determined wills, a rather tenuous basis upon which to commit oneself to decisive, intentional action. Meaning is possible only if it is actual. But who is to say that any situation is actually meaningful? The autonomous individual, the culture, the experts, the priests, the scientists—who? Here pure phenomenology tends to run its course, and can only refer to some ontology or theology for further inquiry.

There is no solution to the problem of boredom if the present *is* in fact meaningless or emptied of the values that are as a matter of fact necessary for human fulfillment. Genuine responsiveness to the present is possible only on the basis of the fact that it is in fact full of values to be shared and makes itself known as such. Only if the present is credibly, unambiguously, understandably *revealed* as meaningful is it possible to embrace it meaningfully even amid its apparent blocks to seemingly essential values.

It might seem a facile ploy here to note that it is precisely of such a revelation that the New Testament proclamation speaks. That seems to be the direction toward which a serious phenomenology of boredom tends, however, and we will explore this in greater detail in the following chapter. At this point, how-

[12] Albert Camus, *The Myth of Sisyphus,* trans. Justin O'Brien (Vintage Books, 1959), pp. 3 ff.

ever, we must not neglect to ask what can be learned from the process of effective psychotherapy about the recovery of organismic responsiveness.

Psychotherapy has found that through an intensive encounter with another person who is congruently open to his own experiencing process, the possibility may be given to the compulsively bored individual to risk opening himself up analogously. The congruent therapist or friend may become a role model for responding congruence. Effective therapeutic dialogue proceeds on the basis of the same style of openness to reality which is prototypically seen in the neonate's bodily experience. According to therapists of many different theoretical orientations, the healing process would not function well at all if it did not in some sense nurture a context in which something analogous to neonate organismic experiencing is recovered.

Psychotherapy involves a revolution in self-awareness in which one is increasingly enabled to receive the present moment in its rich multiplicity and taste its unique opportunities. It occurs not by merely talking about the idea of radical responsiveness but only through a concrete relation to a radically responsive person, through which one is enabled in a new way to be born in the moment, to become sensitive to its claims.

34.4 The Hidden Ontological Assumption of Therapeutic Responsiveness. An assumption lying silently beneath such therapeutic effectiveness is that being itself is meaningful. The therapist does not hand out on a silver platter meanings for the deadened individual, but rather only mediates to him a meaning-giving relationship in which he finds himself being reawakened to what is actually there. Absurdity is finally understandable as absurdity only in relation to certain meanings that make it nameable as absurd. Far from viewing himself as the source or ground of meaning, the therapist only points to the source and ground of meaning through his concrete behavior. He is only an inadequate representative of an intelligibility rooted in reality itself. The therapist's task is to show the individual that there is no ground in being itself for his crippled, stunted responsiveness, but that life is to be received passionately and in every moment anew as a great gift.

It is precisely this implicit therapeutic assumption of the hidden meaningfulness of experience that is made explicit in the witness of the Christian community to God's self-disclosure. By his own sharing in time, God himself has bestowed meaning to time. The world's present existence is meaningful because God himself has chosen to participate in it. Every moment is filled with the renewal of God's gift of love and affirmation of his creation. We are given this moment to celebrate God's love in the form of loving others as God has loved us.

If so, it is now not only demanded but permitted that we conceive of the present in a radically new way. It is now possible to relate oneself anew to the present because the present is not what one at first thought it to be. It *is* something quite different. It is the arena for sharing in the multiple simultaneous value actualization of the creative process.

chapter X

THE FULLNESS OF NOW

35. The Messianic Now

35.1 The Awaited Deliverer. The end of the first century
B.C. was a time of accelerating expectations.[1] Many in the ancient
Near East assumed that the end of history was near. The ruins
of the Qumran community, where the Dead Sea scrolls were
found, now bear witness to the fact that many of the faithful had
withdrawn from the ordinary structures of human existence
(family, economic and political orders, etc.) in order to await
this cataclysmic, saving event.

This apocalyptic stance assumed that now was meaningless.
Deliverance was thought to be totally future. If history is hurling
itself toward the destruction of the old order and the emergence
of a new order, then there is little to do but to await that new
order. So many took up a new life-style which viewed occurring
history as quite empty, and indeed rather boring. Their attention
was partially turned backward in time toward the memory of

---

[1] For the entire argument of section 35 I am deeply indebted to Joseph W.
Mathews, cf. "The Christ of History," *Letter to Laymen*, 1961, for his basic per-
spective as well as Rudolf Bultmann, *Jesus and the Word*, trans. L. P. Smith and
E. H. Lantero (New York: Charles Scribner's Sons, 1934).

the ancient deeds of God's deliverance, but more so forward in time to the expected end. The present time was viewed as impotent and vacuous.

Likewise in our time many individuals structure their whole existence around some sentimental memory of past value actualization, or toward some hoped-for messianic situation, yet remain thoroughly bored, sound asleep to the events of occurring history, quite withdrawn from the reality of the now. The businessman yearns for that delivering day when he can pay off the note, capitalize, and expand. The student imprisoned in the droning emptiness of a chemistry lab awaits the fulfillment of graduation day when he will become a real person. The affectionate mother whose children are now grown up remembers when they were small, when her life had meaning, but she experiences the now as a great void longing to be filled with familial reunion.

Such longings have essentially the same form as the Jewish longing for the messiah, or Christ. There is a broad sense in which the longing for the expected deliverer is inevitable and elemental to the human condition. The expectation of the Christ is what every man knows when he knows himself most deeply, if Christ, in a general sense, means the expected deliverer.

35.2 The Reversal of Human Expectations. The decisive expression of human longing for deliverance occurred amid the apocalyptic expectations of late first-century Judaism. It was in the midst of this crescendo of human yearnings that a rabbi named Jesus appeared. From an objective historical point of view, we have only limited knowledge of this person, since the reports of his ministry have been made only by persons who understood their human expectations to have been revolutionized by their encounter with him. Despite all the precariousness of the oral traditions which for almost a quarter of a century mediated our only knowledge of him, there is at least one thing that we know beyond any reasonable doubt about this man, since it was remembered alike by his friend and foe: Jesus constituted a radical crisis in the messianic expectations of the people of Israel.

210

I will limit my attention strictly to the single most obvious and most characteristic thing remembered about his life. He was remembered as one who, through his life-style and the teaching which reflected it, initiated an acute reversal in human expectations. He confronted everyone he met with a simple, radical decision: either live amid the nowness of God's reign, or remain trapped in the old era now hastening to its end.

Against the prevailing trend of idealized messianic expectations, Jesus announced: The reign of God is *at hand!* In direct opposition to those who were bored with present history, Jesus announced: *Now* is the acceptable time! To those who expected God to change the very conditions of human existence, Jesus announced: God is now *with us!* To those whose thoughts were fixed upon a romanticized past or an idealized future, Jesus proclaimed, brutally and offensively: The kingdom of heaven is *in your midst!*

Whether disciple or opponent, all men who met him remembered him as one who called their human expectations radically into question. To the guilty he declared the forgiveness of sins. To the anxious he announced the trustworthiness of God. To the bored he proclaimed that God was at work amid the ambiguities of history and called them to participate responsively in the redemptive process. He seemed to act as if the end of history were indeed at hand. To those who had pinned their hopes upon glorious messianic illusions, Jesus said: This is it. The awaited time is now!

It is understandable that such a person, who challenged the most sacred expectations of a venerable religious tradition, would be regarded as a troublemaker. For to challenge a man's expectations is to challenge his basic self-image. Jesus was essentially saying: What you have been expecting as an event of final deliverance is already here! He understood his own ministry to be the decisive sign of the already impending new age. To persons who had organized their lives around exalted nationalistic or materialistic expectations, such a message certainly would be experienced as a great threat and offense. Persons would understandably feel angry, indignant, robbed of their highest hopes, and affronted at

211

the impudence of such a blasphemous preacher. When human illusions are unmasked, the one who does the unmasking is understandably regarded as an intolerable intruder. The political and religious establishments conspired together to eradicate this obstreperous pretender. Jesus paid for his proclamation with his life.

Curiously enough, it was precisely the events which surrounded his death which came to refocus and give substance to the question his life had raised. Although he did not desire death, and in fact prayed that the cup of suffering might pass from him, he did not flee the prospect of death when it became clear that the only way to live an authentic life was to offer it up in death on behalf of the message of authenticity to which his life had been committed. So it is a strange story that the one who had celebrated life as a radical gift of God accordingly celebrated death itself as an implication of a life lived responsibly.

The expectations of men were shaken to their greatest depth, however, in the events which followed his remarkable death. For in addition to all these unexpected twists in this amazing story, the final irony was yet to come: Jesus was remembered as having been raised from the dead! I will not deal here with the resurrection as an objective historical question, i.e., whether it in fact happened, but rather only with the indisputable fact that it was remembered as having happened. It was this memory of the resurrected Jesus that constituted the fundamental reversal in the Christ expectations of Israel. For his resurrection itself was remembered as the supreme validation of his celebrative life-style. It was remembered as God's own way of affirming his messianic vocation. So the one who had celebrated the nowness of God's reign became himself celebrated as the inaugurator of that reign, the anointed one, the Son of Man, the Servant Messiah. This enabled the remembering community to read the law and prophets in a new way in the light of his life and death. Hidden messianic meanings became clear, under the illumination of his ministry. The prophetic expectations were now understood to have been fulfilled in an unexpected way through him. He was remembered as the lamb slain for many, whose stripes made us whole.[2]

35.3 The Secularization of the Christ Question. We will not soften the shock of the question which the remembering community asked about Jesus. It was an impudent, outrageous, threatening question to the traditional community of Jewish expectations: Is Jesus the Christ? Two thousand years later it may seem easy to ask this question, but in the first-century context it was an abrasive, unthinkable question. It is not surprising that Jesus' proclamation would be regarded as a *scandalon* to those who held more lofty expectations of the Christ. Would not God have something better to offer in history than the now? Those who expected the messiah fundamentally to reestablish the direction of history, especially politically and economically, were shocked and horrified by the offensive question: Is Jesus the Christ?

If that question constituted a revolutionary challenge to apocalyptic expectations in the first century, even so today it remains a revolutionary challenge to our own modern boredom with history and our own secularized expectations of deliverance. For if we mean by the Christ the end of our expectations for deliverance, we too are insulted by the question: Is Jesus the Christ? For that means: Is the now the end of our expectations? Most of our nows seem just as dull as before. We need some hope to justify our courage amid the present situation of limitation which we must endure. Surely if Jesus' life means that our expected deliverance is at hand, then he remains as outrageous and offensive to *us* as he must have been to first-century religious expectations. For if the messianic event is now, then there is no such thing as a messianic event in the sense in which we expected it, and never will be. If the messianic event is now, then our salvation consists in embracing and encountering the unique speech of the now, responding to it as if now were the end-time, as if now were the gift and demand of God himself! No one can an-

[2] Isa. 53.

213

swer for another. No one can suspend judgment and still hear the question at its depth. Either it is radically the case that the living God is acting in the now, or he is yet to be expected. Either/or: there is no middle ground. The fundamental cleavage between Christian faith and unbelief hinges, in our time as in the first century, on the answer to the simple question: Is Jesus the Christ?

This fundamental reversal in human expectations impinges directly upon our discussion of boredom. For if the present is filled with the self-disclosure of the love of God even amid the ambiguities of history, if now is precisely the arena of God's redemptive action, if the reign of God is at hand, then we have no time to waste either lamenting our present limitations or dozing through the excitements of history. There is nothing to be bored about. To put it differently, it is ontologically impossible to be bored before the occurring love of God.

36. The Ontological Impossibility of Boredom Before God

36.1 The Ontology of Responsiveness. Our thesis: If God has disclosed himself as a participator in present history, then it is impossible to be bored amid the full awareness of contemporary events. No matter how absurdly we may subjectively experience boredom and emptiness as we mourn our unactualizable, idolatrized values, the present objectively is a time of intensive, explosive proliferation of values. The divine activity is elemental to the definition of the present. Man cannot live otherwise than amid the eventing, occurring action of God in the present. From this point of view the now is laden with profound meanings, whether or not we experience it as meaningful. This is the thesis we will explore.

Christian responsiveness celebrates the nowness of God's reign[3] and calls all men to participate in that reign, to claim their

[3] It surely will be evident to the perceptive reader that this entire argument in Part III stands in direct tension with the brilliant essay by Jürgen Moltmann on *The Theology of Hope,* which argues that Christian theology speaks of Christ *only*

214

rightful citizenship in it, which means to be free to respond to the gift of reality now. The present is providing us with a unique opportunity to be free from our idolatries. Every moment is a new occasion for the creation and reception of new values, for response to the divine invitation to be co-creators in the process of historical self-determination.

Subjectively I may experience my present circumstance as devoid of significant meanings, but my ontological condition, my being before God, is one in which every moment yields a fresh new constellation of actual meanings and values. I am being called to rely upon my own organismic responses, to trust in the providential character of the now, to savor the delicate taste of each new moment.

A covenant ontology inquires into man's being as he exists before God (cf. 14, 15, 28.1). A reinterpretation of boredom in the light of a covenant ontology would involve a reconceiving of man as he stands amid the nowness of God's reign. From this perspective, meaninglessness has no ontological rootage. Boredom has no ground in being itself. Boredom is a parasite on being, fed only by idolatry. If it should turn out that life can be lived meaningfully without our gods, then we could better perceive the precarious basis of our boredom, and be freed from it.

Even if man wished to be bored before God, he could not, since to know God appropriately is to know his present activity, its relevance for human fulfillment, and to respond to it fittingly. If idolatry could be shown to be impotent and groundless, then boredom would become recognized as absurd. The Christian

---

in "the form of statements of hope and of promises for the future" (p. 17), that "nothing can be 'very good' until 'all things are become new' " (p. 34), that "realism . . . was never a good ally of Christian faith" (p. 34), and which speaks of *agape* as "love to the non-existent" (p. 32). Moltmann sounds too much like Vladimir and Estragon in *Waiting for Godot* when he speaks of a "God with 'future as his essential nature' (as E. Block puts it), as made known in Exodus and in Israelite prophecy, the God whom we therefore cannot really have in us or over us but always only before us, who encounters us in his promises for the future, and whom we therefore cannot 'have' either, but can only await in active hope" (p. 16). However much we may admire Moltmann's attempt to view Christian thinking as eschatological from beginning to end, his case for a *docta spes* suffers from over-statement.

community points to the action of God in the now which makes belief in him possible and reliance upon the gods unnecessary.

This is the same plethora of values to which Christian proclamation points explicitly, which the therapeutic process assumes implicitly in an inconspicuous secular language of relationship. For therapy is constantly attempting to make reality transparent, so that fresh meanings latent in interpersonal situations may be recognized for what they are.

36.2 God's Responsiveness and Man's Responsibility. Although we have usually thought of *responsibility* as something we *ought* to do—fulfilling our duty, obeying some rule, striving for some ideal—now we are called to discover new definitions of responsibility. Instead we are now being invited to learn that responsibility is fundamentally *our response to the reality in which we stand.*

If the reality in which we stand is fundamentally and finally God's own redemptive concern, then responsibility essentially means responding to God's concern for history. Concisely, *human responsibility is at its deepest level our responsiveness to the responsibility which God has taken for us.* God has taken responsibility for us once for all in the Christ event, where Jesus, the responsible man, the man for others, the celebrator of now, acts symbolically for all men in history. The inner meaning of all classical theories of the atonement is that God takes responsibility for us precisely amid our irresponsibilities. Thus, to be a responsible man finally means to be accountable to God's own accounting of the human condition, to be responsive to God's own incomparable act of responsibility.

The therapist certainly attempts to mediate to the troubled a stance of alert, sensitive responsiveness to reality, awakeness to the ever new disclosure of meanings in the now. But the human responsiveness of the therapeutic agent is always a dull, fragmented mirror of the meaningfulness of reality itself to which it seeks to be transparent. Only in a limited way can he be responsive to his own feelings. Only in a limited way can he reflect the profound, hidden meaningfulness dormant in the now situation.

His limited responsiveness, however, is illuminated by the perfect and unconditional responsiveness of God to the human condition. We can best understand the ontological ground upon which human responsiveness stands by viewing it under the analogy of God's own responsiveness toward us.

chapter XI

WAITING FOR GOD

37. The Life of Waiting

Although we have indicated that the phenomenon of boredom is more perceptively grasped in contemporary literature than in philosophy or psychology, we have not until now been able to support that point with any persuasive exhibits. What follows may seem to some an unnecessary excursus. Yet I know of no better way to express the structure of boredom and the call to responsiveness than by reference to Samuel Beckett's intriguing play *Waiting for Godot*. It is especially fitting, at the conclusion of Part III of our argument, to give deliberate attention to this poetic masterpiece, since it gathers together in one dramatic frame the essential cluster of our entire previous discussion embracing guilt, anxiety, and boredom. If it should seem that this play has already suffered from overinterpretation, then I would invite the reader to relax and allow himself to be interpreted by the play itself, rather than try to give some allegedly correct interpretation to it.

37.1 **The Plotless Plot.** The scene: A lonely country road. Two tramps are waiting beside a barren tree for Godot. When

Godot comes they will be saved; their lives will be fulfilled; they will know where they stand.

Darkness is approaching. They wait, they argue, take off their shoes, button their flies, attempt suicide, complain about the rope not being strong enough, fall down, struggle to get up, talk of the four evangelists, sing nonsense songs, eat carrots, assume a foetal posture, sleep, fight, make up, and embrace.

The most important thing that happens in this play is that nothing happens. The play rehearses emptiness. Even though there is a flood of words, one feels a sense of aridity about their meaning.

For what are they waiting? They say Godot. Who is Godot? They are not sure. All they seem to know with certainty is: When Godot comes they will know where they stand. Godot has their future in his hands.

During the course of each of the two acts, two other characters appear, always together, master and slave: Pozzo and Lucky. Pozzo, a brutal country squire, exuding cruelty masked by the most genteel vanities, seems to own some land nearby. Lucky, his slave, is burdened with a picnic basket, a folding stool, and a heavy bag, which we later find has sand in it. Pozzo has tied a long rope around Lucky's neck, which he jerks periodically, causing a running sore. Pozzo treats Lucky like an animal, expecting instant obedience to harsh one-word commands, jerking his rope, cracking his whip. Lucky is dumb and says nothing except on one occasion when he is commanded to think, whereupon he puts on his hat and goes into a tireless rapid-fire harangue of seemingly incoherent fragments of thought on theology, science, sports, and death.

Pozzo persists with his empty prattle, eating his chicken conspicuously before the others, tossing the bones to Estragon, pretentiously playing the role of the generous squire, discussing his pipe, the weather, and his troubles with Lucky, all with disjointed, elegant, sophisticated barbarity. Finally Pozzo and Lucky exit, leaving Vladimir and Estragon alone in the rapidly darkening twilight, waiting for Godot in moods alternating between hopeless despair and desperate hope.

A boy appears to tell them that Godot will not come today, but he will surely come tomorrow. With this assurance, the night quickly falls. Estragon says: "Well, shall we go?" Vladimir: "Yes, let's go." They do not move. The curtain falls.

The second act is much like the first. It seems to happen the next day, although one is not sure. It seems as if all life is a waiting, without beginning or end. The only difference in the scenery is that by now four or five leaves have sprouted on the tree. The same comic routines recur with hats, shoes, carrots, trousers' flies, and suicide. But amid all this confusion, one thing is clear: They are waiting for Godot.

Pozzo and Lucky return, but now the rope is shorter, and Pozzo is blind. The blind master, the dumb slave, now bound more closely together, cannot rise up again by themselves when they fall. After a long struggle they rise, leaving Vladimir and Estragon to wait for Godot.

A boy appears again, announcing that Mr. Godot will not come today, but he will surely come tomorrow. The night falls quickly, enclosing the two clowns in hapless despair. They wish to hang themselves but do not have a rope. The final line recurs: "Well, shall we go?" "Yes, let's go." They do not move.

The curtain falls.

37.2 The Only Happening. This play lends itself to many possible interpretations.[1] From the outset it has defied consistent interpretation from its critics. We get little help from playwright Samuel Beckett in unraveling the poetic symbolism of the play. He meets with silence all questions as to its meaning, leaving the play to speak for itself. My own exegesis should not be taken too seriously as anything more than a subjective impression of the penetrating images of the play. At least it is clear that the style of

---

[1] Certain elements of this interpretation of Godot may be found in Charles S. McCoy's excellent essay, "Waiting for Godot: A Biblical Appraisal," *Religion in Life*, XXVIII (1959), pp. 597 ff. I am even more deeply indebted, however, to a lucid analysis by Edward Craig Hobbs, speaking on Godot to the Texas Methodist Student Movement in 1959. Cf. Allan Lewis, *The Contemporary Theatre* (Crown, 1962), pp. 259 ff.

the play, as well as the content of its dialogue, communicates emptiness, boredom, and despair as powerfully as any literary piece of recent times.

Who are these characters? Even the names are vague and uncertain. Is it Godot, Godin, or Godet for whom they wait? Pozzo answers to Cain and Abel, Estragon answers to Adam and Gogo, and Vladimir to Didi and Mr. Albert. Only one has the same name throughout—Lucky. Is he Lucky because he knows where he stands, as a slave, while the others are waiting to be told where they stand? Or is he Lucky because he is not waiting for Godot? Or is he just called Lucky to underscore the irony of his appalling situation?

However uncertain we may be about their identities, it is at least clear that the characters always appear in contrasting *pairs*, moving in analogous and opposite ways: Vladimir and Estragon stand still and wait, while Pozzo and Lucky are always on the move and do not wait. The former are tied together by their expectations and dependencies; the latter are joined together literally by a rope. Since the play is not done in a realistic style, the characters come through to the hearer as types, with opposite features and contrasting forms of banality. If physical discomfort is focused in Estragon, whose shoes do not fit, spiritual uneasiness is centered in Vladimir, whose hat does not fit. There are no female characters, since if history is caught in a meaningless unending moment, there seems to be no need for continuity of the race.

There is no change. Except for the blindness of Pozzo and the leaves sprouting (and these changes are not seen happening in the play but only appear after they happen), no events happen. Nothing occurs which is recognized by anyone as significant. This, however, is precisely the importance of this play: It captures in style and dialogue the chronic sense of emptiness and ennui which often characterizes human existence.

For we too are bums on the road of history, with our needs for comfort and understanding, with our sufferings and brutality. We too are waiting for a Godot who will never come in the form in which we expect him.

Amid all this waiting, however, one thing actually does happen—only one thing. Someone does appear: Lucky the slave, scourged by Pozzo. Is this a lucky occurrence offering something new to the buffoons, or is it merely another hapless digression amid the tedium of life? Instantly Estragon surmises that Godot has come, but after taking a second look decides he was quite wrong. But at least one thing happens amid their waiting. Someone comes, and, note carefully, he appears in the form of a servant. The only thing the clowns see is a poor man in desperate need of help, in bondage, and pitiable long-suffering. They sympathize with him slightly at first, but do not really respond to his predicament, and finally take sides with Pozzo. For they are intent upon looking for someone else, Godot, who must be quite different from this. Lucky is not even a recognizable event for them, certainly not a lucky event. Immediately after Lucky leaves, however, they learn that the one they have been waiting for will not come today, but surely will come tomorrow.

37.3 The Lingering Question. The question of the play is not merely who Godot is, but has Godot come? For Godot, it seems, is not known until he comes and is known only by his coming.

The two clowns have the vague impression that they have met the travelers before. One gets the impression that all this has happened before. In fact, it probably happens every day! On the same road every day they meet the same pitiable pair, while they wait for Godot. Yet they are not certain they have met.

Has Godot come? Surely not in the sense in which he is expected. But many clues are dropped in the play to suggest that Godot did meet his appointment! He comes every day. Again and again he appears incognito!

For Godot is that event or encounter in which we are being freed to decide who we are in relation to our needy neighbor. Godot offers each day anew the possibility of understanding ourselves as bound up in accountability with and for the neighbor. Godot is that unique opportunity to know our own destiny as linked with the destiny of the neighbor in need, the poor, the oppressed, the bruised, the nameless. Godot comes to those who wait with messianic expectations.

Actually *it is Godot who is waiting*. Every day he awaits our response. When we fail, he sends his messenger to say, it is too late today, but tomorrow he will surely appear again. Godot is a secularized way of talking about the same fulfilling reality for which the Hebrews yearned in the form of a messiah.

38. The Appearing of the Expected One

38.1 The Irony of the Unexpected. Godot has been widely misunderstood as a drama of despair and meaninglessness, a prime exhibit of nihilistic culture. In order to penetrate to the center of this poetic statement, however, we must come to understand it not merely as a desperate and cynical echo of nihilism, but instead a shrewd, penetrating witness to the appearing again and again, amid human insensitivity, of the possibility of fulfillment.

Irony is a use of humor or light sarcasm, the intended implication of which is the opposite of the literal sense of the words. It portrays a state of affairs and a result opposite to and as if in mockery of the appropriate result. But it does this in order to point even more forcefully to the appropriate result. In this sense Godot is an arresting statement of irony. For the intended implication of the play, that God appears every day incognito, is precisely the opposite of the surface theme of the play. It portrays a state of affairs, two clowns endlessly awaiting salvation, which seems to mock the fact that salvation is being revealed. But it does all this in order more powerfully to dramatize the continual reappearing of Godot. Popular nihilistic interpretations of Godot simply fail to reach this level of irony.

The first act may be viewed in four basic phases: (1) the expectation of Godot; (2) the coming of Godot; (3) the speech of Godot; (4) the announcement of Godot's coming again.

38.2 The Expectation of Godot. Scriptural references abound, often deliberately, comically misquoted, but their placement is not accidental. However rambling and disjointed this play may at first seem, on closer inspection everything is in its place, and a very complex dramatic structure is woven together brilliantly. Beckett sets forth his scriptural text [2] like a classical homily at the outset of the play, Proverbs 13:12 in altered version: "Hope deferred maketh the something sick." The actual proverb is: "Hope deferred maketh the heart sick: but when the desire cometh, it is a tree of life." The tree is a central symbol in the church's memory of the event of deliverance. In the first act, the tree appears to be dead (hope is deferred, and the heart is sick); whereas in the second act the tree is alive, the desire (of all nations, Hag. 2:7, a messianic reference) comes, and vitality is seen in new leaf.

Who are Vladimir and Estragon? Their first conversation offers the surest clue. They are discussing the New Testament story of the two thieves beside the cross. Here are two bums whose wasted lives are silhouetted against the empty sky in the presence of the crucified lord, the tree of life. [3]

What is to be done as they wait at their appointed place beside the tree? Kill time. Wait until they know how they stand before Godot. *Then* they will take it or leave it. If Godot would only reveal himself, *then* they could make their decision, but until Godot comes, they cannot decide. Everything is indefinite. They banter indecisively: "What exactly did we ask him for?" "Oh . . . Nothing very definite." "A kind of prayer." "Precisely." "A vague supplication." "Exactly." "And what did he reply?" "That he'd see." "That he couldn't promise anything." "Consult his family." "His friends." "His agents." "His correspondents." "His books." "His bank account." "Before taking a decision." "It's the normal thing." "Is it not?" "I think it is." "I think so too." [4] It is an interim time when nothing is possible, no option is open at the moment. Indecision is the normal thing.

[2] McCoy, "Waiting for Godot: A Biblical Appraisal," 597-98.

[3] Samuel Beckett, *Waiting for Godot* (Evergreen, 1952), pp. 9-10, hereafter WG.

[4] *Ibid.*, p. 13.

38.3 The Coming of the Expected One. As they wait, some-one does come: the brutalized slave and a dehumanizing master. While Pozzo eats his chicken, the clowns examine Lucky's sore, note his slobbering, observe that he is a half-wit.[5] While waiting for Godot, they are met only by this slave in agonizing bondage. They remark, "It's inevitable!" They describe the suffering ser-vant as a "scandal"![6]

Pozzo, who boasts that he is "made in God's image,"[7] finishes his chicken, allows Estragon the honor of the bone, checks his watch, lights his pipe, and after much elegant folderol broaches the question about Godot. He does not know Godot. He wonders what would happen if Godot should miss his ap-pointment.

Later we discover Pozzo's plans for Lucky. Instead of ruth-lessly kicking him out, Pozzo is now generously taking Lucky to the fair to try to get a decent price for him.[8] Before Pozzo leaves, he magnanimously states that, since it is his nature to be liberal and generous, and since they have been civil to him, he would be glad to do something for them.

He could even have Lucky do a trick for them, perhaps dance or sing or recite or think. A dance is requested. Lucky puts down the bag and makes an attempt. They all agree it was poorly executed. Then they play a game of trying to name the dance of the suffering servant. Estragon names it "The Scapegoat's Agony,"[9] which suggests the agony of another scapegoat, dancing as it were, writhing on the cross.

38.4 The Word of the Expected One. Since the dance was poorly received, they impatiently order Lucky to do something else entertaining. They decide to ask him to *think* for them. A totally unexpected climactic hurricane is about to thunder in upon them. He must have his hat to think. Pozzo commands: "Stand back! Think, pig!"[10] Then in a machine-gun style, Lucky shouts: "Given the existence as uttered forth in the public works of Puncher and Wattmann of a personal God quaquaquaqua

[5] *Ibid.*, p. 17.   [7] *Ibid.*, p. 15.   [9] *Ibid.*, p. 27.
[6] *Ibid.*, p. 18.   [8] *Ibid.*, p. 21.   [10] *Ibid.*, p. 28.

with white beard quaquaquaqua outside time without extension who from the heights of divine apathia divine athambia divine aphasia loves us dearly with some exceptions for reasons unknown but time will tell and suffers like the divine Miranda with those who for reasons unknown but time will tell are plunged in torment . . . " [11] and that continues without a comma, breath, or interruption at a frantic pace for about a thousand words. If carefully considered, however, this speech contains the great surprise of the play and may be understood as a summary of Godot's own message.

Although Lucky's speech at first looks like an incoherent jumble of phrases, we find in it several strands of intelligible continuity and a forceful sequence of thought: Given the existence of a personal God, outside time and without extension, who from the heights of divine transcendence loves us dearly with some exceptions for reasons unknown but time will tell. He suffers like the divine Miranda with those who for reasons unknown but time will tell are plunged in torment, whose fire flames the firmament, that is to say, blasts hell to heaven.

The predicament of man is revealed in the labors left unfinished by the Academy of Anthropometry, the science of the measure of man, of Essy-in-Possy, i.e., of man's essence which consists in his possibility.[12] Many experts are quoted who have established beyond doubt their views, for reasons unknown but time will tell. Among the experts quoted are Fartov and Belcher, whose names suggest ways of releasing gas from the stomach, and Feckham, Peckham, Fulham, Clapham, Peterman, Testew, and Puncher, all phallic and orgasmic symbols. That all these authorities have phallic nuances connected with their names seems to indicate that we are now talking about man's creative powers. In spite of all of man's potentialities, however, death is certain. The skull is the end. Man's work is unfinished. Man fades away, despite whatever strides are made even in digestive elimination and physical comfort. Man wastes and pines, in spite of his tennis, cycling, football, golf, penicillin. In a word, the dead loss per head

[11] Ibid.,   [12] Heidegger, BT, pp. 274 ff.

226

since the death of Bishop Berkeley comes to the tune of one ounce per head. The Academy of Anthropometry has actually measured the dead loss at one inch four ounce per head approximately, by and large, more or less, to the nearest decimal good measure round figures stark naked. What is more grave, in the light of the lost labors of Steinweg and Peterman, is that everywhere—in the plains, the mountains, by the seas, the rivers, the air, the earth, the abode of stones—everywhere there is death and great cold at last. There has always been this death. All the facts are there. Man's labors are abandoned unfinished, and at last there is nothing but the skull.

Admittedly this is a rambling, multifaceted poetic explosion, but I take the heart of it to be: Given the existence of God, we are all loved dearly for reasons unknown but time will tell. God suffers with those who are plunged into torment, and this blasts hell to heaven. In all of man's vitality we can see, supported by many learned studies, that in spite of all contemporary achievement and culture, man fades away and dies, and you can measure the amount of dust left over from all of man's achievements. Even the whole of nature is in the process of dying, and always has been, ever since the year of the lord 600 or something. What we are finally left with is the skull, the fading away, concurrently and simultaneously with all that it. But in spite of all this, God still loves us dearly and suffers with those who are tormented.[13]

Since the word of Godot is so unbearable, the other three attack Lucky and force him to the ground. His hat is taken away. Subsequently all have trouble getting up from their fallenness.

38.5 The Immanent Coming Again of the Expected One. The bums return to their project of killing time. Vladimir remembers having seen the pair before. "I too pretended not to recognize them." [14]

A voice from offstage cries, "Mister Albert . . ." A boy enters and timidly announces that he has a message from Mr. Godot. "Mr. Godot told me to tell you he won't come this evening but

---

[13] Beckett, WG, pp. 28-29. [14] *Ibid.*, p. 32.

surely to-morrow." Valdimir: "You work for Mr. Godot?" Boy: "Yes Sir." Vladimir: "What do you do?" Boy: "I mind the goats, Sir." Vladimir: "Is he good to you?" Boy: "Yes Sir." Vladimir: "He doesn't beat you?" Boy: "No Sir, not me." Vladimir: "Whom does he beat?" Boy: "He beats my brother, Sir." [15] It is clear that the boy and his brother mind sheep and goats. Who is the brother? Is he Lucky, who is beaten? Is Lucky Godot's son? Whoever he is, he is being beaten, as Lucky is being beaten and as Estragon is soon to be. Night falls quickly. Comparing himself to Christ, Estragon takes off his uncomfortable boots and goes barefooted. They consider suicide as they look at the tree, but they do not have a rope. They wonder if it is good for them to be together. They are uncertain. Vladimir says, "Yes, let's go." They do not move. It seems that man is stuck in this place, waiting for the Christ to come.

38.6 Salvation Is Nearer Than When We First Believed. The second act is structured, similar to the first act, in three phases: Godot is expected, Godot appears, and it is announced that Godot may be expected again tomorrow.

It seems as though there are bones all around now. The implication is that there are thousands and thousands, billions of corpses here of people who had been waiting at this place for Godot. Estragon is beaten in the intervening night by unknown assailants. When Pozzo and Lucky return, Pozzo is blind, in utter misery, the opposite of his previous fortune. Lucky is burdened as before, but the rope is much shorter, so that Pozzo may follow more easily. Lucky stumbles and brings everything down with him. They lie helpless among the scattered baggage. Lucky goes to sleep. All Pozzo can say is "Help!" Is Godot appearing today in the form of Pozzo? Vladimir and Estragon stay hidden, debating whether Godot has come.

"To all mankind," philosophizes Vladimir, "they were addressed, those cries for help still ringing in our ears! But at this place, at this moment of time, all mankind is us, whether we like

[15] *Ibid.*, pp. 32-33.

it or not. Let us make the most of it, before it is too late! Let us represent worthily for once the foul brood to which a cruel fate consigned us! What do you say? (*Estragon says nothing.*) It is true that when with folded arms we weigh the pros and cons we are no less a credit to our species." [16]

To Pozzo's "Help!" Vladimir replies, "We have kept our appointment and that's an end to that. We are not saints, but we have kept our appointment. How many people can boast as much?" To which Estragon replies, "Billions." [17] They bargain with Pozzo finally to pick him up for a hundred francs. No not enough; two hundred is required. But when they finally try to pick him up, they find it impossible. When Valdimir kicks Pozzo in the crotch, they try to find a name to call him back and hope that eventually they will find the right one. They try Abel! Abel! Cain! Cain! Cain! Finally Estragon observes, "He's all humanity." [18] When they do finally get up, they admit that it is "simply a question of will power." [19]

The central issue is framed, after Pozzo and Lucky leave unrecognized a second time, in Vladimir's plaintive question: "Was I sleeping, while the others suffered? Am I sleeping now? Tomorrow, when I wake, or think I do, what shall I say of to-day? That with Estragon my friend, at this place, until the fall of night, I waited for Godot? That Pozzo passed, with his carrier, and that he spoke to us? Probably. But in all that what truth will there be?" [20] This will all happen again. Pozzo will not verify his memory, and Estragon will not remember that this has happened again and again. Again tomorrow Estragon will tell him about the beating he received the night before, and he will give him a carrot. It will all happen over again. No third act is necessary in this play, since it would be the same as the first. Finally his soliloquy concludes: "Astride of a grave and a difficult birth. Down in the hole, lingeringly, the gravedigger puts on the forceps. We have time to grow old. The air is full of our cries. But habit is a great deadener." [21] Even out of the grave something is being formed. In

---

[16] *Ibid.*, p. 51.   [18] *Ibid.*, pp. 53-54.   [20] *Ibid.*, p. 58.
[17] *Ibid.*   [19] *Ibid.*, p. 54.   [21] *Ibid.*

the midst of all this death, this skull hill, something is being born. The gravedigger stands astride the grave as a midwife with forceps.

The question: Are we asleep to the reality of birth and death which is taking place constantly in our midst? Are we asleep to the crucified and resurrected Christ daily present in our midst? Are we alert to the constant coming and going of Godot, who meets us in the form of our suffering neighbor in need?

It is not inconceivable that Beckett had in mind Paul's extraordinary letter to Rome: "The commandments," he says, ". . . are summed up in this sentence, 'You shall love your neighbor as yourself.' Love does no wrong to a neighbor; therefore love is the fulfilling of the law. Besides this you know what hour it is, how it is full time now for you to wake from sleep. For salvation is nearer to us now than when we first believed; the night is far gone, the day is at hand." (Rom. 13:9-12.)

part four

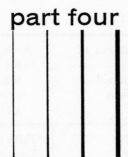

toward a field theory of authenticity

AWARENESS OF BEING

Inclusive Existential Relationships Toward Being or Beings	The Predicament of Man— Dysfunctional Awareness	Authenticity, Full-Functioning, Self-Actualizing Awareness
God and the gods, Transpersonal (I-Thou) relationships	*Idolatry* absolutizing of relative values	*Faith* in God beyond the gods
Self, I, Intrapersonal (I-I) relationship	*Despair* self-loss identity diffusion	*Self-Affirmation*, self-discovery, recovery of identity
Neighbor, other persons, Interpersonal (I-you) relationships	*Alienation* overdependency, depersonalization, withdrawal, aggression	*Love*, responsive care for the neighbor, overcoming alienation
World, nonhuman creation, nature, subpersonal (I-it) relationships	*Desecration* abuse, defilement of natural environment	*Consecration* of things to the neighbor under God, reclamation, new creation

INTRODUCTION

Having dealt with man's awareness of *time*, I now turn to man's awareness of *being*. With respect to the diagram in the Introduction (p. 15), it may seem strange that we have thus far taken the bulkier portion of this book to discuss only the first three of seven categories. All our attention has concentrated upon the three temporal categories, leaving the four remaining dimensions to be condensed together in this last part. It would appear to be a prodigiously complex task to treat each one of the four remaining categories with the same detail that we have given to the previous three. In order to spare the reader unnecessary argumentation and repetitiousness, I will merely summarize the skeletal features of the remaining categories, leaving it to the imagination of the reader to apply the analogical patterns we have already established. The four remaining sections will clarify the awareness of being as illustrated in the chart on the facing page.

I am trying to be as spare as possible, omitting all irrelevancies, in exploring the four essential being relationships in which man always exists as he moves through time. Strictly speaking I am not introducing entirely new conceptualities, since all these have appeared peripherally in our discussion of man's encounter with time. Although these four dimensions are less symmetrical, less commensurable, less balanced than the three previous temporal categories, they nevertheless may be seen in their interaction as inclusive being relationships, just as the past, present, and future are inclusive time relationships. The seven categories together constitute an attempt at inclusive reflection on the self in its basic existential relationships. I am attempting to see the human predicament and possibility in seven inescapable modes which embrace all other possible modalities, so that all subcategories of the human predicament and possibility may be understood as some combination or modification of one or more of these seven modes. It is in this sense that our anthropology (both in its dysfunctional and functional aspects) emerges directly out of the basic dimensions of the spacio-temporal and ontological situation in which man exists. Whether in glory or misery, every man lives with himself, his neighbors, the nonhuman creation, and the ground of being, as well as past, present, and future. He cannot be defined apart from these relationships. If any attempt is made to understand him without these relationships, he is not fully understood.

It is in this sense that I think of this project as a search for a *field theory of authenticity*, understanding authenticity as genuine human self-actualization, full-functioning human health (*salvus*), involving maximum responsiveness to reality in each of its basic modes. These seven modes are precisely the *field*, the arena, the total setting of man's inauthentic and authentic relationships.

To be authentic is to be fully human, to be whole, to be a self-actualizing person. The saving deed of God, to which Christian proclamation witnesses, invites men into authentic existence. Although such wholeness may be reflected in fragmented ways throughout the human situation prior to faith, and although authenticity may be a formal possibility in principle for every man in every now, it is the intention of the Christian community actually to bring men into authentic life in each of these seven modes. It is in this sense that I think of this project as a *secular soteriology*, an effort to understand man's salvation, or authentic self-actualization, in secular categories. Each dimension of the life of faith admittedly has analogues in the life which is lived prior to faith, but faith hopes to bring to full blossom the seed of genuine humanity which is latent in every human existence.

In each of these seven modes we will attempt to state briefly the structure of the human predicament and then to clarify the shape of the authentic life as it is illuminated by the Word to which Christian preaching witnesses.[1]

[1] Cf. Oden, *The Crisis of the World and the Word of God* (Nashville: Methodist Student Movement, 1962), a limited-distribution Bible study in which portions of the argument of Part IV appeared in proto-formation.

chapter XII

THE TRAGEDY OF OUR GODS

39. The Structure of Idolatry

39.1 Absolutizing the Relative. Amid our struggle with an anxious future, a guilty past, and an empty present, we have sought to achieve self-fulfillment through the elevation of limited causes and creaturely goods to the level of ultimate sources of meaning and value. In our glorification of and devotion to these causes as our gods and deliverers, we have increasingly stood at enmity with the source of all things and the end of all things, the original and the final word about life, the void out of which all creaturely things come and the future into which they return, the giver and the slayer of all our finite values and causes.[1]

Every man exists in relation to the one who gives him life. Our very "being here" implies that some reality brought us into being. No man or creature has ever had the slightest capacity to

[1] For the main lines of the argument of Chapter XII I am especially indebted to H. R. Niebuhr, "Faith in Gods and in God," *RMWC*; "The Center of Value," *Moral Principles of Action: Man's Ethical Imperative*, ed. R. N. Anshen (Harper, 1952), pp. 162-75; "Value Theory and Theology," *The Nature of Religious Experience*, ed. J. A. Bixler, R. L. Calhoun, H. R. Niebuhr (Harper, 1937), pp. 93-116.

call himself into being or to remain in being forever. Life is given to us, whether we accept it or not. Life is taken away from us, whether we like it or not. No man can avoid being related to the one who gives him being and calls him out of being. We do not raise the question of the ground of being merely because we are Christians, but because we are human beings. Although there may be many vantage points from which men ask about that reality to which they are ultimately accountable, we begin not with the abstract, speculative question of whether God exists, but rather with the personal question of what we entrust to bestow meaning upon our existence.

Broadly defined, a god is a value enthroned, a loyalty which one cannot do without, that upon which a man counts to render his life meaningful. Luther set both the question of God and of the gods in an intimate relation to trust or faith: "What does it mean to have a god, or what is God? I answer: a god is that from which we are to expect everything good and to which we are to take refuge in all times of need. Therefore to have a god is simply to trust and believe in him. It is . . . only the heart's confidence and faith that make both God and an idol . . . for these two, faith and God, are correlative concepts. Therefore I say that your god in reality is that around which you entwine your heart and on which you place your confidence." [2]

Since man is a valuing being and since choices of value always presuppose some center of value,[3] in a general sense human life is always lived toward some god or hierarchy of values. Both the just and the unjust live by faith that something makes life worth living. Even suicide, which seems to be a totally desperate negation of all value, always presupposes and pursues certain values, such as the release of death, the elimination of guilt, or the attempt to strike back at a cruel environment; and therefore it assumes some specific orientation toward some center of value.

Absolutizing relative values, idolatry becomes the hub of much human anguish, the hidden root of dysfunctional anxiety

[2] *Luther's Large Catechism* (2nd ed.; Augsburg, 1935), p. 44.
[3] H. R. Niebuhr, "The Center of Value," pp. 162 ff.; "Faith in Gods and in God," pp. 115 ff.

THE STRUCTURE OF IDOLATRY

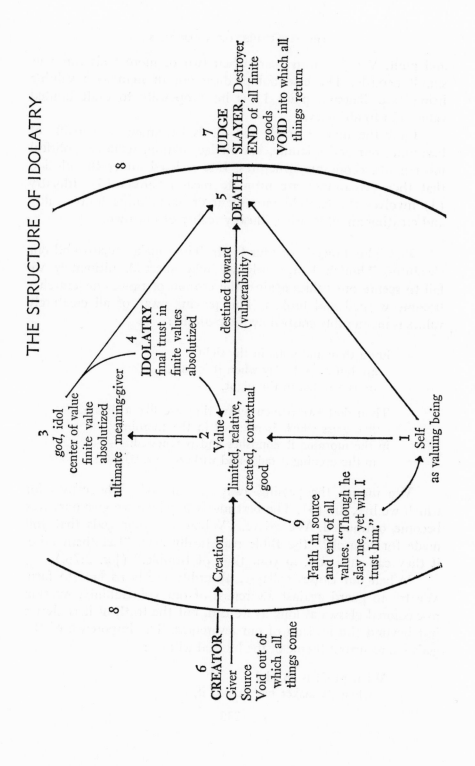

6 CREATOR Giver Source Void out of which all things come

8

→ Creation

2 Value limited, relative, created, contextual good

9 Faith in source and end of all values. "Though he slay me, yet will I trust him,"

1 Self as valuing being

3 *god,* idol center of value finite value absolutized ultimate meaning-giver

4 IDOLATRY final trust in finite values absolutized

destined toward (vulnerability)

5 DEATH

8

7 JUDGE SLAYER, Destroyer **END** of all finite goods **VOID** into which all things return and guilt. We feel torn apart when two or more gods claim us simultaneously. The essential predicament of man as a valuing being (see diagram, point 1) is his propensity to exalt limited values (2) to ultimacy.

Only the highest goods and ideals we know are capable of becoming our gods: family, knowledge, nation, security, political movements, economic structures. Life is lived under the illusion that they (creatures) are ultimate meaning-givers (3). Idolatry (4) involves the twofold movement of abandoning finite reality and creating an alternative, illusory reality of our own.

39.2 The Tragedy of Our Gods. Time makes relative all our absolutes. Though temporarily we may succeed, ultimately we fail to secure our values against the erosion of time. Our crutches become warped and broken. This passing away of all creaturely values is memorably grasped by the psalmist:

> For a thousand years in thy sight
> > are but as yesterday when it is past,
> > or as a watch in the night.
>
> Thou dost sweep men away; they are like a dream,
> > like grass which is renewed in the morning:
> in the morning it flourishes and is renewed;
> > in the evening it fades and withers. (Ps. 90:4-6.)

We mourn the passing away of our gods. The causes for which we live, die (5). The best ideals to which we give ourselves become outmoded. We grieve. "Where are your gods that you made for yourself?" the Bible realistically asks. "Let them arise, if they can save you, in your time of trouble." (Jer. 2:28.)

When our causes collapse, absurdity meets us face to face. We try to guard against awareness of our vulnerability, wearing rose-colored glasses as long as we can, but the truth of it is always just beyond the horizon of our awareness. The impotence of the gods is a recurrent theme of the biblical witness:

> What profit is an idol
> > when its maker has shaped it,

a metal image, a teacher of lies?
For the workman trusts in his own creation
  when he makes dumb idols!
Woe to him who says to a wooden thing, Awake;
  to a dumb stone, Arise! (Hab. 2:18-19.)

Life itself presses the question: What awesome reality swallows up all our human efforts? What dread power overwhelms our gods, what dooms our best causes to frustration and failure? Call it fate or "reality" or just "the way things are." Call it what you wish, but recognize that this is in one way or another the final reality to which every man is accountable. Suppose we do not even attempt to give this reality a name. Let us call it merely "X." Let us speak only of the unknown *void* out of which all things come (6), and the "unknown *future* into which all things return" (7). Call it the "out of which" and the "into which." Call it the source and end of all things, the original and final word about life. Call it whatever you wish, but acknowledge that it is there, and against it there is no defense. Man's life is lived within a great parenthesis (8) in which all created things are enclosed and circumscribed by this final reality.[4]

40. Faith in God

40.1 The Slayer of Our Gods. There is a community of men who have come to understand this slayer of their causes in a wholly surprising way, as faithful to them. There is much about this final reality that we do not know, but this we know has happened: There has come into being a community of men, the Judeo-Christian tradition, who witness to this final enemy of our causes as having made itself known as ultimate friend! The confidence of this community has come to cling not to creaturely goods or finite causes, but to that enigmatic reality from which all our values come and into which they all return. Amazingly, they have stood aface this destroyer of all things to celebrate: "Though he slay me, yet will I trust him" (9). Strange as it may

[4] Niebuhr, *RMWC*, pp. 122-24.

seem, this curious community of men, spanning history almost from its remotest beginnings to the present, have come to put their final reliance, not in limited values that pass away, but precisely in this opponent of our values, this antagonist of our gods! This community has learned to love this final reality as a lover thinks of his beloved, and to celebrate all lesser loves in relation to this final love.

To have confidence in this one is to understand that all other confidences are rooted finally in despair. To trust in this one is to trust in one who stands on the far side of all our anxieties and guilts. To obey this one is to respond freely to the self-disclosing now, to receive its limited value, but without pretending that any historical good is the final good.

But what enables this terrifying destroyer to be recognized as friend? It does not happen without a deepening of human awareness, through which man becomes increasingly awake to his vulnerabilities and value negations. It does not happen without a struggle of reason and conscience, wherein man discovers the phoniness of his gods and the way in which they tear him apart. But according to the memory of this community of celebration, there is another factor in the transition from idolatry to faith: it is their meeting with historical events in which this final one has allegedly made himself known, through the deliverance of the Hebrews from Egypt, through the fulfillment of messianic expectations, and through his continuing self-disclosure in history. Faith in this one is not self-generated or merely fabricated out of the deprived longings of one's own experience. Faith in God is possible only as a response to his concrete self-disclosure. Radical confidence in this enemy of our gods may have occasional manifestations apart from the story of Israel, but this community remembers it as having been prototypically given in certain events through which the meaning of the whole of history is clarified. Since faith in God has the character of response of God's action, this community does not say that faith is something men ought to have, but rather that when it is given it is an incomparable gift, a treasure hidden in a field, for which one might sell all that he has in order to enjoy that prize.

240

40.2 Transvaluation of Our Values. Faith makes relative all those values which our idolatry made absolute. All life can now be valued anew in the light of the giver and slayer of creaturely values. That God has reduced our gods to ashes does not imply that we should despair over the good and beautiful things in this world. Our best causes (no longer hoped-for deliverers) become more deeply significant, not less. They are not gods, so they can now be valued as a part of contextually good created order. We can value them realistically and work hard for their realization. Genuine devotion becomes possible in a real and relative sense.

Confidence in God puts an end to the conflict of our gods. All things in creation may be valued anew in the light of the giver and slayer of value. One comes freshly to see new worth in what was once considered vulgar or valueless. That which was once considered threatening and unchallengeable is now welcomed as less than finally threatening. We are called to value all of life anew in relation to the ground, giver, and judge of value.

chapter XIII

THE BONDAGE OF THE SELF

41. The Structure of Despair

In a few spare pages, this chapter seeks to present a condensed statement of the predicament of the self in relation to itself, i.e., the structure of despair. If the argument suffers from a lack of incisive illustration, it is because, by a deliberate decision, these last four chapters intend to provide only a skeletal outline of the essential structure of dysfunctional and functional awareness in each of the four essential phases of the awareness of being, the second of which is the I-I relation, to which we now turn.

41.1 Self-loss. When I perceive myself as sick in relation to the threat of the idolatrized future, the burden of the idolatrized past, and the godless emptiness of the present, I despair that this unhealthy state is the permanent condition of my life. Bondage to nonfulfillment seems unalterable. Despair is the sickness unto death, since it is that sickness which is aware of the intransigence of all other sicknesses. "Let the day perish wherein I was born," cried Job. "Why did I not die at birth, come forth from the womb and expire? . . . Why is light given to him that is in misery, and life to the bitter in soul, who long for death, but it comes not, and dig for it more than for hid treasures. . . . Why is light given to a man whose way is hid, whom God has hedged in?" (Job. 3:3-23.)

In despair I wish, despairingly, to be something other than I am. I am convinced that there is no hope for a new self-relation in which I could affirm myself as finitely free. No ray of hope remains for the real self to be brought back, redeemed, repurchased. I experience myself as "sold" to inauthenticity, a condition well known in Scripture: "The whole head is sick, and the whole heart faint. From the sole of the foot even to the head, there is no soundness in it" (Isa. 1:5-6.) "I am carnal, sold under sin. I do not understand my own actions. For I do not do what I want, but I do the very thing I hate. . . . So then it is no longer I that do it, but sin which dwells within me." (Rom. 7:14-17.)

The ultimately absurd expression of this despair is the taking of one's own life, supposedly "solving" the problem of man by eliminating man himself. The occasional desire to end suffering by ending life itself is universally experienced by spirit-filled men who from time to time become painfully aware of their finite limitations. Even the greatest heroes of the faith of Israel occasionally gave expression to this ultimate despair: "Cursed be the day on which I was born!" Jeremiah laments. "Why did I come forth from the womb to see toil and sorrow, and to spend my days in shame?" (Jer. 20:14, 18.) Under threat for his life, Elijah "went a day's journey into the wilderness, and came and sat down under a broom tree; and he asked that he might die, saying, 'It is enough; now, O Lord, take away my life; for I am no better than my fathers' " (I Kings 19:4).

Despair is a profound malady of man's spirit, since it is over ourselves that we despair, not something outside ourselves. "It is an unhappy business that God has given to the sons of man to be busy with," writes the despairing preacher of Ecclesiastes. "I have seen everything that is done under the sun; and behold, all is vanity and a striving after wind. I said to myself, 'Come now, I will make a test of pleasure; enjoy yourself.' But behold, this

243

also was vanity. . . . I made great works; I built houses and planted vineyards for myself. . . . I had also great possessions of herds and flocks, more than any who had been before me in Jerusalem. . . . I got singers, both men and women, and many concubines, man's delight. So I became great and surpassed all who were before me in Jerusalem. . . . And whatever my eyes desired I did not keep from them; I kept my heart from no pleasure, for my heart found pleasure in all my toil, and this was my reward for all my toil. Then I considered all that my hands had done and the toil I had spent in doing it, and behold, all was vanity and a striving after wind, and there was nothing to be gained under the sun." (Eccl. 1:13–2:11.) Since one cannot run away from oneself, if one's very self is sick, then every relationship in which the self exists tends to become infected.[1]

41.2 The Movement of Despair Through Time. Since the self exists in time, despair may be seen in three temporal phases. The complicity of despair in other modes of human brokenness may be seen as follows:

	Guilt	Anxiety	Boredom
Despair⟶	Guilt-creating Despair	Anxious Despair	The Despair of Boredom

(a) *The Despair of Guilt.* Despair is spawned by the memory of what one has been. The despair of guilt is the awareness that my past is intolerably burdened with unfulfilled self-expectations. Paradigmatic guilt is the sudden dawning of the despair of guilt. The other side of the despair of guilt is a deepened sense of guilt that I am indeed in bondage to an alien self-understanding.

(b) *The Despair of Anxiety.* Despair exists not only as a relation to memory, but as a relation to possibility. Despair and

[1] S. Kierkegaard, *Fear and Trembling and The Sickness Unto Death,* trans. Walter Lowrie (Anchor Books; Doubleday, 1955), pp. 144 ff.

THE STRUCTURE OF DESPAIR

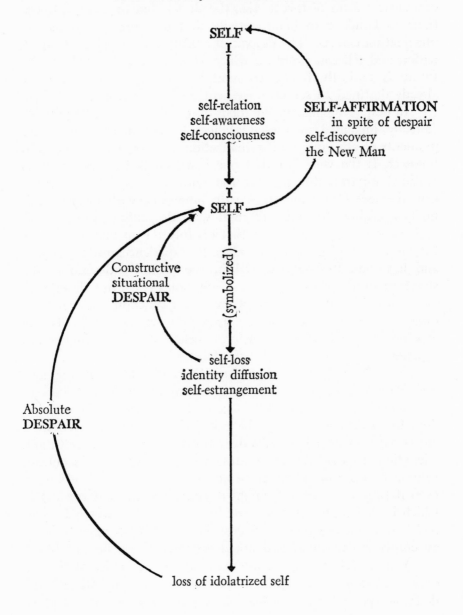

SELF

I

self-relation
self-awareness
self-consciousness

SELF-AFFIRMATION
in spite of despair
self-discovery
the New Man

I
SELF

(symbolized)

Constructive
situational
DESPAIR

Absolute
DESPAIR

self-loss
identity diffusion
self-estrangement

loss of idolatrized self

anxiety join together in a despairing anxiety which is keenly aware of a special form of threat; viz., the threat that the self will continue in bondage to inauthenticity in the future, as far as the imagination can see. The despair of anxiety is a coalition of imagination and self-consciousness which imagines that the self in the future is radically bound to nonfulfillment. The future seems already destined to self-estrangement, fated to perpetual self-loss.

In despairing anxiety the focus of anxiety is upon the possible (already imagined as probable) loss of self-identity in future moments of attempted self-actualization. The pain of the despair, however, is the very fact that one is a finitely free man who is destined interminably to bear the burden of anxiety. I despair over the fact that I am stuck with humanity, with myself! It is understandable that man respond with despairing anxiety, *if* it appears to him to be the case that his future is in fact laden with the same kind of crippling bondage he experiences in the present and has too often experienced in the past. By describing the structure of despairing anxiety I am not castigating those who experience it, but rather simply reporting phenomenologically a dimension of the structure of awareness which I have keenly experienced, and which I assume other self-aware individuals experience with varying modes of intensity.

(c) *The Despair of Boredom.* Despair emerges in dialogue not only with memory and imagination, but also with current experience. Despair can easily coalesce with the dynamics of boredom to awaken what might be called the despair of boredom. I am bored because I have already lost myself in anxiety, guilt, and alienation from others. I am conscious of the vacuum in current value actualization. There is no active "I" to lay hold of values, even if they were there. I might remember some past context in which I felt free, or imagine some future context in which I might feel free again, but now I am despairing over what appears to be an empty environment and bored over my despairing condition.

We are rehearsing the interweaving of the modes of the human predicament not just to punish the reader with morose descriptions, but to describe the curious complexity of these modes, how they reinforce one another and coalesce to intensify

246

the bonds that bind man to unfulfillment. We have described despair as the awareness of bondage to inauthenticity in three modes: despairing guilt, despairing anxiety, and despairing boredom. I am aware either that I have not been myself, or will not be myself, or cannot now be myself, and in each of these temporal modes I answer behaviorally with despair. My whole encounter with time presents the possibility of the loss, not merely of my values, but of my self, my freedom, my capacity for self-direction toward fulfillment.

42. The Ontological Impossibility of Despair

42.1 The New Man. Having viewed despair from the perspective of man's limited self-perception, we now turn to an attempt to understand despair from an entirely different point of view, namely, God's perception of the self. It is the audacity of theology to ask not merely about how man identifies himself, but how God has chosen to relate himself to man in such a way that a new human identity is visible.

Covenant ontology, which is an ontology and inquires into man's being as he exists before God, as distinguished from phenomenology, puts a fundamentally different question to the despair of man. For instead of asking how man is experiencing himself, it asks how man is being experienced by God. Indeed its special temerity is to ask who (before God) *is* man, amid all his ambiguous and fragmented attempts to identify himself. The question of identity is crucial for covenant ontology. For only if we can speak with some confidence of who man *is* can we then speak more assuredly of what he is called to *do* in order to express who he is.

Our thesis: It is impossible to despair over ourselves before God, if God is understood as the one who addresses us as his covenant partner ever anew in the now.[2] The psychological experience of despair is now perceived to be rooted in an ontological impossibility, however much I may experience it as if it were a response to reality. Insofar as I stand before the God who speaks

[2] *Ibid.*, pp. 208 ff.

freshly in every now, there is no time or ground for despair. My task is to learn to identify myself in a new way, on the basis of God's own naming of me as son.

Amid the despair of history a divine word is being spoken which enables and calls man to understand himself as a new creature in the light of God's new creation. A new possibility for self-affirmation has been given us. God has chosen to affirm us. We are called to affirm ourselves.

Since God regards our past as forgiven, secures our future, invests our present with meaning, and loves us amid the collapse of our idolatries, we can now understand ourselves as new men, freed from bondage to despair. In the language of Christian hope: "We rejoice in our hope of sharing the glory of God. More than that, we rejoice in our sufferings, knowing that suffering produces endurance, and endurance produces character and character produces hope, and hope does not disappoint us, because God's love has been poured into our hearts through the Holy Spirit which has been given to us." (Rom. 5:2-5.)

We are valued precisely amid our demoralized self-valuation! Accepted amid our inacceptability! Affirmed amid our incapacity to affirm ourselves! Despair is annulled! Our incurable disease is now known to be curable. "If God is for us, who is against us?" (Rom. 8:31.)

A new age has been inaugurated! We are called to conceive of ourselves in a new way—as participants in the coming (already begun) reign of God's love. It is God who has chosen to be *for* us, even though we continually and absurdly choose to be against ourselves.

In the New Testament proclamation concentrated symbols are pressed to the service of clarifying this new reality in which the self stands. *Adam* is the shorthand sign for the old age of man's despair. It is "old" because it is now undercut by the event of God's love. The era in which we stood as rebels against God and therefore against ourselves is a dying era, although its vestiges are still everywhere evident. The critical victory has been won, though the war rages on. *Christ* is the concentrated sign of God's reclaiming of all his perverted creation, reconstituting the human self, identifying it as his own. For "as one man's trespass led to condemnation for all men, so one man's act of righteousness leads to acquittal and life for all men" (Rom. 5:18). Death has reigned through the whole story of mankind (Adam). *Death* means our inability to choose a new way for ourselves. *Life* means a new possibility for recovering our true selves is given.[3]

The Christian community does not remember merely the *idea* of God's concern for the despairing world, but an *event* in which God himself chooses to participate in limited, finite existence. The incarnation is the basis upon which a new style of self-affirmation is born, a new humanism, the humanism of the worldliness of the word of God.[4]

If I abstract myself out of my covenant relation, it is still possible to despair over my condition; but if I stand every moment afresh in an unnegatable divine-human covenant, then it is impossible to despair over my *self*. I can only despair over an abstract image of myself. This places the question of despair firmly in the context of ontology; that is, if I pursue the question of my own being to its depth, the very question of despair must be revised to accord with the self-disclosing nature of reality itself. To live abstractly *as if* I were not a valued and valuable being, to live as if finite freedom and fate-laden limitation were not embraceable and affirmable, is to live on the basis of an absurdity.

Finally, there is only one thing that is not possible for me, and that is to cease to be who I am. To flee my being as one who is created, claimed, judged, and redeemed by God is never finally within my power, although I may make a stubborn effort toward it. I may view myself *as if* I were abstracted out of my concrete covenant relation with God and neighbor, but finally that view can be little more than an abstraction. If the covenant is renewed by God's own determination, then an ignorant and absurd human self-determination can never finally negate it. Although the cove-

[3] Rudolf Bultmann, "Adam and Christ in Romans 5," *The Old and New Man*, trans. Keith R. Crim (John Knox Press, 1967), pp. 49 ff.; Karl Barth, *Christ and Adam*, trans. T. A. Smail (Harper, 1957).

[4] Dietrich Bonhoeffer, *Ethics*, ed. Eberhard Bethge, trans. Neville H. Smith (Macmillan, 1955), pp. 57 ff., 188 ff., 318 ff., 354 ff.; Barth, *The Humanity of God*, pp. 37 ff.

nant calls for our free response, it is never finally and precariously dependent upon it.

The new man is not a *possibility* which man is being called to actualize, but already is an *actuality* in which man stands, and which he is being called to decide upon for himself. Thus the question of human self-identity is not in the last analysis a question of what sort of identity I may or may not give myself, but rather of who I *am*. The identity of man is finally revealed, according to the New Testament, not in the despair of Adam, but in the new man, the man for others, liberated by the love of God for worldly responsibility.

42.2 The Invitation to Self-discovery. The ethical imperative which emerges out of the experience of despair is to become who one is, to become the new self, the new man, the new identity which is being enabled by reality itself. Be who you are as one who has been freed to embrace both finitude and possibility, both your involvement in nature and your capacity for imaginative self-transcendence. The New Testament is not merely a moralistic series of exhortations for man to change his behavior, but an announcement of a new situation in history, a new era, a new being which enables a new form of doing.

chapter XIV

THE PROBLEM OF THE NEIGHBOR

43. The Structure of Interpersonal Alienation

43.1 Meeting the Neighbor. Every person exists in a relation with other persons. No man can be born, grow, or survive without interpersonal care. Human existence is existence with others.[1] Among our basic existential relationships (to past, present, and future; God, self, neighbor, and world), none is more sensitive to hurt and frustration than is this relation to others.

Our essential predicament with others, interpersonal alienation, is intricately interwoven with other previously described modes of the human predicament. Amid the intensity of my inner struggle with anxiety, guilt, boredom, and despair, I grow estranged from my neighbor in isolation and withdrawal, or despairingly toward him in a clinging relation of overdependence. To the extent that I am alienated from myself, I find it difficult to care for and share with the neighbor. In my pride and self-concern I am offended at his obstinate intrusion in my private

[1] Martin Buber, *I and Thou*, trans. R. G. Smith (2nd ed.; Scribner's, 1958); Rudolf Bultmann, "Das christliche Gebot der Nächstenliebe," *Glauben und Verstehen*, I (J. C. B. Mohr, 1933), 230-35.

world. I break the intended relation of trust and mutual confidence, so that both my neighbor and I must live in loneliness without communicating our need for each other.

"The neighbor" is a shorthand term meaning the next one, the person whom I encounter concretely, the one given to be at this moment near me, whether I like it or not, the one who meets me currently with his gifts and claims, needs and possibilities.[2]

The neighbor always meets me both as a person and an office. Every person exists in multiple offices at the same time. I now exist as a father, a teacher, a citizen, a son, a husband, simultaneously. I encounter my son as a father, and he meets me as a son, and our personal relationship is molded by that official relationship, or in the context of our social roles and stations in life. Whenever the neighbor meets me, he meets me *clothed* in the office in which he exists.

Even though I may be created with a deep hunger for intimacy, I sense a strange vulnerability in risking real closeness with others. I learn to keep a distance from my neighbor. I have experienced all too painfully the barriers he erects against me. I am constantly reminded of my radical inadequacy to give and receive love freely, without seeking to secure love as a possession. Alien and desolate, I stand at a distance from those whom I most love, and from whom I most need comfort and intimacy.

I ought to love my neighbor as I have been loved, but since I find myself preoccupied with the threatening future, the burdensome past, and the empty present, I have no time or strength for the neighbor's needs.

All the wretched geography of the human predicament conspires to reinforce my loneliness and hostility. Anxious before the future, I strive competitively to achieve security by using my neighbor as a ladder for my self-elevation, disregarding the price he must pay for my petty achievements. As feelings of guilt and despair increase, I am drawn into a neighbor-evading syndrome of self-pity and self-loathing. Out of long experience with self-deception, I learn how to deceive the neighbor. Double-mindedly

[2] Bultmann, "Das christliche Gebot der Nächstenliebe," pp. 231-34.

preoccupied with the already and the not yet, my ears are deafened to the call of the neighbor in the now. His needs merely bore me. Proudly imagining I can live without others, my pride itself becomes a fantastic, self-destructive barrier against achieving the intimacy for which I yearn. Bored and despairing over my caughtness in self-concern, I lose interest in the bestowing and receiving of love which would mean authentic life.

Worst of all, my radical self-assertiveness makes me blind to the very fact of my own persistent self-assertion. Out of the poverty of my being unloved I have no riches to give. This is the bondage of the will: being who I am as self-assertive men, I cannot escape the self-assertiveness which makes me think I can escape it.

43.2 Re-Imaging, Pre-Imaging, and Experiencing the Neighbor. Since my neighbor always meets me only in a temporal continuum, a processive time sequence, the alienation I experience may be seen in a movement of three phases: my relation with (1) the remembered neighbor who intensifies my guilt over past value negations; (2) the imagined neighbor who intensifies my anxiety over future value negations; and (3) the experienced neighbor who intensifies my boredom over current value negation.

Interpersonal alienation is deeply bound up with *guilt*, since my past is a past with others. Just as interpersonal alienation reinforces guilt, guilt reinforces interpersonal alienation. For I wish desperately not to be recognized as a negator of values shared with those whom I value. Consequently, guilt drives me away from interpersonal intimacy and self-disclosure.

Interpersonal alienation is bound up with *anxiety*, since the future I face is a future with others. I am painfully aware that my neighbor often has my future in his hands, that I will depend upon him, am responsible to him, and must share a future with him—all of which makes me experience the neighbor as a threat to my potential value actualization. Anxiety is always bound up in those for whom I *care*. Just as interpersonal alienation intensifies anxiety, so also does anxiety drive me away from my neighbor in further isolation. Anxiety burdens communication, invites withdrawal, frustrates intimacy.

It is precisely the absence of needed or desired persons in my now environment which makes me *bored*. In the situation in which I now exist, the caring, fulfilling, desirable people with whom I yearn to share my existence are now absent. Other neighbors may be here, but I could care less. To the extent that I have idolatrized the absent neighbor, I will experience the now as demonically devoid of experienceable value. Just as interpersonal alienation intensifies boredom, however, so also does boredom intensify interpersonal alienation. When I become acclimated to the torpor of the present, I come to assume that no neighbor is ever going to present himself to me as significant. As Vladimir says in *Godot*, "Habit is a great deadener." [3] I become thoroughly desensitized to the call of the neighbor in the moment, to his special gifts and tasks for me.

The movement of man through time thus presents the possibility of interpersonal alienation at every turn. The human predicament can never be seen only in a single mode, but rather in the interaction of complex modes, each of which affects and complicates the others.

43.3 Dependency, Depersonalization, Withdrawal, and Aggression. The self is surrounded by four basic types of encounter with others, which I shall call the neighbor above me, the neighbor under me, the neighbor before me, and the neighbor against me.[4] In each of these four forms I may find myself enmeshed in distorted relationships with those with whom I am called to live.

(a) *Overdependency upon the Neighbor Above Me.* Although a condition of mutual interdependency is healthy, from time to time my neighbor becomes overvalued so much that I am forced into the curious stratagems of *overdependency*. The neighbor above me is the neighbor upon whom I have allowed myself to become absurdly, idolatrously dependent. Our relation becomes distorted by submissiveness, paternalism, patronizing, clinging. I offer myself as a rug underneath his feet. I gladly reduce myself to nothing in order to obtain his slightest favor. Any threat

[3] Beckett, *WG*, p. 58.
[4] Horney, *NHG*, *passim*.

254

to our relationship is absurdly anxiety-creating. Overdependency is the child of idolatry. The neighbor has become too necessary for my well-being, a god. My future is in his hands.

Although the experience of seeing our gods collapse is a painful one, it is nevertheless a potentially liberating one. As life or time or history (which is to say God) teaches us of the vulnerability of all finite, created, human, and historical relationships, it intends to make us free from overdependence upon the neighbor above. For that slaying of our gods, which the Judeo-Christian tradition calls the judgment of God, enables a transvaluation of all our values in such a way that I can now receive the neighbor as a creaturely, contextual good, but no longer as an imagined ultimate source of all goods. I am permitted to see my neighbor as a valued person, and yet not the final source of value for me. I relate to my superiors with respect, but not with the final respect which is due only to God. I am free to enter into interdependent covenants with other finite persons who serve in their various offices, but not on the assumption that any office is beyond appeal or any person indispensable to history. It is in this way that the slayer of our gods presents a liberating possibility to men who are caught in absurd, infantile overdependencies.

(b) *Depersonalization of the Neighbor Under Me.* Whereas I distort my relation to the neighbor above me by *over*valuing his actual importance, I distort my relation to the neighbor under me by failing to recognize his actual importance. I treat him like a thing. The neighbor under me is the unneeded neighbor, the inferior underling, the low man on the totem pole, beneath me in the official pecking order. He is any other person whom I wish to manipulate and control for my own ends, as the older sibling may deal with the younger, or as the sergeant may deal with the corporal, or as the district manager may deal with the assistant district manager.

My alienation from the neighbor under me consists essentially in the fact that from time to time I symbolize this valuable person as merely an instrument for my value actualization, a tool to be used to get something I want. He is not valued for himself, but only for his instrumental value. I dehumanize, *depersonalize*

255

THE STRUCTURES OF INTERPERSONAL ALIENATION

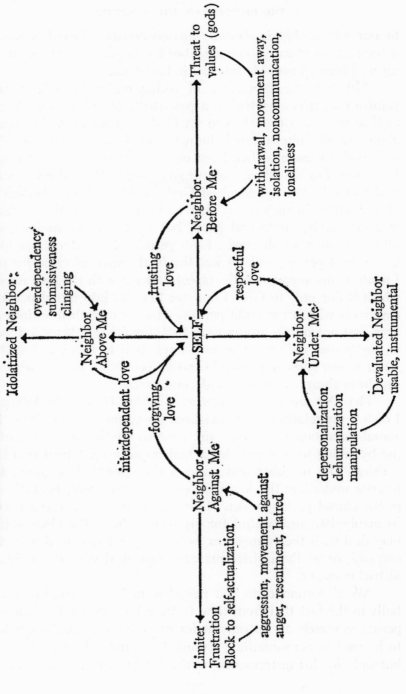

the neighbor, reducing our meeting into an I-it relationship. He is only a means.

Christianity speaks of the radical worth of the most lowly neighbor—not of his intrinsic or ultimate worth, but of his personal worth. Even the lowliest of neighbors is to be honored, because he has been honored by God himself, who was born in a manger of poor folk. The dignity of the neighbor is no less than the dignity of his being the bearer of the claim of God upon me and the recipient of the redemptive love of God! Insofar as we responsively serve the least of these our lowliest brothers, we do special service to the source and end of all creaturely gifts (Matt. 25). The self-presentation of God comes no closer to us than the nearest neighbor in need.

(c) *Withdrawal from the Neighbor Before Me.* The neighbor before me is the one with whom I share my future, the one who encounters me in the realm of possibility. When the future meeting with the neighbor is symbolized as a threat to my value structure, then my understandable response is *defensiveness.* It is in defense of my vulnerable orientation toward life that I tend to withdraw either as a momentary or a chronic life stance. I want to protect myself from the dangerous meeting with the anxiety-creating neighbor. Psychotic forms of withdrawal dramatically illustrate the extent to which defensive mechanisms can drive a person into his own world of internal communication, away from actual relationships with real people. For if safety lies only in noncommunication or bugged communication, then it seems reasonable to keep a distance from whoever represents a threat.

But authentic human existence is an existence with others, a being-in-covenant, in mutual interdependence and accountability. The neighbor is the precondition of my full humanity. I am being invited to learn limited ways of realistically living with my only partly trustable neighbor, trusting him at the level of his trustworthiness, sharing my existence with him, planning and risking relationship with him within certain boundaries in which both his interests and mine are mutually protected and enhanced. That the future is finally in God's hands and not the neighbor's is a liberating word which frees me to deal openly with him, trust-

ing in the God who continues to offer both of us rich value possibilities, even in spite of the values that my neighbor destroys,
undermines, or threatens. To trust God in spite of my neighbor's
untrustworthiness is to learn to view the neighbor in a less threatening way, as a source of contextual good for me and I for him.

(d) *Aggression Toward the Neighbor Against Me.* Frequently the neighbor meets me as a limiter of my freedom, a source of
frustration, a block to my self-fulfillment. I may respond with
anger, hostility, aggression. A variety of types of interpersonal
alienation emerges out of the frustration-aggression pattern, each
of which may carry the seeds of destructiveness and estrangement.

Aggression moves *against* the neighbor, trying to find ways of
striking back at the neighbor's damaging blow. The neighbor
against me is my adversary, against whom I feel that I must fight
in order not to be in some way destroyed.

44. The Ontology of Liberating Love

44.1 The Occurring Love of God. How is the predicament
of interpersonal alienation overcome? How is it possible to recover
covenant trust, openness, and intimacy with the estranged neighbor? The therapeutic traditions, both religious and secular, agree:
I can only experience the freedom to love if I understand myself
to be loved. The capacity to love is the gift of being loved. Love
exists only as a response to being loved. I cannot love out of the
poverty of my lovelessness. I cannot love merely in response to the
idea of being loved, but only to the event, the reality of actually
being loved.[5]

Clinically it is known that when persons who have been
trapped in overdependency, withdrawal, and hatred begin to
experience empathetic, unconditional positive regard, things begin to change. Constructive behavior tends to ensue.[6] Whenever
genuine, empathetic love occurs in therapeutic relationships, it
occurs only on the basis of a larger, perhaps unnoticed ontological
assumption that reality itself is the ground of love, care, and

[5] Erich Fromm, *The Art of Loving* (Harper, 1956); Bultmann, *KM*, p. 31.
[6] Rogers, *OBP*, pp. 59-107.

acceptance. The therapeutic agent, whether in the form of an understanding friend over a coffee cup or a professional counselor, mediates a caring concern which is somehow rooted in reality itself, a care which would be present even if the therapeutic agent were to die, a healing intiative which is embedded in the cosmic process itself. Quite apart from specifically Christian language, such love is undoubtedly mediated through so-called secular relationships.

It is precisely this implicit assumption about being itself as the ground of all loving, caring concern that is the explicit subject of the Christian proclamation. For Christian worship celebrates an event in which the source and end of all human values has allegedly made itself known in history as one who loves and cares unconditionally for estranged humanity, even and precisely amid its hostility, fragmentation, and loneliness. That unconditional love which is only vaguely knowable, as through a broken mirror, amid our human loving and caring is now allegedly knowable in its deeper sense as an *event* in history! It is now possible to respond not only to the abstract concept of unconditional love, but to an event in which the whole of humanity is as a matter of fact unconditionally loved!

Christian worship celebrates the presence of God's love even in spite of the absence of human love. Of course the responsible man is being called to mediate God's own love through his interpersonal encounters, but whether he mediates it through his finite human hands and words or not, it is there.

Do I learn of God's love by first experiencing human love? Rather, the deeper meaning of the limited, imperfect, conditional love which men give and receive is illuminated in the light of the unconditional, radical love of God for humanity. It is always only in a limited sense that we are capable of loving and caring for one another. Even when human intimacy is at its deepest and interpersonal care at its best, still we experience ourselves as caught in all sorts of ambiguous, deceitful, insensitive forms of self-assertion and distorted motivation. Even when I know my best love as impure, fragmentary, and self-assertive, however, I can nevertheless understand it as a fragmented and broken reflection

259

of the love of God. That is the meaning of man as *imago dei*, an imager of God, one who is capable (even and precisely amid his sinfulness) of reflecting the unconditional love of God. There is none good but God, as Jesus himself said, but our goods from time to time may reflect the goodness of God, which finally is nothing more or less than love.

Love is impossible in the radical sense so long as God has not revealed his love. The anxious and guilty man can only love out of his anxieties and guilts. What he calls "love" is still self-assertion so long as he does not actually understand himself to have been loved with an infinite forgiving love, embracing him precisely amid all forms of human rejection. Only God's love could be such a love.

44.2 The Ontological Impossibility of Hatred. Are overdependency, withdrawal, manipulation, and hatred thereby banished from the created order, expurgated from the vocabulary of actual being? At least we can say that estrangement is ontologically groundless. It is as impossible ontologically speaking to be isolated from my neighbor as it is to hate him, insofar as we both stand before God in covenant. I am being called to honor the neighbor as he has been honored by God. If I hate, distrust, abuse, and withdraw from the neighbor, then I am attempting to embody and make historical that which before God is simply groundless, absurd, ontologically impossible, since I am attempting to escape the covenant relationship in which I actually exist. I am trying to be something other than what I *am* (as covenant partner with the neighbor before God). When I experience the neighbor as valueless, or as an ultimate threat, then I simply live under an illusion. Subjectively and psychologically I may continue to experience intense forms of detachment, aggression, and overdependency, but my ontological condition, how I *am* in reality and before God, is as one who is given the neighbor as a partner in dialogue for mutual accountability, trust, love, care, and responsibility.

Indeed it is possible for me to hate an abstract image of my neighbor, i.e., abstracted out of the covenant relationship. I can

260

hate what I imagine him to be, but I cannot hate him insofar as I know him as he is, namely, as one who is valued by God and given to me for responsible co-humanity. When I speak of the ontological impossibility of hatred, I am not suggesting that the emotion of hatred is impossible, but rather asking whether that emotion has its ground in the nature of things, the actual condition of being, the real being of the neighbor. I am asking, regardless of how I might happen to *feel* about my neighbor, who he *is* before God. He is one who embodies the hidden Christ, and who images the love of God to me, even beyond his self-assertiveness.

The biblical witness does not merely exhort us to love the neighbor. This would be hopelessly unconvincing moralism. Rather, it addresses us with the hopeful word that God has loved us and calls us to love in response. Man cannot help being a lover. Human existence is a loving existence. The question is: How can our contextual human loves actually mirror, embody, and mediate the loving, caring concern of reality itself? Faith reasons by analogy. God's own freedom for the neighbor enables authentic human freedom for the neighbor. "In this is love, *not* that we loved God but that he loved us and sent his Son to be the expiation for our sins. Beloved, if God so loved us, we also ought to love one another." (I John 4:10, 11.)

chapter XV

THE ABUSE OF NATURE

45. The Structure of Desecration

45.1 The Nonhuman Creation. Every man exists in a relation with the nonhuman creation, the natural environment in which selfhood is spawned. No man exists without this spaciophysical arena which serves as the cosmic setting for the drama of history. Human life is lived in companionship with the cow, the mollusk, the sea, the endless galaxies—i.e., the natural order.

To be a man is to take up an attitude toward this complex, vital, threatening, awesome setting. Wherever I meet my neighbor, it is always in a context involving organic and inorganic matter: stone, soil, steel, shrimp, sand, light, color, texture, bread, and wine. To be a man is to stand amid these living and dead organisms and elements, responding to them, utilizing them in various ways, struggling against their threatening dimensions, enjoying their beauty. Although man creates history, history itself is created in the milieu of another, more massive creation, the creative processes of nature. It is this unfathomably complex, cosmic totality which we are calling "the nonhuman creation," or sometimes for the sake of brevity simply "the world." Every man exists in an intense, never ending, elemental, existential relation with this non-personal order of things, and it is with that relation that I am now concerned. I am not thinking only of objects or inorganic "things," since that would not include the animal creation, with which man lives in a significant relation of interdependency. Although somewhat proudly anthropocentric, the category of "the non-human creation" points most adequately to the total range of organic and inorganic matter (aside from other persons) with which the self lives in constant companionship, trial, challenge, and dialogue.[1]

The essential predicament of man in his dealings with non-human creation is most powerfully caught up in the term *desecration*.[2] To desecrate is to profane, to abuse, to defile, to violate the actual value of something. Desecrate is the opposite of consecrate. To desecrate is to vulgarize the intended purpose of something of value.

The original, intended, good function of organic and inorganic matter is best expressed by the concept of *utility*. The things of this world are intended and given in order to be *useful* toward the humanizing of man. Instead of using persons as a means of obtaining things, man is being called to use things as a means to serve human ends. The predicament of man amid the nonhuman creation is his tendency to *abuse* the gifts of creation which are given to be used toward the humanizing process.

45.2 Intersecting Modes of the Abuse of Things. The abuse of the created order may be seen in six phases corresponding with other focal points of the human predicament: idolatry (before God), despair (over oneself), alienation (from the neighbor),

[1] Teilhard de Chardin, *The Divine Milieu* (Collins Fontana Books, 1964), pp. 112 ff.; Barth, *CD*, III/1-4, *passim*; G. A. F. Knight, A *Christian Theology of the Old Testament* (SCM Press, 1959), pp. 99-137.

[2] Although *desecration* is often taken to mean the desacralization only of things sacred, I am following a broader priestly and prophetic tradition in viewing desecration as the failure to perceive the presence of God precisely in the secular, the worldly, quite apart from ambiguous distinctions between sacred and secular. Whereas Cox [*The Secular City* (Macmillan, 1964), 25 ff.] regards desacralization as a virtue, I am employing the term desecration as a vicious denial of the value of the secular.

THE STRUCTURE OF DESECRATION

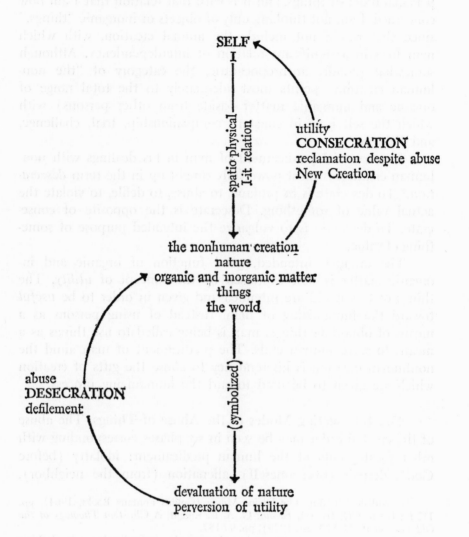

SELF
I

spatio physical
I-it relation

utility
CONSECRATION
reclamation despite abuse
New Creation

the nonhuman creation
nature
organic and inorganic matter
things
the world

abuse
DESECRATION
defilement

(symbolized)

devaluation of nature
perversion of utility

guilt (over the past), anxiety (toward the future), and boredom (in the present). Briefly we will show how the predicament of man amid the nonhuman creation intersects with his predicament in each of these six dimensions.

The created order is abused by *idolatry*, since idolatry refuses to meet and embrace finitude for what it is; namely, relatively, contextually valuable, but soon to pass away. In our pretending that limited values are absolutes, that natural or historical beings are ultimate sources of meaning or value, the created order is desecrated. The key biblical picture of the desecration of nature is that of taking natural objects, wood or metal or stone, and carving or molding them into idols to be worshiped. To absurdly deify a finite object is to vulgarize and defile it, to miss its real value. Paradoxically, in overvaluing the finite object, idolatry bypasses and undervalues its actual, functional, contextual value.

Despair is itself a kind of self-desecration. To despair is to experience oneself as trapped in and indebted to a finite order of things which is always in the midst of passing away. It is in this way that the very presence of the nonhuman creation as an arena for decision comes to intensify despair, while despair in time turns to desecrate the natural environment wherein it has experienced itself as lost.

It is amid interpersonal relationships that the tragic abuse of the creaturely environment begins to take on its most destructive, dehumanizing aspects. How is the desecration of the world enmeshed with *interpersonal alienation?* The created order is given in order to be used toward the humanizing of man (Gen. 1–3). I am being called to use things as a *means* to the *end* of interpersonal fulfillment, the love of the neighbor. But amid my idolatries and anxieties this order of priorities easily becomes turned around, so that I learn to *use* persons as a means of obtaining things.[3] I desecrate the world by valuing its impersonal objects more than the personal reality of my neighbor. I abuse and misplace the unique gift of the nonhuman creation, which is its capacity to serve toward the building of human community.

[3] Reuel L. Howe, *Man's Need and God's Action* (Seabury Press, 1953), p. 24.

If material things embody an exceptional power to disrupt interpersonal growth, then they obviously have the power to intensify *guilt*. For I bear within me not only the memory of my life with things, but also the memory of the barriers which created things have erected between me and my neighbor. Much of the memory of guilt attaches itself to the symbols and physical concretions of interpersonal estrangement. Our idolatrized loves and competing aspirations for creaturely things are deeply implicated in interpersonal guilt.

The nonhuman creation becomes an endless source of potential *anxiety*, since our deepest values are often tied with objects and artifacts of our spacio-temporal environment. For if things are valuable, and if values are vulnerable, then anxiety is deeply enmeshed with the question of the value of things. By intensifying idolatry and interpersonal alienation, anxiety itself plays a key role in activating desecration, the despoiling of certain creaturely goods in anxious pursuit of others.

There is finally a significant confluence of *boredom* with the desecration of the natural environment. For boredom is the lack of attentiveness toward the special gifts and demands of the creation, the failure to embrace present options. Boredom is the dialectical opposite of idolatry (which overvalues the limited good), since boredom *under*values the resources of the now situation. Thus it amounts to a denial of the world, an unintended asceticism, a withdrawal from its unfolding gifts of being and value, an unnatural flight from creation. It is in this way that boredom indirectly desecrates the created order: by ignoring, dismissing its current potentiality, turning aside from its now gifts which are only once given and then forever withdrawn into the irretrievability of the past.

The structure of desecration, as the essential predicament of man in relation to the nonhuman creation, is thus seen in its tragic intermeshing with the other forms of the human predicament: the created order is abused by idolatry, which misjudges its actual contextual value. Despair over oneself tends to become projected toward all things. Instead of using things as a means to interpersonal growth, we use persons amid our love for things, intensifying interpersonal alienation. Since the nonhuman creation is valuable, its defilement by man is guilt-creating. Since its finite goods are idolatrized, the vulnerability of those goods become anxiety-creating. Finally the boredom which is inattentive to the gifts of the now amounts to a denial of the world, an absurd asceticism toward the unfolding spatio-temporal environment. In each case the intended relation of *using* the nonhuman environment, receiving, enjoying, and employing its resources toward fuller humanization, is undercut by other dynamics of the human predicament.

46. The New Creation

46.1 The Reclamation of Covenant Creation. Having described the predicament of man as he stands before the nonhuman creation, wasting, abusing, prostituting, profanizing, desecrating, defiling its created values, we now ask how God himself addresses this predicament, according to the Judeo-Christian memory. Although it is usually thought that the Christian proclamation has more to say about the redemption of history than of nature, it should not be forgotten that the New Testament pictures the world, this whole nonhuman creation, as groaning in travail eagerly waiting for redemption, as if the early Christian community were hoping that not just human history but the total cosmic history would finally share in the redemptive process (Rom. 8:18-25). How does the Christian witness call for a reconceiving of the very being of the created order so that even man's prodigal abuse of created things is finally circumscribed by the judgment and grace of God? In what sense has the God of Christian celebration taken up an attitude not just toward human history, but toward all organic and inorganic matter, plant and animal creation, the physical universe from neutrons to nebulas?

Our thesis: Not only the historical but the natural order exists in covenant.[4] All creation is covenant creation. We have dis-

---

[4] Barth, *CD*, III/1, *passim*.

cussed the covenant essentially as a relation between God and Israel, and therefore prototypically with all humanity, wherein God chooses to be the God of this people, even in the midst of their ignorance, neglect, and denial of the covenant. It might seem difficult to apply such a bond to the created order, since covenant presumably calls for responsibility, or some kind of responsiveness to it, in that it asks us to be who we are as covenant partners. The hypothesis of process philosophy, concerning the panpsychic nature of all reality, even inorganic matter, presents an exciting prospect to a Christian theology of creation in covenant. This hypothesis argues that the totality of the created order possesses a certain awareness, that everything shares in a kind of protoconsciousness. Even the rocks and molecular processes, which ostensibly seem to be the farthest removed from any overt consciousness in the human sense, nevertheless exist at the atomic level in a kind of elementary responsiveness to reality, so that the whole scope of nonhuman creation, and not merely human history, is thought to exist in an unending continuum of responsive interaction with every other part of cosmic history.[5] The increasing acceptance of this hypothesis lends credibility to the extrapolation of the concept of covenant toward the whole of nonhuman creation, a thought which has been anticipated not only by the New Testament writers, but also by the prophetic and priestly literature of the Old Testament.[6]

If the world of things exists in covenant, then we are called to honor it as it is. If the nonhuman creation *is* valued by the ground and giver of values, then we are being called to value it accordingly; neither to idolatrize or desecrate it, but to receive its contextual values as they appear and disappear in processive time. We are being addressed with the divine calling and divine permission to lay hold of the world, the secular, the created order of things, to utilize its gifts toward humanization, to be attentive to its address, to receive its relative values for what they are, and

[5] Charles Hartshorne, *Man's Vision of God and the Logic of Theism* (Archon Books, 1964), pp. 154 ff.

[6] Walther Eichrodt, *Theology of the Old Testament*, I, trans. J. A. Baker (Westminster Press, 1961), 410 ff.; Heinrich Schlier, *Principalities and Powers in the New Testament* (Herder, 1961).

to rejoice even amid their death and destruction, giving thanks to the one Lord, creator, consummator, who gives and who takes away.

Perhaps the image of *reclamation,* so often used with respect to the recovery of wasted physical resources, might be an appropriate image to speak analogously of redemption at the level of the nonhuman creation. In the red clay plains of the mid-American prairies which have been plowed up by men and eroded by furious streams of lengthening time, we see deep gashes in the balance of nature, with valuable soil rushing seaward. The reclamation of that land involves damming, reseeding, working to reconstitute the soil and make it again what it originally was prior to the invasion of history. Something like this seems to be at work in the natural order. Quietly God is at work reclaiming the natural order, so it may serve more adequately its functional purpose of being the arena for the humanizing process. We ourselves are being called to share in that process of reclamation in response to God's own reclaiming activity. Something of this quiet natural process of reclamation is reflected in Sandburg's poem "Grass":

Pile the bodies high at Austerlitz and Waterloo.
Shovel them under and let me work—
I am the grass; I cover all.[7]

The natural processes are at work healing over the wounds of history. The most awful tragedies of human history, the most absurd value negations of man, Auschwitz or whatever, will be overtaken by time. Nature will outlast history. This leads us directly to our next affirmation, parallel to the previous hypotheses of a covenant ontology.

46.2 The Ontological Impossibility of Desecration. If creation is covenant creation, then no matter how we waste or desecrate, prostitute or defile it, our abuse of creaturely things is rooted in

---

[7] From *Cornhuskers* by Carl Sandburg. Copyright 1918 by Holt, Rinehart and Winston, Inc. Copyright 1946 by Carl Sandburg. Reprinted by permission of Holt, Rinehart and Winston, Inc.

an ontological impossibility; i.e., we cannot change the essential being of nature by our human and historical distortions. Our disordering of nature has no invited place in the order of creation. Desecration is absurdity. It cannot *be*. For by definition it is that which being has passed by. In all its violence it is asleep to being, and lives in a dream world. The feast of being to which it is invited to awaken is covenant creation. What *is*, what is going on in the nonhuman creation, is finally not man's unbeing and undoing, but God's being and doing with and for man in his environment.

This indicative calls for an imperative. If God is continually in the process of reaffirming his covenant with the plethora of created beings, then we too are called to do so, to be constantly resensitized in reverence for life (Schweitzer),[8] to value life—not finally, not ultimately, not idolatrously—but contextually, in its own created condition, as it is!

Faith's analogical reasoning embraces the nonhuman creation in the confidence that God himself has embraced it. If God is concerned constantly to renew the creation in covenant, then man is being called to share in that renewal. God's freedom for the world enables human freedom for it. That does not mean that the nonhuman creation suddenly loses its capacity to threaten or frustrate the value actualizations of man. The world will remain what it is, namely, the natural, spatio-temporal arena in which history moves. But the faithful man moves within this awesome setting in a keen awareness of its source and limit, the ground on which it stands and the end to which it returns, even the creator and consummator of time.

---

[8] Albert Schweitzer, *Out of My Life and Thought*, trans. C. T. Campion (Henry Holt & Co., 1933), pp. 159-60; Barth, *CD*, III/4, section 55.

47. EPILOGUE

47.1. Systematic Reconstruction in an Era of Post-Radical Theology. Whatever one might think of this complex effort, it is at least clear that the search for structure in experiencing is basic to its total character. There would have been nothing to report had there not been a consistent and intelligible structure which reveals itself in phenomenological self-examination.

Perhaps an expression of sympathy is due, not only to the patient reader who has followed this long path with me, but also to the bewildered librarians who are forced to make decisions about where an exercise of this sort fits into the spectrum of humanistic studies. For cataloging an argument of this sort raises special problems, about which I am tempted to comment. Is this essentially a study in anthropology—a doctrine of man—since it focuses on the theme of human awareness; or does it belong more directly to the field of ontology or phenomenology (or even ethics, since it attempts to speak of the good life)? To others it might seem more akin to the psychology of religion or practical theology. My closest critics have already advised me that I have given it a title which delimits it, which doubtless is true, but what do you do when you find yourself grasped by a structure of experiencing which is broader than any single title? Despite my earlier inclinations, however, as I try to locate this exercise in the spectrum of academic disciplines, I must confess that it comes closer to the range of concerns of systematic theology than any other field I can identify, even though I do not think of myself as a systematic theologian and never once imagined as I began to develop this project that I was writing a systematic theology. This admission is a telling one, however, since system-building in theology has been almost taboo since the beginnings of the existentialist influence on theology.

271

Note the sequence: This study began as a phenomenological inquiry into the contents of my own consciousness. A structure emerged, which demanded broad analogical pursuit. Only then did it become necessary, as a demand of phenomenology itself, to bring to bear the resources of the Judeo-Christian tradition to reformulate a deeper perception of the structure of awareness. Far from intending to write a systematic theology, I meant only to account for the structure of my own experiencing; but to my surprise I have discovered that in the very process of phenomenological analysis a system has been revealed, a structure has emerged, a series of analogies has been unfolded, which exhibit intelligibility and consistency and which demand theological assessment. It is not I who have constructed the system. I have only tried to see what is actually there.

Regrettably, the discipline of systematic theology has been barely surviving some very lean years. Following the strident mood of necrotheology,[1] the mainstream of theology in diaspora has been meandering, searching for its misplaced identity amid rapid secularization. There may indeed be fresh demands in our time for sharp, judicious polemical theology which deliberately forces encounter with sloppy pop theology. Even more so, however, the secularizing context calls us to clear, consistent, systematic theological reconstruction. We can no longer get by with uncritical utopian messianism, any more than we can escape into esoteric historicism. There is no future for culture-absorbing dilettantism, any more than there is for the kind of methodological treadmilling which we have seen so much of in the last decade.

I find myself keenly disappointed in my own generation, amid our general ennui toward the systematic structuring of reflection. We have produced pitiably little that could be called even the beginnings of a systematic theology for the emerging generation. My shelves are full of the systematic reflections of the era of Tillich, Barth, Aulen, the Niebuhrs, Gogarten—all old

[1] Cf. Thomas Altizer and William Hamilton, *Radical Theology and the Death of God* (Indianapolis: Bobbs-Merrill, 1966); Oden, "The Lack of Radicality in 'Radical Theology'," *Christian Advocate*, XI (1967), 87- ; "Radical Theology— Which Way Now?" *motive*, XVIII (1967), 3.

enough to be my grandfather—but where are the constructive efforts of my own generation? Of course I do not expect theologians now in their thirties to already have completed systems, but what does disturb me is the general lack of interest and motivation to do systematic reconstruction. Admittedly, the recent contributions of Macquarrie and Kaufman are welcome exceptions to the larger pattern.

We have lived too long in the lengthening shadow of our grandfathers, and out of the less illustrious labors of our fathers' generation. The tendency of the current theological generation to be content with the tightly delineated essay, the report of others' efforts, the groping intuition, the headline-attracting phrase, fails to satisfy the hunger of the emerging generation for inclusive, consistent, synthesizing reflection.

This is not to suggest that the tentative, probing efforts of this discussion are adequate to the demand for fresh, constructive theological integration. Rather, I am merely expressing my own surprise that the procedure I have followed has led me unexpectedly and yet unavoidably from pure phenomenology precisely to systematic theology (12, 13, 26, 27, 35.3, 42.2) in an era in which theological systematization is atrophied and defensive.

To admit that we are living in an uncertain, timid, languishing era of systematic theology does not imply that we lack brilliant, astute minds at work in this field. It would be difficult to find a period of theology with more sheer intellectual acumen and brilliance than the current generation; but it is ironic that all this theological firepower has produced such a meager result in substantial systematic reconstruction for our time. It seems quite a dodge, to me, even an unconscionable evasion, to retort that this is not an age for system-building, that we are still in an era of groping, and that it is premature to attempt any encompassing efforts at systematic construction. Paul Tillich shrewdly observed that "some of the most passionate foes of the system are most systematic in the totality of their utterances. And it often happens that those who attack the systematic form are very impatient when they discover an inconsistency in someone else's thought." [2]

[2] Tillich, *Systematic Theology*, I, 65.

273

We can see developing in certain quarters, however, some exciting new initiatives in holistic theological reflection. I am thinking particularly of Protestants Moltmann, Pannenberg, and Richardson, and a radiant cluster of Roman Catholic theologians who are determined both to stand responsibly amid their historic traditions and yet to do their own original reflection amid the newness of the modern world. However great Bultmann's contribution, the post-Bultmannian era may be remembered as a low ebb of Protestant theology, with its esoteric, parasitical, and self-congratulatory style. The emerging generation may be much more promising, with the integrative philosophical thinking of Pannenberg and Richardson, and the imaginative spirit of Moltmann cutting the initial channels. However much I may differ with Pannenberg's exaggerated historical objectivism or with Richardson's eclectic pneumaticism or with Moltmann's uncritical futurism, it is nevertheless with the bold spirit of their probing that I feel a sense of comradeship. They constitute the cutting edge of theology today.[3]

47.2. The Quest for Structure in Experience. Reality presents itself as intelligible. Experience has structure. It is not a coercion of reality, or a projection of our structures onto it, to look for the intelligibility and consistency structured into reality itself. It is for this structure that we have been searching, and for language faithfully to embrace and reflect it. This sort of synthesizing, synoptic anthropological reflection is a part of the intellectual challenge of each new era, our own included, and when we dodge it, we evade a demand implicit in reality itself.

In any event, it is in the service of this sort of integral reflection, the overarching attempt to give a systematic, cohesive account of the structure of my own experiencing, both as a human being and as a recipient of the Judeo-Christian tradition, that this effort has been undertaken. Actually my stronger motivation for working through this exercise, however, has had less to do with

[3] See Jürgen Moltmann, *Perspektiven der Theologie* (Munich: Chr. Kaiser, 1968); Wolfhart Pannenberg, *Was ist der Mensch?* (Göttingen: Vanderhoeck und Ruprecht, 1962); Herbert W. Richardson, *Toward an American Theology* (New York: Harper & Row, 1967).

the current lacuna in systematic theology, than with my own personal, internal concern for self-clarification. For even when I have deliberately tried to throw this structure away, dismiss it and go on to something different, it has kept calling me to accountability, insisting that I give it my attention.

We hear much bold talk these days about new mutations in human history resulting from technology. Affirming the exciting promise of man's new technological environment, I nevertheless find this talk easily exaggerated and often unconvincing, if we are thinking of the core modes of the human predicament such as guilt and anxiety.

The yet-to-be twenty-first-century man, no less than the primitive man of the twenty-first century B.C., must face possibility, live with his past, and experience his present. That has not changed one iota, and will not change as long as man lives in time. Post-modern man, as well as ancient man, will remain a valuing being with temptations to idolatrize his limited values. He must live with others and with himself, however crude or advanced his technology. As far ahead as I can see into the future, and as far back as I can see into the past, man always has experienced these seven basic modes of existential relationship—and always will. Each is unavoidably written into the very marrow of the human situation. I cannot envision any human mutation or any technological environment which would exempt man from being in time or living with himself, others, nature, and finally before the source and end of being itself.

index of scripture references

277

index of subjects

Abraham, 183-84
absolutizing, 64-66, 148-50, 197-99, 235-39
abuse of nature, 262-70
acceptance, 77, 80-81
acculturation, 39, 76
aggression, 258
Albee, Edward, 191
alienation, interpersonal, 251-58, 263, 265
Altizer, Thomas, 272*n*
analogy, 18, 25-27, 41, 50-55, 80, 140-41, 144, 188, 207, 271-75; *see also* gatefold "Strata of Analogies"
anamnesis, 125-26
anxiety, 26, 50-54, 74, 132, 237, 244, 246, 253, 263, 266, Part Two *passim*
    analogue of guilt, 25-27, 50-54, 132-33, 144
    consequence of guilt, 53-54

anxiety—*cont'd*
    constructive and destructive, 150-51
    current literature, 133
    definition of, 26, 141
    demonic forms of, 155, 175, 178
    idolatrous intensification of, 147
    images of, 145-46
    inevitability of, 155-56
    limits of, 27, 53, 152
    ontology of, 133-35
    paradigmatic, 146-47, 153
    situational, 143-44
    structure of, 131-58
    universality of, 156
Augustine, 71
authenticity, 27, 48, 77, 125, 194-95, 200, 212, 232, 253
authority, sources of theological, 87-89

279

DATE DUE

6-12-70			
OCT 1 9 1973			
SEP 2 9 1975			
JA 3 '84			
GAYLORD			PRINTED IN U.S.A.